A NOTE ON THE AUTHOR

KWASI KWARTENG was born in London to Ghanaian parents.
He has a PhD in History from Cambridge University and is the Member
of Parliament for Spelthorne in Surrey. He is the author
of the critically acclaimed *Ghosts of Empire* and *War and Gold*.
Thatcher's Trial is his third book.

@kwasikwarteng

THATCHER'S TRIAL

SIX MONTHS THAT DEFINED A LEADER

KWASI KWARTENG

BLOOMSBURY

LONDON · OXFORD · NEW YORK · NEW DELHI · SYDNEY

Bloomsbury Paperbacks
An imprint of Bloomsbury Publishing Plc

50 Bedford Square
London
WC1B 3DP
UK

1385 Broadway
New York
NY 10018
USA

www.bloomsbury.com

BLOOMSBURY and the Diana logo are trademarks of Bloomsbury Publishing Plc

First published in Great Britain 2015
This paperback edition first published in 2016

British Library Cataloguing-in-Publication Data
A catalogue record for this book is available from the British Library.

ISBN: HB: 978-1-4088-5917-9
PB: 978-1-4088-5918-6
ePub: 978-1-4088-5919-3

2 4 6 8 10 9 7 5 3 1

Typeset by Newgen Knowledge Works (P) Ltd., Chennai, India
Printed and bound in Great Britain by CPI Group (UK) Ltd, Croydon CR0 4YY

To find out more about our authors and books visit www.bloomsbury.com.
Here you will find extracts, author interviews, details of forthcoming
events and the option to sign up for our newsletters.

David English sees some similarity between his early struggles to establish the new *Daily Mail* and the trial of my Government during its first two years. Just as he kept his nerve, so we shall keep ours – and win through.

Margaret Thatcher, 1 May 1981, at the Celebration Dinner on the occasion of the 10th Anniversary of the new *Daily Mail* at Claridge's

Contents

Preface   ix

1 Portrait of a Lady   1
2 Friends, Foes and the '81 Budget   40
3 Civil War on the Left   68
4 Death in Ireland   98
5 Riots   130
6 'Among Friends'   154
7 Purge of the 'Wets'   180

Epilogue   208

Notes   219
Bibliography   235
Acknowledgements   239
Index   241

Preface

This book is about a leader beset by troubles. Margaret Thatcher was elected in 1979. She had made history as the first woman to lead a government in the Western world. Her style was regarded as shrill and unreasonable. After the general election, there was initial excitement at the prospect of a new dynamic figure at the head of British politics. Nineteen-seventy-nine was a significant year across the world: the fall of the Shah of Iran in January ushered in an age of Islamic control in that country; the death of Pope John Paul after his papacy of only one month led to the election of the first non-Italian pope in 500 years; at the end of the year, the Soviet Union invaded Afghanistan, which marked the start of a nine-year conflict.

In Britain, there was a widespread feeling of change which Thatcher seemed to represent. May 1979 was indeed a watershed. It was apparent even to people at the time that something new had happened. Newspaper editorials spoke of 'a policy sea change' in which the focus on the state would be replaced by a new emphasis on the individual.[1] It was also appreciated that Thatcher marked a break from the patrician Tory leadership style represented by Macmillan, Eden and, to a lesser extent, Heath.

Of course, the most obvious difference was that she was a woman. Less obviously, as a consequence of her gender Thatcher had not been initiated in the traditional breeding grounds of the Tory establishment. Among post-war Conservative leaders up to 1979, she was the only one, with the exception of Heath, not to have attended an exclusive public school. Unlike Heath, she had not served in the armed forces and had absolutely no military experience. As a woman, she was excluded from many of the social clubs – the St James's gentlemen's clubs – which featured so prominently in High Tory circles of the time.

Thatcher's background was different in more subtle ways. Her father was a Methodist lay preacher. This religious foundation gave her thinking a particular intensity. As a leader, she constantly referred to her upbringing as the daughter of a preacher. Her imagery was infused with Low Church Christian references to the Bible, in particular to the New Testament and parables.

Thatcher saw the world in basic, even simplistic, terms. This binary approach to life was at the core of her being. For her, the conduct of affairs was a series of conflicts between good and evil, between the free market and socialism, between 'people like us' and enemies. This Manichaean mentality was in many ways the source of her conviction and self-belief.

By March 1981 it appeared that her government would fail. Unemployment had risen to 3 million and public expenditure had increased, as had the public deficit. Within her own party, Thatcher's position was insecure. Many of the leading Conservatives were precisely those patrician figures – Old Etonians, landed gentry and wealthy figures from the world of business – who had dominated the party since the end of the Second World War.

Thatcher's Trial is a short account of the six months which defined Thatcher as a leader. These six months started with the budget delivered on 10 March 1981 and ended with the reshuffle of her government which took place on 14 September. During this period, Margaret Thatcher showed herself to be inflexible, tough minded and courageous. Her judgements were clear but often wayward; her self-belief sometimes faltered, although publicly she never let any hesitation blunt her message. She always conveyed an image of utter certainty, even when some of her closest allies openly expressed reservations. As Norman

Fowler, a member of her first government, remembered, in 1981 'we had one challenge after another'.[2]

An important source has, naturally enough, been Thatcher's own utterances, particularly her public speeches. Speeches were of great significance to Margaret Thatcher. She made no attempt to hide this in her own memoirs: 'As one of my speech writers said, "no one writes speeches for Mrs Thatcher; they write speeches with Mrs Thatcher". Every written word goes through the mincing machine of my criticism before it gets into a speech.'[3] She placed a heavy emphasis on the spoken word. It took on an almost sacred quality. She was one of those politicians who believed fervidly that words mattered.

Thatcher in 1981 was, in many ways, a weak and fragile political leader. The mere fact of a woman prime minister was itself regarded as an experiment, something which her own experience would either justify or condemn.

This book is set out in seven chapters. An introductory chapter briefly recounts Thatcher's background, the circumstances of her winning the Conservative leadership in 1975, and the general election of 1979. The 1981 budget was the most controversial of her premiership. While her government was beset by troubles in Northern Ireland, civil unrest spread across many cities of Britain. Nineteen-eighty-one marked the final split in the Labour party as the moderates left to form the new Social Democratic party, launched on 26 March 1981.

By September 1981 everyone had had enough. It was clear that Margaret Thatcher would have to reassert control over her Cabinet. She did this in a characteristically brutal and uncompromising fashion. Most notably, Lord Soames, none other than the son-in-law of Sir Winston Churchill, was summarily dismissed. People said this was because he had been right when Thatcher had misjudged the mood during civil service strikes. To replace Soames and Ian Gilmour, two easy-going Old Etonians, Thatcher promoted men such as Norman Tebbit, Cecil Parkinson and Nigel Lawson. These were younger men with energy, but without the grand social backgrounds enjoyed by Soames and Gilmour.

Margaret Thatcher was the most controversial post-war British Prime Minister. To her opponents, she was tough, harsh, uncaring and dogmatic. They believe she made Britain a more unequal, more materialistic and more brutal place. To her supporters, she simply saved a Britain which was heading towards the condition of an ungovernable socialist state. Both opponents and supporters agreed, however, that she was a driven, powerful political figure, motivated by ideas and with a certain well-defined view of the world.

It was the Labour leader Ed Miliband, the son of a Marxist sociologist, who said these words about her in the House of Commons, in April 2013: 'You can disagree with Margaret Thatcher, but it is important to understand the kind of political leader she was. What was unusual was that she sought to be rooted in people's daily lives, but she also believed that ideology mattered. Not for her the contempt sometimes heaped on ideas and new thinking in political life.'[4] Thatcher believed that ideas were essential in politics.

This book looks at Thatcher as a leader, examining a difficult six-month period which saw her reassert her authority, while still lagging behind in opinion polls. The book relates those difficult months to core ideas, to which Thatcher returned continually to confront the challenges thrown up at her. 'Freedom', the 'rule of law', 'good and evil' were a few of the basic principal notions, the compass points that she used to navigate those turbid waters of 1981.

Margaret Thatcher was a passionate and intense figure. This book aims to capture her unique quality as a leader in some of the most adverse conditions facing any statesman in modern peacetime.

Kwasi Kwarteng

May 2015

Portrait of a Lady

Wednesday 4 March 1981 – The church was full and lavishly furnished. It was an expression of the wealth and pride of the City of London. Thatcher, Prime Minister for two years, was in her most fulsome and high-sounding mood. 'Two years ago in this church, I spoke as both a Christian and a politician about how I found my religious convictions affecting the way I approached the responsibility of government.' St Lawrence Jewry is a church in the heart of the City of London. It stands beside the Guildhall and is the official church of the Lord Mayor of London and the City of London Corporation, the people who had been running the City for nearly 800 years. The Prime Minister gave thanks for having been brought up in a 'Christian family' and for having 'learned the message of the Christian faith'.[1]

At this moment, seven young people, mostly in their teens and dressed in suits, stood up and began to shout; they said the Prime Minister should spend less money on armaments and more on jobs. Much of what they said was inaudible. One young man took over the pulpit and started shouting at Mrs Thatcher directly, as she stood by the lectern at the head of the aisle, where she had started her address. The rector of the church, the Rev. Basil Watson, appealed for calm. He got no response. A little later, the seven, believed to be supporters of the Young Communist League, were led out of the church. They were booed and hissed by the congregation. 'Now you see why I fight these people,' intoned Thatcher. The congregation, about 550 strong, a solidly respectable crowd of elderly ladies in fur and tweed coats,

alongside young City types in Jermyn Street trenchcoats, were firmly
behind the Prime Minister.[2] It was typical that she should identify her
enemy in human form; the young left-wing activists were the embodiment of everything she was against.

Thatcher proceeded to deliver her homily to the respectable congregation. A homily, defined as a 'religious discourse which is intended
primarily for spiritual edification', is exactly the word to describe the
mixture of lecture, sermon and moral encouragement which had
become the hallmark of her style. 'The concept of the nation is at the
heart of Old Testament Judaism.' This concept, the congregation were
perhaps surprised to learn, was also one 'which those who wrote the New
Testament accepted'. More fundamental than the idea of the nation
was, in Thatcher's words, 'the idea of personal moral responsibility'.

The 4 March address was one of the most extraordinary ever given
by a British prime minister to an errant congregation. 'Of course, we
can deduce from the teachings of the Bible principles of public as well
as private morality.' The Bible, Thatcher urged, remained an important
source of inspiration in the Britain of 1981. Even though 'there are
considerable religious minorities in Britain, most people would accept
that we have a national way of life and that is founded on Biblical principles'. After the 'twilight of medieval times, when for many life was
characterised by tyranny, injustice and cruelty', Britain had become
what J. R. Green, the late Victorian liberal historian, had described as
'the people of a book and that book was the Bible'.[3]

As history, Margaret Thatcher's thesis was questionable. As inspiration and as a picture of her mind, the references to the Bible and to
J. R. Green were typical. Green himself was an 'advanced liberal', whose
A Short History of the English People had sold 500,000 copies in the fifty
years after its publication in 1874. He was popular with liberals because
he rejected the traditional view of British history as a parade of kings
and queens and battles, and sought to write about the life of ordinary
people. To do this in 1874 was radical, even revolutionary.[4] It is highly

likely that such a book would have been known to Margaret Thatcher's father, Alfred, himself a liberal who was reputed to be the 'best-read man in Grantham'. The young Margaret used to collect 'armfuls of books' for her father every week.[5] Even though Thatcher got considerable help in the St Lawrence Jewry speech from the right-wing journalist T. E. Utley and others, its sentiments were wholly characteristic of the mature Thatcher style.

What was perhaps striking to the congregation in March 1981 was the identification the Prime Minister clearly felt with biblical figures. Thatcher stressed the need for a 'national purpose'. In this vein, she asserted that 'unless the spirit of the nation' is renewed, 'our national way of life will perish'. Whose responsibility was it to ensure that this way of life did not perish? 'Who is to undertake this task?' the Prime Minister asked her supportive audience. Her answer was simple, if breathtaking in its implications. 'It has always been the few who took the lead: a few who see visions and dream dreams.' In ancient times, the Prime Minister continued, 'there were the prophets in the Old Testament, the Apostles in the New, and the reformers in both Church and State'. There was no doubting that she saw herself in this role, as a renewer of the 'spirit of the nation'. 'If we as a nation fail to produce such people,' she continued, 'then I am afraid the spirit of the nation which has hitherto sustained us, will slowly die.'

The heady mixture of national pride, Bible-based scripture, individual morality and basic liberal political philosophy all came together that March day. Thatcher defined her sense of limited government. Generosity, she declared, 'is born in the hearts of men and women'. It 'cannot be manufactured by politicians'. To think that the 'exercise of compassion can be left to officials' was an 'illusion'. It is difficult to imagine what the tweedcoat-wearing congregation thought of Thatcher's address. There was no doubting the grandeur of her imagination and the ambition of her vision. 'Let me sum up. I believe the spirit of this nation is a Christian one. The values which sustain our way of life have by no means disappeared but they are in danger of being undermined.' She finished with a rousing anthem to British pride and self-congratulation. Quoting John Newton, an evangelical preacher of the eighteenth century, she said, 'Though the Island of Great Britain exhibits but a small spot upon a map of the globe, it makes a splendid appearance in the history of mankind, and for a long space of time has been signally under the protection of God and a seat of peace, liberty and truth.'[6]

Earlier in her premiership, in 1980, Thatcher had already publicly expressed her conviction that the City of London's success owed much to the moral qualities of Englishmen. At a dinner marking her twenty-one-years as MP for Finchley, held at the Intercontinental Hotel by Hyde Park Corner on 18 October, she had decried the 'lack of will by successive governments to tell the people the truth about the situation'. This had 'sapped the British will to work and their traditional pride in a job well done'. More specifically, 'the City of London became the world's great financial centre more because of its reputation for honesty rather than for any geographical or political reasons'. In short, in Thatcher's moral nationalism, for want of a better phrase, 'Englishmen were famous for their hard work, thrift, reliability, honesty, initiative, intellectual curiosity, philosophical and scientific pre-eminence'. Furthermore, the Prime Minister asserted, 'Moral qualities were the secret of our economic success.'[7]

Such words would more likely be heard in a US president's State of the Union address, something that J. F. Kennedy or Ronald Reagan might have said about the American people. The strength of moral virtue within Americans had long been a theme of American exceptionalism, but to hear such phrases from a British prime minister was rare. This is not how Prime Ministers had spoken since the nineteenth century. Thatcher's strident nationalism was so entirely in character that probably nobody thought it strange that she could make such bold claims on behalf of 'Englishmen'.

That Margaret Thatcher could utter such sentiments without the faintest twinge of embarrassment was testament to her upbringing and early experiences. Famously brought up in the flat above her father's grocer's shop, she was steeped in the Methodism which her father preached every Sunday. The basic themes of individualism and national pride, commingled with Christian ethics, the absolute value of right and wrong, were ideas to which she would return repeatedly. There was always, in this form of preaching, a hint of British, perhaps even more narrowly English, exceptionalism.

Thatcher's upbringing had by her own admission been 'very strict'. The young Margaret, born in 1925, and her elder sister Muriel were 'never allowed to go to a cinema on a Sunday'. They were even forbidden to play any games such as snakes and ladders. Church, more specifically the Methodist Church, 'played quite a large part in our lives', Thatcher remembered. She also vividly recalled 'going to morning Sunday school at ten, then to the Church service at eleven, then to afternoon Sunday School at 2.30 where I was responsible for doing the musical accompaniment and generally to the service at six'.[8] Even by the standards of 1930s England, two Sunday School lessons and two services amounted to an impressive degree of religious devotion.

The Methodist Church at Finkin Street in Grantham is a fine building, dating from the 1840s, in a Tuscan style. It was here that Margaret Thatcher worshipped and played the piano accompaniment to the hymns which lay at the heart of Methodist worship. Alfred Roberts, Margaret's father, was a powerful, imposing figure, standing at six foot two inches, with wavy blond hair. His approach to church was straightforward and, as is evident from Margaret's exercise books, in which he wrote notes for his sermons, he presented a tough, practical version of Christianity. Indeed, his daughter's sermon at St Lawrence Jewry in March 1981 could have been written by Alfred himself. He had the same certainties, the same instinctual belief in faith and nation which animated his daughter when she was Prime Minister. 'If as a nation we allow, through neglect and indifference, the roots of Christian inspiration . . . to wither and die, then the fruits of the spirit must wither and die also.'

There is no doubt that the mixture of piety, self-righteousness and stubbornness which political enemies felt to be the sure hallmarks of Thatcher's mature style were developed at her father's knee. 'God', the Methodist lay preacher wrote in her exercise book in 1941, 'wants no faint hearts for his ambassadors. He wants men, who having communed with heaven can never be intimidated by the world.' Beyond the putative wishes of the Deity, Roberts explicitly referred, like many Protestants before him, from Martin Luther to John Bunyan and John Wesley, to the 'spark within' which every one of us 'must kindle'. All this came in a sermon entitled 'Strength comes from within'. Once we had discovered 'the light within ourselves we have to project that light' in 'every department of our living' in order that we might 'develop our own power'.[9]

Roberts's sermons, if the notes are in any way indicative, were forthright and powerful utterances. A common theme was the power of the individual to realise himself and influence others. He told his congregation that 'you must yourself believe intensely and with total conviction if you are to persuade others to believe'. In another emphatic comment in the notebook, Roberts asserted, perhaps with more enthusiasm than orthodoxy, that the 'Kingdom of God is within you'.[10] He was a tough, principled individual who was in essence a self-made man. Born in 1892, he was very much a late Victorian in outlook and mentality. His Methodism was a primary motivating force in his politics. He served as a councillor and alderman in Grantham and was elected Mayor of Grantham from 1945 to 1946.

Methodism as a political force had an interesting history, associated with liberal causes. Throughout the nineteenth century, and throughout Alfred Roberts's youth, the Methodist Church had been overwhelmingly on the side of the Liberal party. One writer in the 1940s pointed to the founding of the *Methodist Times* in 1885 as a 'convenient date for marking the beginnings of a dominant Liberalism within the Methodist Church'. As that publication observed in its issue of 30 June 1892, 'Out of thirty-five Methodist Parliamentary candidates, not one supported Salisbury [the Conservative Prime Minister].' The article suggested that 'without exception, they supported Gladstone'. When Gladstone died, Hugh Price Hughes, the founder editor of the monthly, wrote a striking editorial article for the issue of 26 May 1898. Hughes boldly claimed that Gladstone would never have become Prime Minister but for Methodist votes.[11] At the 1918 election, only seven years before Margaret's birth, there were eighty-two Methodist candidates standing for parliament. Of these candidates, only seven stood as Conservatives, thirty-seven were Liberals, twelve were Coalition Liberals, personally loyal to the Prime Minister, David Lloyd George, while the remaining twenty-six were members of the recently formed Labour party.[12]

Paradoxically perhaps, as the young Margaret Roberts was growing up, Methodism took on a more left-wing character. As elections went by, an 'increasing number of Methodists' became Labour parliamentary candidates, even though the majority were 'still Liberal', ever more dismayed by the disunity of the Liberal party.[13] Whatever their political persuasion, Methodists consistently maintained hostility to the opening of public places on the 'Lord's day'. Alfred Roberts, when serving as a Grantham councillor, had objected to the opening of parks for games on Sundays. He believed that, even though there was 'no such thing as compulsory Christianity', there was 'such a thing as drifting into a life which was absolutely and totally devoid of any spiritual inspiration'. These were strict views.[14] As Margaret Thatcher remembered, 'Everything had to be clean and systematic. We were Methodists and Methodist means method.'[15]

The influence on Methodist thought and practice was strong throughout Thatcher's subsequent career.[16] One aspect of this religious background which can easily be overlooked is the extent to which the certainties of the Finkin Street pulpit reduced problems to basic binary propositions. All through her life Thatcher revelled in bold, concrete and binary thinking. There would be no compromise, no shades of grey in her forthright world view. There was freedom and slavery, justice and injustice, right and wrong. This binary thinking was perhaps the most fundamental legacy of her strong Bible-based upbringing. Such dualism – the tendency to think in strictly black-and-white terms, without any hint of grey – is more characteristic of American political discourse than anything in Britain.

Manichaeism is an odd word describing a simple idea. Deriving their inspiration from a third-century Persian holy man named Mani who believed that there existed two kingdoms, one of darkness and one of light, Manichaeans saw the world as a field of perpetual conflict between good and evil. They were dualists. The two rival powers, in their view of the universe, were easily understood: 'Good and Evil, Spirit and Matter, the Kingdom of Light and the Kingdom of Darkness'. Such dualism has been described as a feature of US politics, where an analogy has been recognised 'between the ancient Manichaeans and the Radical Right'.[17] Thatcher's convictions were always based on an almost religious sense of moral righteousness, on the absolute certainty of what was right and what was wrong. Once this essential feature of her thought is grasped, it comes as no surprise that she applied it to her own Cabinet, listing different members under the headings 'for us' and 'against us'; perhaps characteristically, in a list dating from 1982 the numbers 'against us', in her view, were more than double those 'for us', her stalwarts in Cabinet.[18]

It was these certainties which sustained her at the most difficult points of her career. Such 'truths' gave her the confidence which inspired her friends and infuriated her enemies. All her political life, Thatcher believed she practised the kind of leadership which her father had preached in the Grantham of the 1930s and 1940s. As Alfred Roberts wrote in one of her exercise books, employing unusually convoluted language, 'a religion of veracity must always be rooted in spiritual inwardness'. It was the 'spirit within' which gave a person capacity for leadership. 'If you are going to kindle a flame in the heart of your hearers, you have to keep the flame burning on your own altar' was another of his insights into conviction leadership.[19] When Thatcher described herself as a 'conviction politician', she may well have been consciously emulating her father's example and stated beliefs.

After graduating from Oxford in 1947, Thatcher seemed bent on a political career, but worked in various jobs before getting married to Denis in 1951 and training to become a barrister in London. Her subject at Oxford was Chemistry, perhaps a surprising choice for an aspirant politician. This scientific training with its empirical, analytical emphasis was something Thatcher would take pride in later, when she became Prime Minister; science, with its clear definitions and 'modern' appeal, would be something that would define her as Prime Minister. Indeed a letter to the *Economist*, written after she had reached Downing Street in May 1979, contributed to the debate about the scientific training of the new premier, as against the more literary, humanistic educational backgrounds of so many of her predecessors.

Against the charge that her scientific mindset gave her a narrow intellectual approach, the correspondent, one H. A. Martin from Dunmow in Essex, protested, 'How can anyone say, as you report her colleagues saying, that Mrs Thatcher's non-humanist education has given her non-lateral thinking without historical depth?' Martin went on to say that it was 'precisely because she graduated in science that she has a more open mind, and an acute awareness that unforeseen and new problems might occur'. He continued, 'A training in science is the perfect base from which to tackle any situation, especially if fortified by one in Law.' By contrast, 'classicists are perpetually fighting Greek battles, in a world where technology rules, and the clear thinking of Mrs Thatcher is not hampered by the rigid strait-jacket of the outdated ivory-tower "humanists"'.[20] Science was innovative and dynamic.

She had become an MP at the relatively young age of thirty-four in October 1959.[21] More remarkably, she was one of a handful of women elected to the British parliament in that election. Among 630 MPs returned, only twenty-five, just over 4 per cent, were women. Thatcher herself was one of twelve Conservative women elected in a parliamentary party of 345 MPs. From the start sex, in the narrow sense of gender, was a defining part of Margaret Thatcher's political character. Of the twelve female Tory MPs, Thatcher was not only the youngest, she was also the most media friendly – a young professional woman with two small children.

Thatcher's career until 1975, when she seized the leadership of the Conservative party, had been more or less conventional. She had been the only woman in Prime Minister Edward Heath's Cabinet from 1970 to 1974. She had been a junior minister at the end of the 1959–64 Conservative government, but none of these appointments presaged the dynamic and polarising figure she would become. Despite the relatively humdrum but competent start to her career, Thatcher did occasionally give public pronouncements and speeches which, in a tentative though unmistakable way, expressed her thoughts. Those thoughts often harked back to her father's world view, his stress on the individual's moral responsibility.

As early as 1968, Thatcher gave a lecture at a meeting held during the Conservative party conference. It was entitled 'What's Wrong with Politics?' She argued that 'the great mistake of the last few years has been for the government to provide or to legislate for almost everything'. For her, the result of this general activity was that 'the emphasis in political debate ceased to be about people and became about economics'. She praised her own Conservative party for reducing 'the rates of taxation'. This was an expression more of a wish than the reality of the Conservative governments from 1951 to 1964. In Thatcher's view, such tax reduction had stemmed 'from the real belief that government intervention and control tends to reduce the role of the individual, his importance and the desirability that he should be primarily responsible for his own future'. This was a clear statement of the individualism she would preach throughout her career. Thatcher had a clear message. 'Money is not an end in itself,' she insisted, but it did enable one 'to live the kind of life of one's choosing'. Referring to a parable which she would often come back to, she also noticed that 'even the good Samaritan had to have the money to help, otherwise he too would have had to pass on the other side'.[22]

Even at this relatively early date, only a couple of weeks before her forty-third birthday, Thatcher – a new member of Heath's shadow Cabinet – gave a good impression of the kind of politician she would become. Already she was openly expressing her doubts about 'consensus politics': 'There are dangers in consensus: it could be an attempt to satisfy people holding no particular views about anything.' She went on to say, 'It seems more important to have a philosophy and policy which because they are good appeal to sufficient people to secure a majority.' Thatcher finished off her conference speech with the observation that 'No great party can survive except on the basis of firm beliefs about what it wants to do.' In words which would form the bedrock of her 'conviction politics' for more than two decades, she observed that it was 'not enough to have reluctant support. We want people's enthusiasm as well.'

Those words could have been said by Margaret Thatcher at any stage of her period as Prime Minister. That such a clear and articulate expression of her view of politics had been given in 1968 suggests that she had a few fixed beliefs which were unchanging and constant. In many ways her mind was rigid and unbending. As a politician, she seemed to be fully formed at a remarkably early age, even before she was elected to parliament, and she simply harped on the same themes over and over again: the rule of law, individual freedom, government not being the answer to everything. She constantly repeated these very basic principles.

Of course in 1968 the speech of a junior member of the shadow Cabinet at a fringe event of the party conference would have attracted little attention. Nevertheless the themes of 'individual responsibility', 'low taxes', 'less government', 'firm beliefs', the appeal to 'people's enthusiasm', all bore the hallmarks of Thatcher's mature political style. She had simply grafted her Grantham views on to the Conservative party, but she remained an outsider. It was her Methodist, nonconformist background which gave to her the feeling that she was outside the traditional Conservative party, with its strong identification with hierarchy and its solidly Anglican establishment roots. This general sense of being an outsider was, in part, a feature of her electoral appeal.

In the meantime, Thatcher seemed to be a capable, though unexciting, prospect as a future political heavyweight. She got promotions, but there was always the suspicion that her ascent owed much to her being the token woman, not to any inherent ability. During Heath's 1970–4 government, Thatcher had been a dutiful, if somewhat controversial, Education Secretary. Her opportunity to aim for the leadership of the party arose from the second defeat of the Conservatives in 1974 at the October election (Harold Wilson had narrowly beaten Heath at the February election). During the contest, Thatcher was portrayed as a plucky if implausible challenger. Her champions were initially journalists on the fringes of the Tory right, with the inimitable Patrick Cosgrave writing in the *Spectator* of 14 December 1974 that Edward Heath had been 'the most unsuccessful political leader of modern times'. Cosgrave believed that 'Thatcher could hardly fail to be a better leader than Mr Heath.'[23]

The thirty-three-year-old Patrick Cosgrave, an impetuous and often inebriated Irishman, was exactly the kind of outsider figure that was attracted by Thatcher. That December, he was political correspondent and deputy editor of the *Spectator*. His later antics included notorious bouts of drinking which led *Private Eye* to allege that he had lost his post as Mrs Thatcher's adviser 'because he had been sick over her in a taxi'.[24] He praised Thatcher's 'quality of courage and endurance under fire'.[25]

Ronald Butt, writing in the *Sunday Times* at the end of 1974, also agreed that a Thatcher leadership of the Conservatives would be something 'very different in style and also in the emphasis in its politics'. Her leadership would, in the view of this journalist, 'answer better to public opinion which, under a Liberal–Tory establishment, has been too often ignored'. This December 1974 opinion piece also managed to identify the source of Thatcher's appeal. 'Mrs Thatcher has always, rightly, been a champion of what one might call the classless middle-classes concerned not with their origin but with their achievement and their sense of personal responsibility.' At this rather early date, before the actual leadership contest itself which took place in January 1975, *The Times* was less hopeful about Thatcher's prospects as party leader, although it acknowledged in a perhaps backhanded compliment that it would 'certainly be a safe bet that in the fullness of time she will become the first woman Chancellor of the Exchequer'.[26]

The press was intrigued by Thatcher's relative youth. At forty-nine, she was a young dynamic force, with potentially a long career ahead of her. The *Evening Standard* on 27 December 1974 reported that she hoped 'to stay in politics for another 15 to 20 years' and that when she retired 'possibly in 1994, as she approached 70', she would attend 'bookbinding classes': one of her first jobs would to be to 're-bind 30 ragged volumes of Kipling she has at home'. The feature even claimed that Thatcher was 'something of a do-it-yourself handywoman'.[27] Thatcher's passion for Kipling was genuine, though it is doubtful whether she did any more than rely on the poems she had learnt in her youth, which had been kept in her capacious memory. The notion that she nursed a passion for bookbinding, or even home improvements and DIY, was strictly for the newspapers and the colour supplements in the immediate context of a leadership election, where candidates are encouraged to show their interests in order to demonstrate that they are 'well-rounded' characters who do not, contrary to the correct public perception, obsess about politics.

Thatcher's hinterland, beyond the Methodism of her childhood and a predilection for powerful sermons and poems, was notoriously limited. Her fascination for a weary public in 1974 did not derive from her interests, pretended or otherwise, but from her actual person and from her sex. 'At 49 she is attractive in the way good-looking women become as they grow older,' a column in the *Scotsman* could observe without any seeming embarrassment in January 1975. Her 'skin is pale and smooth, her hair a pretty blonde, if not entirely as nature intended it, and she wears little make-up'. In this profile, the newspaper observed that the problem Thatcher had was with her own sex, who had undermined her aspirations to genuine leadership. 'A male politician, a Minister even, can take his drink too seriously, even his women, but a woman politician, in the absence of anything worse, is sneered at for her hats, her hair or her housekeeping, invariably by other women.' The same article, referring to her tenure as Education Secretary, rightly observed that 'Mrs Thatcher has been tarred with museum charges and milk snatching, but who remembers the name of the Minister who deprived the over elevens of milk in the 60s?'[28]

All through December 1974 and January 1975, as the Conservative leadership battle became more intense, profiles and articles spewed forth assessing the Thatcher leadership bid. While some criticised her 'unfortunate manner' and her inability to relax which led to her taking 'her job so seriously', others hailed her as a Messiah.[29]

Even at this early stage, Thatcher became a symbol and a heroine for some of the Conservative right who yearned for a more 'authentic' and, to their mind, more 'principled' articulation of what it meant to be a Conservative. As Cosgrave asserted, 'It is the conviction that she stands for something recognisable as Conservatism which has gained so much support for her in recent weeks, not merely on the right of the party but in the solid centre.' In his stark analysis, 'unless it is different, the Tory party is nothing'. Thatcher was the saviour writers like him and the right of the party were looking for. Her detractors were incoherent misogynists according to this way of thinking. Mrs Thatcher was 'different', and 'all the arguments against her are made up of the most outworn and negative prejudices': she was a woman, her opponents would argue, 'she cannot do this, that or the other'; she would 'not get the men's votes', she would 'not get the women's vote etc., ad infinitum'.[30]

For the right of the Tory party, as expressed by the trenchant pen of Patrick Cosgrave, the problem for the Conservatives was simply one of definition and clarity of objective. It 'cannot be too often said that, until the party decides where it wants to go, and what it stands for, it is unlikely to get any votes at all'.[31]

Other editorial writers did not share this view. Most saw the Thatcher phenomenon as something not only novel but frightening. All seemed to agree that Mrs Thatcher would mark a radical departure from what had gone before, however ill defined that might be. For the London *Evening Standard*'s gossip column 'Londoner's Diary', Thatcher wanted 'to get back to Tory principles of encouraging individual enterprise and hard work'. It was a measure of the confusion about Tory principles that the paper implied that those principles had somehow been abandoned. According to this column, which represented a mainstream, slightly right-of-centre view, Thatcher seemed to be saying to the party, 'Let's fight as Tories. If we lose, let's lose at [sic] Tories.'[32]

Thatcher's appeal on the right was obvious enough. They felt that Heath had compromised too much. In his attempt to be 'all things to all men', he had reduced the party to an incoherent blancmange of opportunism and broken promises, with absolutely no strategic direction. Lord Coleraine, the son of the notably hardline Conservative Prime Minister Andrew Bonar Law, pointed out in a letter to the *Daily Telegraph* that 'the fatal weakening of the Conservative Party arose from the attempt to be all things to all men'. Coleraine, briefly an Education

Minister, now in his seventies, claimed that what was needed 'to appeal to the floating voters was the ability to inspire them with a sense of conviction'. Of course, in his view, Thatcher was the only candidate who could do this. Those of Coleraine's opinions would have enjoyed his citation of the opinion of Lord Salisbury, a traditional hero of the right wing of the party, who provided the classic argument for the 'core-vote strategy'. Salisbury had believed that the party 'would lose more by alarming its normal supporters than it would ever gain by bidding for the gratitude of those who were not'. Salisbury had also said, 'You may say that they cannot vote against you, but they won't vote for you, and they won't work for you, and you'll find it out at the polls.'[33]

As a rousing figure for the Tory right, Thatcher was clearly a godsend to the Labour party, which still had ambivalent attitudes to women in politics at all levels. The left-leaning *Daily Mirror* had reported that 'Labour leaders would like to see Mrs Thatcher not only mangle Heath on the first ballot but actually win the run-off. They believe she would be a certain winner at the Dispatch Box in the Commons. And an equally certain loser at the next election in the country.'[34] The idea that, as a woman, she could not be a credible contender for the highest office was something which dogged her campaign in the weeks before the first round of voting in the Tory leadership contest on 4 February. Her communication skills were also under scrutiny, with Woodrow Wyatt, a former Labour MP, now a newspaper column-ist and later a keen supporter, dismissing her in comparison with Mr Heath. Wyatt described as 'ludicrous' the idea that the Conservatives should make Thatcher leader on the grounds that Heath was 'too inhu-man to communicate'. Heath was, as far as Wyatt was concerned, 'a hot water geyser, compared with Mrs Thatcher's iceberg'.[35] Wyatt's article was even entitled 'Would you cry on her shoulder?', hinting implicitly that Thatcher's tough masculine style was not the warm, comforting support one might expect from a woman.

To what extent such criticism was made because of her gender is, of course, impossible to say. Commentators talked endlessly of her fighting qualities and her determination, but there still lingered doubts about her general appeal. As Wyatt was prepared to acknowledge, Thatcher was 'a very capable woman', who was 'tough' and who 'glories in fighting for beliefs'. The *Observer*, for which Wyatt was writing, made the same point in its editorial on 2 February, two days before the first round: despite Thatcher's 'high abilities' and 'the drive and determination she has shown throughout her political career', her leadership 'would make no sense'. Despite coming from a background similar to Ted Heath's, Thatcher had according to the left-wing *Observer* the 'unfortunate and probably unfair image of a gracious middle-class matron who lives remote from the dust and toil of industrial Britain'. She was a middle-class woman from the South-east, in short, who had no empathy for the industrial Midlands: that was the subtext of this patronising and, to twenty-first-century ears, slightly sexist judgement.[36]

Being seen as a Southern middle-class suburbanite and, perhaps more damagingly for the time, being a woman on top of it all were supposed impediments that Thatcher had to fight against in the course of the leadership campaign. Indeed, the extent to which commentators, largely from among her opponents, played up and even ridiculed her suburban housewife image was a major feature of the campaign. The origin of the snobbery that many journalists and politicians, of all political persuasions, felt towards the suburbs is somewhat inexplicable. Hugh Dalton, the Labour Chancellor of the Exchequer of the 1940s, had once boomed in the direction of a Conservative MP, 'What's that suburbanite looking at me for?'[37] Certainly such feelings of disdain were still strong in the mid-1970s. In the *Western Mail*, Nora Beloff gave a withering if typical assessment of Thatcher as she appeared in 1975 to so many of her outwardly more sophisticated contemporaries in the worlds of politics and journalism. Thatcher was simply 'a suburban wife whose genuine interest and expertise in Dresden china and old porcelain might be the sum total of her outside interests'. Again, it was noticeable how female journalists were often readier to stress elements of Thatcher's appearance than their male counterparts. Beloff, a fifty-six-year-old journalist, referred with a hint of envy to Thatcher's 'generally unruffled appearance, fresh complexion, fresh cheeks and meticulously waved and tinted blonde hair'. These somewhat irritatingly perfect features gave an 'outward impression of coldness'. They also gave the impression of a 'protected middle-class lady far removed from the hardships of working-class life'.[38]

As a woman with strong political beliefs and, her detractors would suggest, an underdeveloped sense of humour, Thatcher was easily ridiculed and underestimated. When Denis Healey in the House of Commons denounced her as 'La Pasionaria of Privilege' at the end of January 1975, the former Oxford classical scholar was cleverly pointing out two of Thatcher's weak points in one telling phrase. La Pasionaria, as many of the parliamentarians would know in 1975, was the vocal young woman who had roused the Republicans in their fight against General Franco during the Spanish Civil War of the late 1930s. The original La Pasionaria, the nickname given to one Dolores Ibárruri, had been a passionate champion of workers' rights and devoted supporter of left-wing causes. Thatcher, of course, was the opposite. She was, yes obviously, a woman, but she was also seen at the time as being very right wing.

Thatcher's response to Healey's jibe was sharp, direct and aggressive. It was not witty. 'Some Chancellors are macro-economic, some chancellors are fiscal but this one is just plain cheap.' It didn't match Healey for verbal flair; nor did her response reflect the international and historical range of the original comment. However, she gave the strong impression that she wasn't going to be pushed around by clever, older, more culturally sophisticated men.[39] By the time the leadership campaign was approaching a conclusion, at the end of January 1975, she had developed a tough exterior. As she proceeded, there was the inevitable 'stop Thatcher' campaign mounted by the Conservative party old guard.

Those who have observed Conservative leadership contests over the years will recognise the desperate urge that arises during the campaign to 'stop' a supposed front runner. Such campaigns are always framed in negative terms, to prevent a certain candidate from winning the prize and thereby, in the view of that candidate's detractors, making the party unelectable. In 1975, it was Margaret Thatcher's turn to suffer attack from the habitual nay-sayers who, without any constructive ideas themselves, have dedicated their energies to preventing another candidate who seems likely, for the time being, to prove victorious. It was on 24 January 1975 that a *Daily Mail* headline screamed, 'Top Tories in Stop Maggie Thatcher bid'. The true nature and seriousness of such a 'bid' can be questioned, but the newspaper confidently, if sensationally, reported that 'Mrs Margaret Thatcher's bid for the Tory leadership is gathering so much momentum that near panic has broken out among the party's top people.'

Without naming the 'top people', the report suggested that these shadowy grandees (another cliché of newspaper reporting about the Conservative party) were distinctly 'worried at the possibility of her beating Mr Edward Heath' in the first round. Only 'a coalition of the Tory left and the centre now seems capable of halting an extraordinary surge in popularity for the Tories' senior Lady'. The 'coalition of the Tory left and the centre' did not in fact stop Thatcher's advance, but the phrase clearly identified Thatcher as a right-winger.

This label and the fact that she was a woman, and implicitly an unknown quantity, were the two charges Thatcher constantly encountered during the campaign. It would seem that the charge of being a woman managed to get under her skin as the campaign wore on. 'Forget I'm a woman,' Margaret Thatcher exclaimed, as reported by the *Daily Express* on 1 February, the Saturday before the first round of the leadership contest. 'Forget the accusations that I am a Right-winger defending privilege. I had precious little privilege in my early days,' she protested.[40]

Despite not being overtly cerebral, she had by her side Sir Keith Joseph, a rather donnish, reflective and complex Jewish intellectual, as 'her personal think tank'. Her political philosophy was 'simple and trad', observed the *Economist* at the very beginning of February. Thatcher 'values ability, hard work and enterprise, and believes in individual liberty, thrift and application'. While believing in 'meritocracy she finds it hard to notice the claims of the non-meritocrats'. All this was written in the week before she became leader. Nothing in this description would have seemed odd or discordant to Mrs Thatcher or any of her supporters at any stage in her subsequent career. If Bismarck once described Napoleon III as a Sphinx without a riddle, Thatcher was even more simple, monolithic and unchanging than that bombastic, though ultimately bland, French emperor. Of all leading politicians in Britain in the twentieth century, she arguably developed the least and showed the least change over the course of her career.

The complexities of a Macmillan, the wanderings across parties of a Churchill, were something quite foreign to Thatcher's make-up. It is remarkable to what degree the lineaments of her character and her mature style, even after she had been Prime Minister for a decade, were observable in those early days of 1975, before she won the leadership of her party. You might even say that Thatcher was fully formed as a political character by the time she left Grantham for Oxford in the autumn of 1943.

Walter Bagehot – the celebrated editor of the *Economist* – once described Robert Peel as 'a man of common opinions and uncommon abilities'. This glib phrase is only partially correct in its application to Thatcher: her opinions, based on Methodism, a respect for law and order, and a passionate belief in liberty were simple, but not 'desperately common' in the Britain of 1975. Thatcher had stamina, a 'prodigious' appetite for work. She liked taking decisions and was clearly comfortable with power. She also had an instinctive sense of her supporters and her base. The *Economist* observed that 'Mr Macmillan's motto used to be "look out for your base".' This was an unusual motto for a man who would later be regarded as a patrician 'wet', a centrist who was guided only by pragmatism; Thatcher's motto seemed to the writers of the *Economist* to be 'look after your supporters'. This was at the heart of a phenomenon which was observed right to the end of her career. That was why 'she is so popular at Tory party conferences', among the grass roots of the party who tended to inhabit a provincial England far removed from London.[41]

The upshot of the contest was a shock defeat for Ted Heath on 4 February 1975. The first round was over, and the second would take place in the next week. In the meantime, despite the hints at plots revealed in the *Daily Mail*, the political world still reeled from the shock of Heath's defeat. He had been leader of the party for nearly ten years and, despite poor interpersonal skills and a mediocre election record, he projected authority and a certain managerial competence. In an editorial entitled 'Snow White and the Tory Dwarfs' published on 5 February, the morning after Heath's defeat, the *Daily Mirror* crudely asserted: 'suddenly Mrs Thatcher stands out among the Tory dwarfs like a life-size Snow White'.

Thatcher was a 'very tough Snow White', but she was essentially too right wing for popular support. The consequences of a Thatcher leadership were obvious for this left-leaning newspaper: 'If the Tories do make Mrs Thatcher their final choice – and it will take a very muscular dwarf to stop her now – they will commit themselves to a more right-wing image than they have had for years.' Despite his solidly working-class background – his father had been a carpenter and his mother a domestic servant – Heath projected the values and beliefs of the old patrician Tory ruling class. Thatcher, interestingly, in the superfine class distinctions which dominated British society for much of the twentieth century, was more lower-middle class than working class. Heath had needed an organ scholarship to get through Oxford, while Thatcher, though desperately hard up as a student, paid her own way, without any academic awards.

Thatcher would lead a 'narrow-based party', the *Mirror* continued, while her nearest rival William Whitelaw, a Cumbrian squire who had been educated at Winchester and Cambridge, represented a 'broader-based party'. The objection to Thatcher was all too familiar; she projected an image that would be 'dominatingly middle class'. Once again, it was held against her that she was 'suburban' and 'anti-union'. As usual, her geographical bias was held against her as well. The party, under her leadership, would be even 'more Southern English than it is now'. Yet, despite all these obvious failings, the paper acknowledged that her victory over Heath, by 130 votes to 119, had been an 'astonishing triumph'.[42]

As a consequence of this triumph, Thatcher now became a menacing figure. In an article which appeared the morning after Heath's humiliation, entitled 'The Iron Maiden', Marjorie Proops, an editorial writer on the *Daily Mirror*, warned Thatcher's opponents that 'she will not easily be deflected from her chosen course'. The phrase 'Iron Maiden', which never gained the popularity of the 'Iron Lady' bestowed upon her by the Soviets in 1976, reflected what many people thought about Thatcher. Those who 'send her up' – and there were, and would continue to be, many such people – 'about her hats and her hairdos, her well-stocked cupboard and the pinny-in-the-kitchen suburban personality she projects' would inevitably 'find themselves with egg on their faces'.[43]

Backbench Tory MPs were attracted by Thatcher's aggressive, combative style, as she herself put it, when interviewed on Granada Television's *World in Action* programme, shortly before the first round of the leadership contest: when asked why she thought MPs would vote for her, she replied, 'They know I don't flinch from attack. I can, and do, attack quite vigorously when it is needed.'[44] In an editorial piece the morning after Heath's defeat, the *Daily Telegraph* identified her weaknesses in the eyes of her opponents, namely that she was a woman, with a limited, 'suburban' appeal. Yet the newspaper praised her achievement. She had waged her campaign 'amid assurances that no woman could get to lead the Tory party', and she had been the victim of snobbish jibes about 'suburbia'. The suburban theme had been a strong current during the campaign, but her success was due to her combativeness and decisiveness. Above all, according to the *Telegraph*, 'almost alone among her party's present Front Bench she has shown the ability to prosecute coherent opposition to socialism'.[45]

In the second round of the contest, Thatcher obtained 146 votes, an improvement on the 130 she had gathered in the first round. This increase in support reflected more the perception that she was a winner than any fresh enthusiasm for her or for the causes she espoused. On the announcement of her victory, Thatcher gave a measured and cool press conference in the Grand Committee Room of the House of Commons, which is just adjacent to Westminster Hall. For this conference, she wore a 'magnificent black silk costume', showing the fascination with glamorous clothes which would later mark her period as Prime Minister.[46] She stressed that 'a good deal would have to be done in the economics sphere and in particular to win back the industrial areas of the Midlands'. Interestingly, Labour MPs were happy with her success. Thatcher was constantly accused of being an unelectable right-winger. Within an hour of her election as Conservative leader she had to deny these accusations, which had come 'not only from delighted Labour MPs, some of whom regard her election as guaranteeing a Labour government for years ahead, but also from some Conservative MPs, including moderates and some members of the old Harold Macmillan school'.[47]

Most Conservative MPs, however, were enthusiastic, given the confrontational style of the new leader. These MPs, by emphatically supporting Thatcher, felt that they had 'shown not only Mr. Heath but

also his closest supporters what they thought about the Heath administration'.[48] Many in the party simply wanted a change of direction.
There was also a feeling, naturally enough, that it was a remarkable
thing that had happened for a woman to be leading the Conservative
party, or any major party for that matter, in 1975. Of course the novelty
and progress represented by Thatcher being a woman was tempered
by the acknowledgement and even the fear that there was something
distinctly unsettling about her political views. The *Guardian* political
commentator Ian Aitken in a piece entitled 'First Lady will put the
Tories right', wrote that 'The Conservative party yesterday shut its
eyes, pinched its nose, and jumped into the deep end of the women's
liberation movement with an overwhelming vote of confidence for
Mrs Margaret Thatcher'. This, however, was a 'speculative step' which
would result in a 'distinct shift to the Right in the Party's centre of
gravity'.

Shirley Williams, the forty-five-year-old Labour Cabinet minister, made much the same point. She was 'pleased to see that in the
Tory Party of all parties a woman has now broken through'. It was,
Williams admitted, a 'staggering thing for them'. Williams's worry, if
the concern of a political opponent can be described in these terms,
was that it would mean taking the Tory party 'to the right', which
wouldn't be 'a good thing for the country'.[49] The Labour MP Joyce
Butler, a sixty-four-year old stalwart of the cooperative movement and
MP for Wood Green in London, was even more ecstatic. She viewed
Thatcher's success as 'absolutely splendid'. It was time 'we had women
in the top jobs'. Unlike many of her Labour colleagues, Butler was
not only 'very pleased about it', she thought it would give 'the Tories
a tremendous electoral advantage'. Another of Labour's eighteen
female MPs, Gwyneth Dunwoody, the member for Crewe, suggested
that Thatcher's triumph was a 'very interesting example of how men
have frequently under-estimated women's ability', while Renée Short,
Labour MP for Wolverhampton North East, was incredulous: 'Fancy

that, with all the male chauvinism in the Conservative Party. It is a staggering result and she has done very well.'[50]

As Leader of the Opposition, Thatcher projected the fighting, embattled character which, arguably, had won her the leadership of the Conservative party in the first place. She believed in her mission and would be strident in her statements. The impression she gave, however, was of someone trying very hard to engage with new ideas, but her intellectual rigidity did not make her attempts to be a philosopher politician very convincing. In a patronising editorial of July 1977, the *Economist* described her as 'Britain's very probably next prime minister' who in 'the past ten days' had attempted to cast herself as 'her Tory party's philosopher queen'. Thatcher, the magazine argued, was 'no Disraeli'. On the contrary, there was an impression 'that an awful lot of learning is being crammed rather dangerously quickly into that handsome fair head'.[51]

The grammar-school scholarship girl, cramming facts into her head, always desperate to try and do the right thing was, of course, a role which Thatcher continued to play, and one which journalists were always either mocking or observing with praise. Back in 1975, Marjorie Proops, the *Daily Mirror* writer, had observed that Thatcher was a woman who wanted to do the right thing. Both the journalist and Thatcher had attended a Jewish memorial service at Finchley in north-west London, the heart of Margaret Thatcher's parliamentary constituency. 'I hope you'll tell me', Thatcher whispered, 'exactly what I must do. When I should stand or sit. I do want to be careful not to make any mistakes.'[52]

Thatcher's appeal and strengths were obvious. Yet, throughout her period as Leader of the Opposition, there were doubts about her ability to appeal beyond a narrow base of Conservative support. She was shrill; she didn't listen; she was too ideological. She talked about 'freedom' as if it was something personal and simply defined. It was all so clear-cut and obvious in the basic, some would say crude, framework of her mind. 'Individual freedom' became almost a watchword for Thatcher in the months and years following her election to the Conservative leadership in February 1975. In that very month, before the election, Peregrine Worsthorne, a somewhat fogeyish journalist in his fifties, had identified this aspect of Thatcher's view. 'If Mrs Thatcher were elected leader,' he wrote, 'the party would become genuinely interested in the cause of individual freedom for the first time in its long history.'[53] Whatever the truth of that statement, there have been few candidates for the leadership of any political party about whom such a bold claim could be made.

In the meantime, of course, Thatcher had to convince the country and her party that she could be a prime minister. The evidence suggests that neither the country nor the Conservatives were particularly well disposed towards the Grantham grocer's daughter. Throughout the 1979 general election campaign, there were doubts about her 'extreme' personality, doubts which she was especially sensitive about. In deflecting such criticism, she often reverted to the Manichaean certainties of her world view. At the start of the campaign on 11 April, Thatcher spoke at length in her customary clear and uncompromising style to her constituency association in Finchley. The remarkable aspect of this speech was how trenchant and dogmatic it turned out to be. After a period in which the Labour government had tried to 'control every detail of our lives', Thatcher said that the answer was 'not an overnight return to what (a little unjustly) people call Victorian discipline. What we must return to is a simple belief that, when you have made all possible allowances for our misfortunes, every one of us has a choice between good and evil from which nothing can absolve us.'

'Good and evil'. Nothing could be simpler, and you didn't need an advanced degree in Theology to understand that the idea of absolution might have something to do with religion. It was no surprise that in her published election address to her constituents the same day, Thatcher yet again appealed to one of her favourite themes, the battle between good and evil, right and wrong: 'I want a Britain where children are taught that there is a real and absolute difference between right and wrong.'[54] The whole of her Finchley adoption speech on 11 April was drenched in Thatcherite certainties and commonplace observations. The address was suffused with the oratorical style of the pulpit, of Low Church sermons and copybook sayings. 'The state that tries to do everything ends by doing nothing well' was one. 'I want to live in a land of law and order' was another clear, if bland, statement of her priorities. The end of the speech showed a characteristic flash of aggression, which she adopted instinctively. 'I seek confrontation with no one. But I will always strenuously oppose those at home whose aim is to disrupt our society and paralyse our economy . . .' The enemy within – unruly unions, strikers, criminals – would be resisted, just as surely as 'those who threaten our nation and its allies with attack from abroad'. In this unusually wide-ranging adoption speech, Thatcher spoke of Lord Nuffield, the founder of Morris Motors, and pointed out that, although 'he may have become rich himself', he created a new and flourishing business that gave 'jobs and prosperity to thousands of people who would never had had them otherwise'. This was, in Thatcher's simple words, 'free enterprise in action'.[55]

The circumstances of the election were unusual. The Labour government had been brought down in March by a no-confidence vote in the House of Commons, though Prime Minister James Callaghan personally retained considerable affection among the wider public. Known as 'Sunny Jim', he was a popular, avuncular figure, respected for his geniality and warmth, but the reassuring personality he projected seemed to many a sign of complacency.

It was long remembered how, in January 1979, Callaghan had returned to a cold Britain after a week in the Caribbean, where he had attended the Guadeloupe summit meeting followed by a few days' rest in Barbados. The damaging headline from the *Sun* had been 'Crisis, what crisis?' What Callaghan had in fact said was the less memorable 'I don't think that other people in the world would share the view that there is mounting chaos.' Unfortunately for Callaghan, most people remembered the *Sun* headline.[56] For Thatcher and the Conservatives, memories of Labour's Winter of Discontent, when Britain came to a standstill and even the gravediggers went on strike, provided endless electoral ammunition. 'Who will forget the sick denied admission to hospital, the rubbish piled high in the streets and squares, the children locked out of their schools, the mourners unable to bury their dead?' Thatcher asked the suburban party faithful of Finchley. This image was not just a 'nightmare dreamed up by some wicked Conservative propagandist'. It was 'Labour Britain last winter', Thatcher proclaimed.[57]

In the course of the 1979 campaign, Thatcher was certain about the kind of politician she was. Which other party leader or presidential candidate, a mere two and a half weeks before the election itself, would compare herself to a preacher or to Old Testament prophets? 'The Old Testament prophets didn't go out into the highways saying, "Brothers, I want consensus." They said, "This is my faith and my vision! This is what I passionately believe!"' This rhetorical flourish was delivered in Cardiff, the Welsh capital. 'Mr Chairman, in politics I've learnt something that you in Wales are born knowing.' This was simply, 'if you've got a message, preach it!'[58] These words are justly famous and have been quoted by all Thatcher's biographers, but their significance in the story of religion in British politics has been underplayed. The language of 'preaching', 'Old Testament prophets', the certainties of 'faith and belief' came naturally from the Methodist lay preacher's daughter when speaking to an audience in Wales, a stronghold of Protestant nonconformity in Britain. Thatcher perhaps missed her true vocation when she entered politics; she was more naturally an evangelical preacher or missionary in her public style.

One feature of the 1979 campaign that would perhaps surprise later generations was the extent to which Thatcher's femininity was emphasised. This was something which the candidate herself was more than happy to play along with. Before the election campaign started in earnest, the *Sun*'s Katherine Hadley, in an interview entitled 'My Face, My Figure, My Diet', revealed Thatcher's rather mundane beauty tips. 'Margaret Thatcher runs herself like a machine.' The feature pointed out the inconsistency of treatment between male and female politicians. It was conscious of the implied sexist conventions of the age. In the late 1970s, nobody complained 'about the cut of Mr Callaghan's trousers', nobody 'tears him to pieces if he sounds like a pompous policeman'. But, the paper asked, 'who would want a dowdy female fatty for Prime Minister'?

Of course the implication was that Margaret Thatcher was no 'dowdy female fatty'. 'Never a doughnut passes her lips, never a sliver of delicious chocolate cake.' The surprising thing perhaps, given her subsequent no-nonsense reputation, was how open and cooperative Thatcher herself was in pandering to such trivialities. 'I have no special dietary regime of meals,' she insisted, 'I just try to eat little.' She added, 'Now and then I eat chocolates, but I find it hard to stop at one,' but the leader of the Conservative party confirmed that 'you can't indulge' in chocolate. 'It will sit on your hips.' The *Sun* feature, of 16 March 1979, about seven weeks before the general election, made the most of trying to portray Thatcher as an ordinary middle-aged woman struggling to maintain her figure and physical appearance. Thatcher 'says she weighs 9½ stone. Yet she is feminine enough to apologise, because it sounds heavy. Most women will know that 9½ stone is a jolly good weight for a woman of her height at 53.' Thatcher was described as '5ft 5in tall' and taking 'size 14 in dresses'.

Thatcher's recipe for the astounding energy she had always shown would perhaps have been less surprising to a generation brought up on wartime austerity: 'Keep yourself hungry and cold. "You're more alert if you've not had too much to eat and you're not too warm."' Thatcher frankly enjoyed being fifty-three. 'You have more mental stamina, more energy, than when you are younger.' The only problem was that 'you must be more figure-conscious. When I was your age, I could eat anything,' she said to the reporter. On being told that she looked 'so much prettier than five years ago' and that this could have been the effect of a face-lift, Thatcher denied that this was the case. She revealed that 'If you lower your chin while giving a speech then you look all double chins.' As a consequence, 'I have to remember to keep my head up all the time.' In a frank interview, Thatcher confessed that she often had 'a tiny whisky and soda, and I make it last a long time'.[59] Her femininity, one might almost say sex appeal, was something which she was never shy to use for political purposes.

Of course, Thatcher, despite one or two wobbles on the campaign trail, proved victorious on election day, 3 May 1979. The excitement about electing the first female Prime Minister in the Western world was something palpably felt on the streets around Whitehall and in Downing Street itself. Thatcher announced her arrival on the world stage with some embarrassing remarks, or so it was felt by some of her entourage, attributed to St Francis of Assisi. 'Where there is discord, may we bring harmony. Where there is error, may we bring truth. Where there is doubt, may we bring faith. And where there is despair, may we bring hope.' There is no evidence that St Francis ever used these words, but the simple dichotomies, the bald opposition between discord and harmony, error and truth, doubt and faith, fitted the Manichaean duality which lay at the core of Thatcher's world view and personality.

At 4.15 p.m. on Friday 4 May, Thatcher entered 10 Downing Street for the first time as Prime Minister. A crowd of more than 1,000 met her with the 'kind of hysterical exultation usually reserved for royalty'. On the same day, she characteristically said that she owed her success to her father, Alfred Roberts. 'I owe everything to my own father. He brought me up to believe in almost everything I believe in and on which I fought the campaign.'[60] The message was as clear as it could be. In Thatcher's own mind she had fought a campaign of which her father

would have been proud, which was straightforward and crystalline in
its certainty and clarity. For her, there had never been any doubt or
subterfuge about the kind of conviction politician she was.

'Mrs Thatcher evokes powerful devotion and equally powerful antipathy,' the *Guardian* editorial recognised on Saturday 5 May, two days
after the general election. 'After almost a full Parliament of dour, struggling Labour Government', Thatcher's Conservatives 'offered a policy
sea change. For the State read the individual.' The campaign may have
been characterised by 'all-embracing vagueness', but the direction was
at least clear.[61] Thatcher's naked appeal to nationalism was also apparent at the time. A Mrs Humphreys from Herne Bay in Kent, it was
reported in the same *Guardian* article, claimed to have four children
'who had all voted Conservative'. 'Mrs Thatcher will make Britain
great,' she said. 'We must have standards and we must have law and
order.'[62] This aspect of Thatcher's appeal, the stark nationalistic side
had, like so many things concerning Mrs Thatcher, been apparent from
the beginning, at least from her assumption of the leadership of the
Conservative party at the beginning of 1975. 'The history of England
from the sixteenth century to 1945 (or 1914?) was one of extraordinary continuing success, of a steady increase in power and glory. This
made the English into nationalists, but of a generally civilised kind,'
an editorial in the *Economist* declaimed in October 1975. Thatcher
appealed to such 'nationalist and patriotic sentiments', largely because
she shared them passionately. Such sentiments had traditionally been
centred on 'the pageants of crown and defender of the faith, then on
the gloriously expanding empire on which the sun never set, and then
on the knowledge that all sensible people recognised that anything
manufactured in Britain was best'. These feelings were 'in some sense
spiritual values'. They were 'larger than the individual and outside'. By
the 1970s, the people of Britain felt less self-assured. The main loss of
British self-confidence 'has not come through the transfer of empire to
commonwealth'. It had occurred because of the 'appearance of relative

impoverishment at home'.[63] It was just at the moment when British self-confidence seemed to have plumbed its lowest depths that Thatcher had emerged as a potential national leader, espousing Old Testament evangelical certainties and powerful narratives of national resurgence coupled with dogmatic simplicity.

Thatcher herself adopted the high-flown rhetoric of nationalist myth-making two days before the election itself. She was a preacher, national myth-maker and prophet rolled into one. In Bolton on 1 May, she openly adopted the mantle of Jeremiah, or one of the other Old Testament prophets with whom she sometimes identified: 'Unless we change our ways and our direction, our greatness as a nation will soon be a footnote in the history books, a distant memory of an offshore island lost in the mists of time – like Camelot remembered kindly for its noble past.'[64] Only Thatcher in recent history could, without any irony, appeal to the myth of King Arthur while employing the minatory language of an Old Testament prophet.

In the meantime, despite winning an impressive personal mandate, Thatcher had to construct a government. Her instincts may have been those of a 'conviction' politician, but she had to make do with the materials she had within the upper ranks of the Conservative party. Contrary to much vaunted ideas about the 'Thatcher Revolution', the upper echelons of the party remained a broad coalition. This was the substance from which Thatcher had to build her team. Eighteen of her twenty-two Cabinet ministers had been office-holders under Ted Heath.[65] Initially, from the point of view of the summer of 1979, Thatcher seemed to be fitting into the mould of traditional Conservative Prime Ministers, except for the obvious difference that she was a woman.

Indeed the aristocratic and gentlemanly air of her first Cabinet was a source of newspaper comment at the time. It seemed that the Lincolnshire grocer's daughter would be restrained by the squires and gentry who had been the traditional, hereditary rulers of the Conservative party for generations. 'Considering that Mrs Thatcher is supposed to head a radical, even revolutionary, government, the social background of her new Cabinet has an extraordinary dated air,' commented Simon Hoggart in the *Guardian* on 7 May, the Monday after her historic victory. Six of Thatcher's Cabinet had been educated at Eton, the proudest and most exclusive of public schools. Another three were products of Winchester College, while the rest 'with the sole exception of Mr John Biffen' had attended 'a variety of expensive schools rich in prestige'. The point about these men, and they were all men, was that they were landowners, barristers, men with City connections, mostly graduates of Oxford and Cambridge. In other words, 'in spite of two world wars and ceaseless social upheaval, the country is now being run by exactly the same people who were running it 100 years ago', observed Hoggart. The 'toffs are back in charge'.[66]

Despite the radicalism of the woman whom some on the left perhaps uncharitably called 'the Tsarina of Finchley', the view was that Thatcher's wildest excesses would be curbed and restrained by the traditional custodians of the Conservative party. There were dangers, however, that some on the left identified. The 'special danger in the size of the Tory triumph', observed one commentator, 'is that she will interpret it as a vote of confidence in her crude notions of self-help and capitalist freedom'. The left also saw her as an authoritarian figure who had boasted that she wouldn't 'waste time having internal arguments'. The 'Tsarina of Finchley' would undoubtedly, 'urged on by her Rasputin, Sir Keith Joseph', continue to press on with 'some of her more loony projects like abolishing the Price Commission' and pushing ahead with 'the promised anti-union legislation'. Thatcher to many on the left, even at the time she became Prime Minister, was an aberration. It was true that she 'clearly prides herself on being a politician of principle rather than compromise'. It was also likely, because of this, that she would persevere in her policies 'rather longer than Mr Heath after 1970'. Yet these policies would not prove popular, since the truth was that a 'broadly Social-Democratic view of the State and its duties is now firmly established in Britain'.[67]

It's important to remember that it was often her opponents on the left who never doubted the strong ideological conviction Thatcher always displayed. This is part of the reason she was so demonised. It was Harold Wilson, the former Labour Prime Minister, who identified this quality in his old sparring partner over the despatch box. As leader of the Labour party, Wilson himself had faced four Conservative leaders, Macmillan, Douglas-Home, Heath and Thatcher, but he was convinced that Thatcher was 'much more ideological than any Conservative leader I've ever known'. This seemed pretty uncontroversial, given the famously pragmatic character of Ted Heath's leadership and the languid, patrician ease of Macmillan and Douglas-Home. Wilson, himself a pragmatist, but one blessed with a sharp academic and analytical mind, identified the core of Thatcher's mental make-up. She was infused with 'both an intellectual and moral ideology. Her belief in free markets and free enterprise is social as well as intellectual.' Wilson also observed the 'strict moral upbringing whose existence depended upon hard work and private enterprise'.[68] These comments all appeared in a book published in 1980. Wilson in the first year of Thatcher's premiership had got to the essence of Margaret Thatcher. Her characteristics were obvious to anybody of Wilson's mental acuity, because she never really changed and, once in a position of authority within her party, she could never hide her visceral convictions.

One issue which put Thatcher outside the circle of her Cabinet was the question of capital punishment. Ever since the abolition of the death penalty for murder in 1965, the issue of capital punishment had been a controversial one in the Conservative party, as well as in the country at large. It quickly became a defining issue which placed any prospective parliamentary candidate in a particular category within the party, with candidates of the political right generally in support, while more moderate Conservatives consistently opposed it. Needless to say, a strong majority of Thatcher's Cabinet colleagues opposed the return to the death penalty which, by 1979, had already been abolished for fourteen years. In July that year, only two months after her election, the House of Commons once again debated whether to reintroduce it. 'It was an extraordinary moment in June [sic] when a solid phalanx of Cabinet heavyweights trooped into the capital punishment division lobby against her.'[69] Such grandees as William Whitelaw, Jim Prior, Francis Pym and even Geoffrey Howe, Thatcher's Chancellor of the Exchequer, opposed reintroducing this ultimate sanction of state power. Thatcher burnished her right-wing credentials by voting for its reintroduction. It was an extraordinary thing for a Prime Minister to oppose most of her Cabinet on such a fundamental issue of conscience.

For Thatcher, isolation from senior colleagues was not something to be avoided. She relished holding strong opinions, even if they conflicted with those of her senior colleagues. After the assassination of Airey Neave, her trusted parliamentary associate, by the IRA on 30 March, Thatcher was particularly bereft of close allies who might support her in power. Her relative isolation was something which was observed at the time. Described as the 'loneliest' Prime Minister since Attlee, Thatcher was 'a very solitary leader' who had 'no party base' and 'since the death of Airey Neave' she had been 'remarkable for the absence of any political confidant among those around her'. This may have been an exaggeration, but it is an indication of how informed opinion saw Thatcher's predicament in the first year of her premiership.[70]

Besides a natural isolation as the only woman in a Cabinet of men who had been educated at the most expensive schools in the land, Thatcher's dogmatism, her natural 'us and them', 'sheep and goats' mentality, intensified the alienation. Such dogmatic clarity was perhaps more suited to opposition than to government. Mrs Thatcher, it was often argued, had 'led the Tory party as a factional leader with more than an element of "he who is not with me is against me"'. By 1979, however, she was the leader of the whole nation. She was warned, in her new position, not to treat the 'large sections of the community against her' as 'enemies'.[71]

Adam Raphael, the *Observer* journalist, pointed out in her first year in Number 10 that 'Thatcher's views on race, social security, capital punishment and a whole range of other social issues' were 'distinct from those of her more aristocratic colleagues'.[72] Thatcher had infuriated elements of the left with her remarks about parts of Britain being 'rather swamped by people with a different culture' in an interview for Granada Television's *World in Action* in January 1978.[73]

As already noted, the world of the traditional Tory rulers involved membership of a range of gentlemen's clubs from which, as a woman, Thatcher was naturally excluded. This is an important but often casually overlooked feature of Thatcher's rule. She had no natural places to unwind, to pick up the gossip and share in-jokes with trusted confidants. In this respect she was similar to Ted Heath, her immediate predecessor as Tory leader, but Heath had served in the Second World War in the Royal Artillery where he had experienced a 'good war', in the conventional phrase, and had learnt at least some of the easy camaraderie which was an essential part of the Conservative politician's armoury in the immediate post-war period. Heath also famously enjoyed music, in which he was a skilled performer, and sailing, another of the interests he flaunted as Prime Minister. Despite his cold and abrupt manner, he had a range of friends from the arts, among other spheres. He inspired a degree of loyalty which, as yet, Thatcher had not been able to command. 'No praetorian guard has emerged of the calibre which surrounded Edward Heath or even Harold Wilson.' This claim can be made against any new leader, but it is reasonable to suppose that as a woman leader, in a House of Commons which in 1979 still had only nineteen female members out of 635 MPs, Thatcher's opportunities to form alliances in bars and clubs were limited. It was perhaps an irony that the Conservative election triumph that year, while bringing Britain's first female Prime Minister to office, had seen a significant reduction in the numbers of female MPs from twenty-seven to nineteen.

Sometimes politically isolated but resolutely sure of her own opinions, Thatcher's personality dominated commentary during that first year of her government. The view was very much that she had been reined in. As Peter Thorneycroft, the Conservative party Chairman, an Old Etonian who had been Harold Macmillan's Chancellor of the Exchequer, remarked, Thatcher had not 'wound up the social services' or 'abolished free education or done anything of that nature'.[74] Her domineering spirit and strident sense of purpose were obvious, but there were conflicting tensions within her government and arguably within her own mind. There was the marked contrast between 'the solitary intellectual iconoclast' and the 'more orthodox Tory pragmatist' right from the beginning of her period as Prime Minister.[75] Such tensions as existed within her government made her feel frustrated and impatient. Despite her frequent lapses into triumphalism, Thatcher was acutely conscious that she was on a kind of probation; in her first House of Commons speech as Prime Minister, she had described her election as a 'watershed', which had delivered a 'decisive result'.[76] Yet she also knew that as a woman she was a novelty, an experiment, who would be summarily dismissed by the traditional party men if anything went wrong.

Despite these constraints, Thatcher was the 'first person anywhere near the top of the Conservative party to acknowledge the existence of the new "radical right" and to produce a programme and political style that appealed to it', observed Hugh Stephenson, the *Times* journalist, in 1980. She knew that her appeal to the traditional leaders of the Conservative party was limited and as a result she carefully cultivated the party's backbenchers. Her relationship with the entire party was 'brittle' and her personal ratings, throughout her period as Leader of the Opposition, lagged behind the ratings of the Conservative party itself.[77]

Political isolation and perhaps a little insecurity about her position, alongside her own domineering personality and self-righteous conviction, led to a certain imperiousness in the Prime Minister. Her own position as the wife of a man who had sold his family paint business to Burmah Oil ensured that she did not have the money worries of many of her backbenchers who balked at her resolution not to increase MPs' pay in 1979.[78] On the whole, though, backbenchers saw her as approachable. It was senior colleagues who bore the brunt of her high-handed manner. In a rare moment of self-deprecating humour, she referred in public to her Foreign Secretary Peter Carrington and herself as 'sweet and sour', 'in that order'.[79] Many of her senior colleagues would have agreed with that assessment. She had 'a capacity for being extremely and gratuitously offensive to people in circumstances where they might otherwise be open to persuasion'.[80]

To civil servants, she sometimes appeared brusque and implacable. 'The relations between her and civil servants are characterized by the uncreative emotion of fear,' as one magazine put it.[81] Among senior mandarins there was consternation as their carefully prepared Cabinet minutes would be returned with 'rude prime ministerial scrawl all over them'. Thatcher was also in the habit of marking the work of senior officials as if they were school essays. She had little taste or regard for diplomacy and showed the same aggression as Prime Minister that she had shown in opposition. As one of her ministers ruefully expressed it, 'unlike her predecessors in Downing Street, she has no need of protection from her ministers; they need protection from her'.[82]

There was also a sense that the unease caused by her leadership stemmed from her own ideological convictions as much as from any doubts about her personal manner. Much of the trouble within the government, ministers freely admitted, stemmed from the fact that, 'for the first time since the war, the party is being led not from the left of its centre but from the right'. For some, Thatcher's credentials as an ideologue were an advantage. Lord Pannell, a Labour peer who would die in March 1980, less than a year after Margaret Thatcher entered Downing Street, had 'no doubt that she is the best leader [of the Conservative party] now because she brings a definitive sense of purpose and a certain hardness to the party'. This had been particularly obvious in her stand on immigration, a stand which Charles Pannell, 'as a lifelong Labour member', had resolutely opposed.[83] While Macmillan and Heath had both shown 'an instinctive sympathy for the Whitehall ethos of social democracy', the government was now being run by 'someone who, while she defers to the bureaucracy organisationally, is wholly out of sympathy with that ethos'.[84]

Friends, Foes and the '81 Budget

Wednesday 11 March 1981 – The scene was the Mansion House, the traditional home of the Lord Mayor of London, a fine eighteenth-century Palladian building at the heart of the City of London. Thatcher was on the offensive. The budget delivered by her Chancellor of the Exchequer, Geoffrey Howe, had been widely reported and denounced.

The criticism directed at the budget was that it was harsh and restrictive. Thatcher was trying to cut spending and many felt she had been over-zealous in this attempt. 'Now what really gets me is this,' she declared, sounding an unusually colloquial note, at the *Guardian* Young Businessman of the Year Awards. The people 'who are most critical of the extra tax are those who were most vociferous in demanding the extra expenditures'. Thatcher was staking her ground as a balanced-budget right-winger. She was quite willing to raise taxes in order to reduce borrowing. As for her opponents, she could scarcely conceal her contempt. 'And I wish some of them had a bit more guts and courage than they have.' One of 'the most immoral things you can do is to pose as the moral politician demanding more for health, for education, more for industry, more housing, more for everything', and then say, 'No, I didn't mean you to pay tax to pay for it, I meant you to borrow more . . .' So when people said it was a 'no-hope Budget', Thatcher could only say to them, 'this Budget is the only hope for Britain's sustained and genuine revival'.[1] The language of revival and renewal tripped easily off Thatcher's tongue.

The budget itself had been delivered naturally enough by Sir Geoffrey Howe, a proud and quiet man, who seemed emollient but hid a pronounced stubbornness. A barrister, Howe seemed to relish the difficulties of his job as Chancellor of the Exchequer, which he held from 1979 to 1983. Like his boss, Margaret Thatcher, he enjoyed the battle, though his style was duller and less explosive. Of a similar age to Thatcher – Howe was fifty-four in March 1981 – he had served as Solicitor General under Heath as well as holding junior ministerial office.

Thatcher and Howe, in their later published reminiscences of the 1981 budget, both claimed responsibility for it. To them it was a success, a proof of the government's toughness and consistency, in the face of seemingly overpowering odds. Howe proudly, and perhaps a little pompously, declared that 1981 was 'the year that witnessed the birth of my most controversial Budget', which he felt had been 'harsh' but 'comparatively straightforward'.[2] He was in an aggressive mood on the day of the budget itself, when his announcement that the government would not seek to boost demand by borrowing and spending money was met with 'groans of despair from the Opposition'. His speech lasted an hour and a half and was delivered in his dry, lawyerly manner. It was observed that his own backbenchers 'sat in fairly glum silence' throughout his performance.[3] 'A change of course now would be fatal,' the Chancellor insisted. These were words which no doubt reflected his own dogmatic and assertive character as much as they reflected the personality of the Prime Minister. 'Just boosting demand would do nothing' to solve the nation's difficulties. Like all Chancellors when faced with bad domestic news, Howe attempted to tie Britain's economic problems to wider world events, the 'world recession' as he called it.

Although the 1981 budget has attracted lots of attention in the memoirs of Thatcher, Howe, Lawson, John Hoskyns (one of Thatcher's principal advisers) and others, its immediate context is often forgotten. Even though Thatcher and her friends portrayed themselves as being steadfast and principled in their determination to stick to their plans, the budget itself had followed a major U-turn.

It was at the end of February 1981 that Thatcher's government had retreated in the face of opposition from the redoubtable NUM, the National Union of Mineworkers. One of Thatcher's informal advisers, John Sparrow, a tough merchant banker at Morgan Grenfell, wrote directly to Thatcher on 20 February 1981, a mere two and a half weeks before the budget: 'You will be aware of the disappointment and, in some places, bitterness that have been caused by Wednesday's decision to retreat in the face of the NUM.' Sparrow, originally an accountant, was one of the people outside the government machine that Thatcher so often liked to consult. Despite being head of the government, her approach remained that of an outsider, always eager to question establishment orthodoxies and searching for external justification to vindicate her opinions.

Sparrow sent weekly letters to Margaret Thatcher throughout her early years as Prime Minister. Appeasing the miners, in his view, was like paying the 'Danegeld' without getting rid of the Danes. Doing a deal with them was 'a severe setback not merely for economic and social policy, but also for your support in the country at large'. Such a letter two weeks before a controversial budget could not have done much to raise Thatcher's morale. Sparrow and his friends in the City, among other people working in the private sector in 1981, were certain that they saw 'a pattern in which the public sector is cushioned against the consequences both of its own follies and the harsh facts of life'. This is a common complaint among private sector businessmen, although, as recent economic events have shown, they are as welcoming of government support in difficult times as any other workers in the economy.[4]

The 'harsh facts of life' had led to the standoff between the government and the miners in February 1981. To Norman Fowler, one of the grammar-school-educated politicians Thatcher trusted, the government was 'badly locked in a dispute with the National Union of Mineworkers'. This had arisen because the National Coal Board, the public body which operated the mines after nationalisation in 1946, wanted to close uneconomic pits. The prospect of a miners' strike early in 1981 was something which Mrs Thatcher's government simply could not countenance. On Wednesday 18 February, David Howell, the youthful Energy Minister, was forced to withdraw the threat of pit closures, after two hours of crisis talks in Whitehall which involved union leaders as well as senior civil servants. The negotiations themselves had been brought forward a few days at the behest of the government.[5] The next morning, Cabinet ministers woke up to a 'dreadful press' accusing the government of 'ignominious surrender'.[6]

Private sector industrialists had mixed feelings. Businessmen were happy that a miners' strike had been avoided. They were concerned, as John Sparrow of course had suggested, that the public sector was once again being treated with indulgence. The miners had gained a total victory. The union leaders wanted the government to reduce coal imports, and the government agreed to reduce them from eight million to five and a half million tonnes over the next year. The miners also demanded more money for the Coal Board, which now struggled after subsidies had been withdrawn by the government in the 1980 Coal Industry Act. The NCB, as a consequence of the Thatcher government's capitulation, dropped the programme of twenty-three pit closures it had announced on 10 February.

The U-turn occurred only four months after Thatcher had famously told the party conference in October, 'You turn if you want to. The lady's not for turning.' Conservative backbenchers were concerned. She described the retreat, without any apparent irony, as 'swift and decisive'. Michael Foot, the Labour leader, mockingly congratulated the beleaguered Prime Minister. What had occurred was 'a great victory for the miners and the nation', he said.[7] Thatcher's equivocations in the House of Commons inspired admiration among some journalists. 'All the talents of Harry Houdini, the great contortionist and escapologist, were being attributed to the Prime Minister.' The government was 'changing the script in the middle of the play'.[8] But Thatcherites were dismayed by the 'sell-out' to the miners. Michael Foot even suggested that he might ask her to dinner by way of celebration.

Against this background, the March budget would always be a trial of strength. In Thatcher's recollection it was a great example of staying the course, of bold, determined leadership. Needless to say, the story of the government's capitulation to the miners the previous month is barely mentioned in her own account of the early months of 1981 in *The Downing Street Years*. The budget acquired a mythical status among Thatcher's most loyal supporters.

The state of the economy in 1981 ensured that any budget of that year would be a highly significant event. Thatcher had made the fight against inflation the centrepiece of her economic strategy. In February 1980, in typically strident and assertive language, she had declared that her 'first priority is to restore sound money and conquer infla-tion'.[9] Inflation in Britain had been over 20 per cent in the mid-1970s and was still over 10 per cent in 1981. The phrase 'conquer inflation' was characteristically Thatcherite in its hint of military, even spiritual, triumphalism. According to one economist with centre-left leanings, a major theme of Thatcher's first three years as Prime Minister was the 'economic and political price the government risked' in order to bring down the rate of inflation.[10] With her dogmatic certainties and self-confidence, Thatcher was determined not to be deflected from the goal of sound money.

About the origins of the budget itself there have been many accounts, allocating blame and praise either to Thatcher and her team of irregular auxiliary advisers, such as Alan Walters and John Hoskyns, or to Geoffrey Howe and his team at the Treasury. In many ways the final responsibility for the character of the budget is irrelevant, since it was Thatcher who was most identified with it and who, it was widely known, had made mastery of the economic brief a central part of her definition as Prime Minister. British Prime Ministers, though techni-cally First Lords of the Treasury, had taken different approaches to their involvement in the formulation and execution of economic policy. Of her predecessors, Churchill, Sir Anthony Eden and Alec Douglas-Home had adopted a somewhat leisurely approach to economic affairs, not really interesting themselves in the minutiae of fiscal policy. Heath, with his technocratic attitude and zest for efficiency, had been more involved in economic management.

Of all Conservative Prime Ministers, Thatcher was perhaps the most obsessed with economic matters. After the budget, she was the most prominent target of press criticism. It was her leadership that was at stake, a fact of which she was only too conscious. The relationship between Margaret Thatcher and Geoffrey Howe was close, but Thatcher often liked to assert her seniority by reminding Howe that she was the First Lord of the Treasury. Howe's approach to Thatcher at this time was likened to that of the 'good country solicitor doing his best for an important client'.[11] This was perhaps unfair, but no one could doubt in whose hands ultimate power lay.

Geoffrey Howe delivered the budget to the House of Commons on Tuesday 10 March, beginning his statement a little past 3.30 in the afternoon. One of his opening remarks could easily have been made by Thatcher herself. The 'economic well-being of the nation owes more . . . to the spirit and vitality of its people than to any single act of government'.[12] The main problem the budget sought to address was the government's borrowing. In the favoured jargon of the time, the PSBR, or the Public Sector Borrowing Requirement, was too large. As Howe said, 'borrowing as much as £14 billion would be irresponsible'. The PSBR was the term used for the deficit. The Chancellor said he had concluded that 'it would be right to provide for a PSBR in 1981–82 of some £10½ billion'. This was 'a little more than 4 per cent of the Gross Domestic Product'. By way of comparison, this figure was 6.6 per cent in 2013–14.

The magical figure of £10.5 billion has entered into the minor mythology of Thatcherism. Thatcher's advisers John Hoskyns and Alan Walters claimed that it was only on their insistence that this 'tough'

figure was finally agreed to. Thatcher herself claimed credit for enforc-
ing this. In her memoirs, she claimed that as late as 24 February Howe
still envisaged a PSBR for 1981–2 of £11.25 billion. She suggested that
she was prepared to accept a penny increase in the standard rate of tax
in order to raise more money to reduce borrowing. It was only if the
PSBR was reduced to 'around £10.5 billion' that it would be possible to
cut interest rates.[13] There was no doubt that Thatcher's kitchen cabinet
of informal economic advisers were pressing for a more severe reduction in the government's borrowing target. Tim Lankester, Thatcher's
Private Secretary, in a note written on 11 February, described Walters as
saying that the 'markets would be disappointed by a PSBR of £11bn', a
low figure the Chancellor believed was unattainable. The PSBR forecast
for 1981–2 had now risen to £13½ to £13¾ billion.[14] Howe simply did
not believe that it 'would be politically possible to adopt a more stringent approach than he had outlined'.

Lankester's account supports the Walters and Hoskyns view that they
backed even more stringent plans than the Chancellor himself. Walters
believed that any kind of softness or half-hearted measures could lead to
'a funding crisis either in the summer or the autumn'.[15] 'Funding crisis'
essentially meant that investors, or 'the market', would stop buying
British government debt, thereby requiring the introduction of some
form of bail-out by the International Monetary Fund (IMF), which
would be a national humiliation. Walters revelled in more severe measures. In a remarkable note to the Prime Minister, dated 20 February,
only two days after the government's rather humiliating climbdown on
the pit closures, he and Hoskyns observed that it was of course easy for
them 'to prescribe a tough budget, when we don't personally have the
responsibility of presenting it'.

The Walters and Hoskyns note also made explicit the connection
between the surrender to the miners' demands and the need for toughness in the coming budget. The note indicated that this connection
was something which had come from the mind of Margaret Thatcher

herself: 'As you have already suggested, the withdrawal of the pit closure plan will inevitably affect the Budget.' The capitulation to the miners could be 'one of the pegs on which to hang a tougher Budget'. The budget could be 'a perfect opportunity – the opposite of a U turn – for the government to reassert authority and regain control of events'.[16]

Alan Walters, Thatcher's principal economic adviser, was a brilliant but difficult man. He had been drafted in by Thatcher to fight her battle against establishment economic orthodoxy, which was broadly Keynesian in so far as it advocated a dynamic role for government to 'manage demand' by borrowing in bad times to prop up the economy. Of course, this was exactly what Thatcher wanted to avoid. Instinctively arguments which required the government to borrow more money seemed to her perverse and self-indulgent. She always thought of the economy in moralistic terms. Walters himself came from a background with which Thatcher identified. He was a self-made man to the extent that he had been born in a working-class district of Leicester, the son of a grocer. He was only about eight months younger than Thatcher herself. Unlike Thatcher, the young Walters had left school at fifteen and found work as a machine operator in a shoe factory. Walters's story, which saw him rise in the world from being a machine operator to becoming a respected economist with an international reputation, represented exactly the kind of upward mobility that the Prime Minister revered.

Walters had been recruited by Mrs Thatcher in 1980, on secondment from Johns Hopkins University, for a two-year stint. He was known for his sharp mind and his disorganised desk, which has been described as 'a chaotic jumble of paper which looked as if a waste-paper basket had been emptied on it'. Undismayed by this apparent disorder in his working habits, Walters possessed a coffee mug inscribed 'Quiet – genius at work', which no doubt accurately reflected his own estimation of his talents. Later he came to believe that he had almost single-handedly persuaded the Prime Minister to stick to a much tougher line in the budget than the Treasury and her Chancellor, Sir Geoffrey Howe, had originally intended.

Walters would later recall that his intervention had led to a charged scene, a few days before the delivery of the budget, in which he spoke to the Prime Minister harshly: 'You are going to Hell and quickly too, and you will be finished.' He claimed that Thatcher's Private Secretary rang him a few hours later to tell him that the Prime Minister had accepted his advice and had ordered Howe to redraft his budget. Naturally enough, Howe remembered no such last-minute intervention, nor any such determination on the part of the Prime Minister to overrule him. In his recollection, the 1981 budget was 'the product of calm deliberation'.[17] Walters would prove a controversial figure throughout his time at Margaret Thatcher's side. He eventually proved too much for her second Chancellor of the Exchequer, Nigel Lawson, who resigned in 1989, citing Walters's undue influence on the Prime Minister, which made it impossible for Lawson to continue doing his job. Walters himself was also forced to resign.

His role and that of John Hoskyns, a self-made computer millionaire, pointed to a characteristic feature of Thatcher's leadership style. She loved to surround herself with maverick thinkers, people who were sceptical of orthodoxies and supremely self-confident in their own abilities to question establishment assumptions. Hoskyns had joined the Army straight after Winchester, without going to university. He then enjoyed a short career at IBM, which he left in 1964, while still in his mid-thirties, to set up his own company. He was very like Thatcher in many of his personal traits. Direct, opinionated and self-assured, he had the determination and clarity of focus often exhibited by his boss. When Thatcher offered him a job in the Prime Minister's Policy Unit, his first words were: 'I'm not here for the beer. When I'm finished I'll go.' Hoskyns's stature as a maverick allowed him a certain latitude when it came to criticising the Prime Minister directly and, sometimes, in unflattering terms.

He was obsessed with the key problems of 'excessive public spending, inflation and trade union power'.[18] Like Walters, he remembered putting pressure on a reluctant Prime Minister and Treasury to be more aggressive in the 1981 budget. He recalled writing a joint resignation note, along with Walters, in case his stringent recommendations were not followed. 'We believe the time has now come for your Number Ten advisers to disband and leave Whitehall. The opportunity to turn the UK economy round, presented by the May 1979 mandate, has passed.' The Hoskyns note was bleakly downbeat: 'The best that can happen now is that the Tories win the next election on the back of Labour's disarray and the UK decline continues in relative terms.'[19]

Five days before the budget, Hoskyns had a dinner at the Centre for Policy Studies, a Thatcherite think tank established in 1974, with Alan Walters and two relatively staunchly Thatcherite MPs, Cecil Parkinson and Norman Lamont. Unprompted, the two MPs launched into an attack on the softness of the government, particularly in regard to the surrender to the miners in February. They were 'appalled' by the state of the government and by 'the all piss and wind mood about Margaret'. There was an air, among some of Thatcher's right-wing supporters, of defeat and resignation. But a week before the budget was due to be delivered, Hoskyns believed that 'we had won the argument, that the Budget was designed to cut the PSBR by £3.5bn'.[20]

The central theme of Howe's budget was the 'fight against inflation': 'If we are to stay on course for lower inflation and lower interest rates, we must borrow less.' In his firm, monotonous voice he asserted that 'Some harsh decisions are inescapable.' The provisions of the budget surprised, even shocked, many in the House of Commons on both the Opposition and government benches. Howe introduced a new oil company tax – the Supplementary Petroleum Duty – at a rate of 20 per cent on the total value of oil and gas produced.[21] A 2.5 per cent tax on bank deposits was expected to raise £400 million.

The Labour Opposition was unusually energetic in its hostility. Michael Foot launched a formidable attack on Howe in the budget debate. The budget, he proclaimed, was a 'no-hope Budget by a no-hope Chancellor'. It would 'only inflict the most serious injury on our country over the year to come'. In a prophetic, and uncannily accurate, statement, he declared that Howe's statement was 'a Budget to produce three million unemployed'. Foot was passionate in his denunciation of Howe's refusal to expand the economy in a time of recession. The Chancellor was 'embarking once again on deflation on a massive scale'.²²

Foot by 1981 was himself an embattled and ageing political leader. Already sixty-seven at the time of the budget, he was a romantic socialist and literary man, who relished debate in the House of Commons, but did not really take to leadership of a major political party. The budget, however, offered him the opportunity to indulge his penchant for the knock-about debating style he had perfected in his days as President of the Oxford Union in the early 1930s. Foot's shadow Chancellor, Peter Shore, was another who had the rather casual, academic manner culti-vated at Oxford and Cambridge universities. In his reply to the Tory budget, Shore lacerated Howe with becoming sarcasm. 'May I offer a word of congratulation?' he asked mischievously. 'After two years of increasing divisiveness in Britain', the Chancellor had succeeded in drawing together 'all the disparate elements of the nation – unions and managers, TUC and CBI, taxpayers, housewives, pensioners, those who smoke and newspapers as varied in style if not in ownership as The Times and The Sun'. All these various groups had been brought together 'in a great collective spirit of total hostility' to what the Chancellor had done.²³ In an able speech, Shore launched a broad critique of Thatcher's economic management. Indirect taxes, principally VAT, would rise, as would taxes on beer and cigarettes, which had a disproportionate effect on those 'with the smallest incomes of all', principally 'the elderly, the sick and the increasing number of unemployed'.

Shore blamed 'Thatcherism', already by 1981 a clearly defined concept, at least in the minds of the Prime Minister's detractors. The increase in unemployment was a consequence of the 'blinkered and aggressive monetarism' to which Britain had been subjected since May 1979. Shore launched a frontal attack on the principal Thatcherite strategy, the continuing fight against inflation whatever the cost. 'Inflation has been the prime target. It has been squeezed, but employment and production have been nearly throttled.'[24]

This debate exposed the differences between Thatcher's approach to economic policy and those of her predecessors. Thatcher had made the fight against inflation her principal target. Neither Heath nor Macmillan, neither Callaghan nor Wilson, had made the battle against inflation into such a titanic, almost moral, mission. They were all pragmatic men of goodwill who wished to keep the social fabric of the nation together. Shore and Foot both grasped the nature of Thatcherism, in its stark ideological purity, in its crusading zeal and in the crude way – in the eyes of men of more pragmatic stripe – that it reduced problems to binary simplicities. Shore absolutely understood the nature of Thatcher's ambition. In this Commons debate he actually quoted Thatcher's speech at St Lawrence Jewry, which had been delivered the previous week.

'To her inflation is an evil. It is morally debilitating,' Shore told the packed chamber. 'In her words, she puts the demise of inflation "at the top of my list of economic priorities. It is in my view, a moral issue not just an economic one."' Neither Thatcher nor any of her ideologically committed supporters would have disagreed with this part of Shore's argument. In his view, Thatcher thought of unemployment as a 'difficulty', a 'problem', but not as an evil. This might have seemed like semantic logic-chopping, but the difference was clear. The Prime Minister had 'got it the wrong way round'. Inflation was the 'problem', while unemployment was 'evil and immoral'.[25]

Like Foot, Peter Shore was a cerebral, even other-worldly figure. Unlike his leader, however, Shore was not adept at the cut and thrust of the House of Commons debating style. His mop of blond-white hair made him seem boyish and perhaps a little insubstantial, though his intellectual self-confidence was high. 'He firmly believed that the world recession [of the late 1970s] could be cured through a combination of socialist and Keynesian techniques . . .'[26] Like so many of the political establishment in both the Conservative and Labour parties, he subscribed almost religiously to the expansionist orthodoxy of the post-war years.

Shore's observation that a range of diverse bodies stood opposed to Thatcher's economic policies was, of course, broadly correct. For the *Financial Times*, the budget was 'an admission of defeat', but it conceded that 'the painful fiscal decisions' had been 'necessary' because the government had lost control of public spending in its first two years. In the *Guardian*, Francis Cripps and Wynne Godley, Cambridge-based academic economists of left-wing sympathies, denounced the 'severely disinflationary budget' which would cause a hyper-slump such as the country 'had never seen before'.[27] On Thursday 12 March, two days after the budget, *The Times* reported that hostility to it 'swept upon the Government from almost all sides of the nation yesterday'. Both the Trades Union Congress (TUC) and the Confederation of British Industry (CBI) deplored the Chancellor's failure 'to give decisive encouragement to industrial expansion'.[28]

In the ensuing days and weeks, there was a chorus of denunciation directed against the budget but, encouragingly for Thatcher, there were signs of support among sections of the popular press. This was exactly the kind of division under which Thatcher thrived. She no doubt would have been thrilled by the *Sun* headline, perhaps auspiciously published on Friday the 13th, 'Be Tougher, Maggie', over an editorial which decried the government's 'only relatively minor cuts in state spending'. Thatcher, in the view of Rupert Murdoch's *Sun*, 'MUST do what her own sound instincts tell her is right'.[29]

The support of the *Sun* at this crucial time was a measure of Thatcher's success in rallying a section of the still influential print media to her side. She inspired loyalty and needed unflinching support against the barrage of criticism and hostility she often faced. 'Our faith in her is unshaken,' the *Sun* proudly asserted at the end of the editorial. 'She has been too patient for too long' was the paper's rather bizarre conclusion.

Sustained by her own sense of righteous duty, excited by the prospect of fighting and defeating a range of enemies, Thatcher seemed to gain a new sense of purpose, a clarity which inspired her own confidence in her mission. The *Economist*, which in its 140 years had never been a friend to socialism, described Howe's statement as a 'Budget with few friends'. Its 'apparent severity' had 'shocked his political supporters and friends'. The reaction of industry, according to the highly prestigious weekly, had been 'instantaneous and furious', while the budget itself had provided 'a tonic for the dispirited Labour parliamentary party'. The CBI's President, the now forgotten Sir Raymond Pennock, denounced the budget in vivid terms. It was 'at best a brush-off, at worst a kick in the teeth'.

Pennock was a man with whom Thatcher should perhaps have had an instinctive sympathy – he was later described as 'a remarkably smooth operator whose deft touch combined with tenacity and guts took him from grammar school to the top of British industry and ultimately into the House of Lords'.[30] Yet he had spent more than thirty years with ICI, at the time Britain's largest industrial company, an enterprise which represented all the lazy corporatism which Thatcher's entourage loathed and believed to be at the root of Britain's post-war economic malaise. Pennock's manner had no doubt been polished by an Oxford degree and a wartime stint in the Royal Artillery, where he had fought a good war, earning a mention in despatches in 1945. Such a career was of course very different from that of the maverick entrepreneurs and academics, like John Hoskyns and Alan Walters, with whom Thatcher liked to surround herself.

Among the opponents of the budget, none were more intellectually respectable, and none were subsequently more reviled among Thatcher's circle, than the 364 economists who signed a letter, published in *The*

Times on 30 March 1981. Nigel Lawson, a junior Treasury minister, gently mocked these academics in his 1,100-page account of his political career, *The View from No. 11*. In Lawson's happy memory, the timing of the letter was 'exquisite', since the British economy 'embarked on a prolonged phase of vigorous growth almost from the moment the letter was published'.[31] The economists themselves were earnest and sincere and comprised virtually the whole academic establishment in the field of economics. A feature, not often mentioned, of this famous letter was that it was organised at Cambridge University, the academic, some might even say spiritual, home of John Maynard Keynes, whose name was inextricably associated not only with his university but with the post-war consensus Thatcher believed herself to be in the process of overthrowing. The Cambridge slant of the letter was remarked on at the time, with one official describing the list of signatories as 'predictable, with a heavy Cambridge bias'.[32]

The Cambridge letter had its origins in the week of the budget itself. On Friday 13 March, the same day as the positive *Sun* editorial, a letter entitled 'Dear Colleague' was sent with the high-sounding letterhead 'Faculty of Economics and Politics – University of Cambridge'. The initial letter, which aimed to be a rallying cry for the economics profession across the country in their fight against Thatcher's policies, was signed by two academics, Frank Hahn and Robert Neild, both respected Keynesians. Hahn and Neild's letter to colleagues was rather disingenuous in stating that 'a large number of economists in British universities, whatever their politics, think the Government's present economic policies to be wrong'. It was time that economists 'all spoke'. Of course, while it may have been true that an overwhelming majority of academic economists were strongly against Thatcher's economic policies, the phrase 'whatever their politics' seemed to stretch things a little too far.

The letter was a deliberate attempt to engage as many academics as possible in a statement which flatly contradicted the basis of government policy. It was an unprecedented exercise in academic futility. The scheme was carefully planned, however. The instigators of the letter wrote that they were sending the letter 'to one senior member in each British university'. The plan was 'to circulate the statement with the list of signatories within ten days'.[33]

The actual letter which appeared in *The Times* was a vintage exercise in academic pomposity, couched in jargon-laden, robotic-sounding prose: 'There is no basis in economic theory or supporting evidence for the Government's belief that by deflating demand they will bring inflation permanently under control and thereby introduce an automatic recovery in output and employment.' Furthermore, Thatcher's policies would 'deepen the depression, erode the industrial base of our economy and threaten its social and political stability'. The Thatcherites themselves had great fun at the expense of the economists, and the 364 economists became part of the mythology of Thatcherism, even adding to the thin volume of jokes spawned by Mrs Thatcher's policies, as Howe memorably described an economist as 'a man who knows 364 ways of making love – but who doesn't know any women'.[34]

There was also disaffection with her economic strategy within Thatcher's own party. On the morning of the budget, three members of the Cabinet – Peter Walker, Jim Prior and Ian Gilmour – met for breakfast. They were self-consciously critical of Thatcher and her gang. They would become known as 'wets', a sobriquet whose precise origin was unknown, but was thought to derive from public-school slang. Thatcher herself enjoyed the term. It appealed to her binary cast of mind, her love of sharply opposing contrasts. She herself defined the term 'wet' in a footnote in the second volume of her exhaustive memoirs, *The Downing Street Years*. For someone not known for her interest in semantics or etymology, her definition is noteworthy. '"Wet" is a public schoolboy term meaning "feeble" or "timid", as in "he is so wet you could shoot snipe off him".'[35] Thatcher's glee in defining the term 'wet' in this way was characteristic of her self-image. Indeed, in the recollection of one of the 'wets' themselves it was she who was 'responsible for pinning this name on to her opponents'.[36] Labelling opponents was something that came easily to Thatcher.

The breakfast that the 'wets' had organised, by contrast, was characterised by timidness and indecision. Jim Prior, the Employment Secretary, a bluff Suffolk farmer with a patrician attitude to politics, remembered how the three Cabinet ministers at that breakfast 'tried to decide what action we could take'. Of course, they did nothing, although Prior 'came very close to resigning'. The helplessness of the 'wets' was a feature of the year. Prior even later admitted that 'a year or so later' he 'regretted very much that I hadn't [resigned]', but, luckily for his immediate career, he felt that 'the resignations of the three of us would not have made much mark'.[37] Gilmour expressed similar regrets at his own lack of resolve in the face of the 1981 budget. He asked himself, 'Why then had I not resigned instead of patiently waiting to be sacked?' The agonised self-questioning of some of the 'wets' showed the extent to which they partially felt, in their hearts, that they had not risen to the level of events. Gilmour later claimed that resigning would have been 'the right thing to do' and it would have made him feel 'much better', but he justified his decision to stay, only a few sentences later, with the phrase, 'just to give up the fight and depart would have been craven'. The confusion in Gilmour's own testimony only reveals the agony of indecision he clearly experienced during this difficult period.[38]

Unlike Thatcher, Gilmour and Prior were not particularly known for their fortitude or resolution. They were naturally men of consensus and compromise. The shrill certainties of Margaret Thatcher's intellectual style were alien to them. Over the next few weeks, they wrestled with their consciences while deciding to stay within a government whose leader they fundamentally opposed both ideologically and temperamentally. There was never any doubt that Thatcher's stance in the 1981 budget was an ideological one, deriving from different premises from those which had underpinned the Keynesian consensus. In her own words, years later, she described the views of her opponents in scathing, somewhat sarcastic terms: 'for those who had not heard that Keynes was dead, the prospect of reducing expenditure and curbing borrowing as we and the world sank into recession was undoubtedly alarming'. In a dismissive phrase she recalled that the 'wets' and others 'put up a hundred and one reasons why any particular cut was out of the question'.[39]

The Cabinet dissensions were public and obvious. During budget week, the print media made great play of the fight within Thatcher's Cabinet and the palpable differences of ideology. It was clear that despite her firmly held, even dogmatic, views Thatcher was prepared to tolerate far more open dissent than would normally be the case in British Cabinets. Conflict, confrontation and vigorous debate were all hallmarks of her leadership style. She relished intellectual combat – provided, of course, that she prevailed. The *Sun* on Friday 13 March, three days after the budget, remarked that Margaret Thatcher 'faced open revolt last night from the Cabinet over the Budget', suggesting that the recriminations continued a while after its delivery. The newspaper recalled how 'Startled Ministers first heard the Budget secrets at 10.30 on Tuesday morning', barely five hours before the statement in the House of Commons.[40]

A number of other senior figures were also concerned about the budget's political and economic impact. Francis Pym, Lord Carrington and Lord Soames were described as 'clearly uneasy', while Mark Carlisle, the Education Secretary, and George Younger, the Secretary of State for Scotland, 'expressed their reservations'.[41] The significant feature of these Cabinet dissensions was, of course, their public nature and the widespread coverage they received in the press. As Prior himself put it, Thatcher's Cabinet 'must have been the most divided Conservative Cabinet ever'.[42] Cabinet disunity, presided over by an ideologically committed and ruthlessly determined leader, became a prominent theme of the newspaper coverage. As Bernard Ingham, Thatcher's loyal press officer, bluntly stated, the day after the budget, 'not all your Cabinet Ministers are behind you'.[43]

Such an open revolt on a central plank of government policy among such high-ranking members of the government was largely 'unknown' in British politics.[44] This dissension at the very highest levels of her government helped to define Thatcher's leadership. The notion of internal dissenters, the 'enemy within', played an important role in her dualistic vision of leadership. Probably in her eyes, and certainly in the view of many of her most ardent supporters, the 'real enemy' were not the 'divided and derided Socialists' who were weak in the country at large, but the 'flat-footed Heathites in her own Party and within her Government'.[45]

The 'wets' themselves had been wrong-footed and shocked by Thatcher's determination and her resolve to break the post-war Keynesian consensus. To her, such a break was necessary; Keynes, a notoriously quick-witted, unconventional secular thinker with a bohemian private life, was everything Thatcher was not. His flashy academic prowess was also something which was alien to Thatcher's rather plodding, even if fastidiously accurate, fact-based mental processes. In a cry of despair, the 'wets' came up with the somewhat extraordinary suggestion that budgets should be decided in Cabinet, effectively by some sort of committee. Bernard Ingham informed Thatcher that Francis Pym, the Leader of the House of Commons, had 'rather deftly applied public pressure for a pre-Budget discussion in Cabinet of economic strategy' during a press conference on the Thursday after the budget.

Division, opposition and conflict were features of the political debate within the Conservative party, not just within the Cabinet. On the floor of the House, the Conservative critics of Mrs Thatcher were equally outspoken during the debate. Most prominent of these was Peter Tapsell, an MP with City connections, a fifty-one-year old former Treasurer of the Oxford Union, who worked at the respected stockbrokers James Capel. Observing the conventions of parliamentary debate, Tapsell denounced Geoffrey Howe's budget as 'economically illiterate' and 'fundamentally wrong in concept and frequently maladroit in detail'. Tapsell, in Howe's recollection, had resigned from the front-bench Treasury team 'without any really convincing explanation, in December 1978'.[46]

One particular object of backbench concern was the 'decision to slap 20p on petrol', particularly among those MPs representing rural constituencies. The backlash was such that journalists were speculating that 'Sir Geoffrey will have to go – and that a rattled Premier will have to try new policies to keep her Government afloat'.[47] The Chancellor's position was also a target for Peter Tapsell, who stated that 'Sir Geoffrey Howe has now lost the confidence of broad sections of the City, of industry and of the Conservative parliamentary party.' Tapsell appealed to Thatcher's patriotism. 'She owes it to the country and to the Conservative Party to find a Chancellor of the Exchequer who will command confidence and offer hope.' This was particularly disingenuous because Tapsell would have known how dominant Thatcher herself was in the formulation of economic policy, and how closely associated with those policies she personally was.

Some members of the Conservative party were even less reserved privately than Peter Tapsell in his bold call for Sir Geoffrey Howe's removal. There were dark hints and rumours that Thatcher's own position was precarious and that she would be ousted by a cabal of establishment figures, the proverbial 'men in grey suits' of later political imagery. John Hoskyns, writing on 19 March, nine days after the delivery of the 1981 budget, referred to a conversation that had taken place between him and Ronnie Millar, a former playwright and actor now employed as a speechwriter for Margaret Thatcher. Millar continued to be worried 'about the way Margaret had lost or allowed the departure of so many supporters', people like Richard Ryder and

Gordon Reece, personal confidants who had gone on to pursue new opportunities. Millar reported a conversation which took place in the US and which had been recounted by Reece, Thatcher's advertising guru. Henry Kissinger, the former Secretary of State, had apparently claimed that his friends in the British Cabinet had said Thatcher would be 'out within a year'. This was all highly circumstantial, dinner-party chat, without any corroborating evidence, but it was indicative of the febrile atmosphere that surrounded the Prime Minister at that time. It is unclear who Kissinger's friends were in the British Cabinet, though it is known that he had some contact with Peter Carrington, the Foreign Secretary.

A rather paranoid atmosphere began to develop around a number of Thatcher's intimate circle. On Friday 20 March Hoskyns and Millar visited 10 Downing Street where they met Thatcher and Ian Gow, her Parliamentary Private Secretary. Gordon Reece came later, when Thatcher had departed, and reported that he had warned her to 'be prepared, in June or July, for Macmillan, Thorneycroft and [Edward] du Cann to tell her to stand down'.[48] Millar was the kind of outsider, with an unusual background, that Thatcher liked to cultivate. She enjoyed mavericks who could think for themselves. Although educated at an independent school and Cambridge, he had enjoyed an unusual career in entertainment, far from politics or the law. He had also spent four years as a screenwriter in Hollywood, which added a certain confidence to his speechwriting. Millar was six years older than the Prime Minister and his varied experience of life, as actor, writer and Royal Navy reservist during the Second World War, gave him a breadth which many political speechwriters notably lacked. Thatcher eventually awarded him the ultimate accolade by describing him as a 'real believer in our whole philosophy'.[49]

Thatcher remained embattled and seemed to enjoy the challenges posed by some of her Cabinet colleagues and her party. The petrol-duty increase of 20p, which had caused such unease among her backbenchers, when more than thirty Tory MPs had rebelled on a motion in the budget, remained firmly in place. She simply told MPs that there was 'no question of abandoning the 20p increase'. In the actual vote, eight Tory MPs voted with the Opposition, while twenty-five abstained. As well as rejecting the idea of a compromise on the petrol-tax increase, Thatcher flatly rejected the idea that there should be pre-budget discussions round the Cabinet table. She told Michael Foot, the Labour leader, 'Budget statements are never discussed in Cabinet.' She could not remember in all her time in Cabinet a budget which was 'discussed by Ministers before being presented'. An observer of this interchange might have remembered that Mrs Thatcher had been in Cabinet for little more than three and a half years before becoming party leader, but this consideration perhaps did not blunt the force of her argument. Yet there still remained the criticisms within her Cabinet and the wider party. Mrs Thatcher, in the view of the *Financial Times*, could ignore her senior colleagues only if she was 'very powerful'. Yet at that moment Thatcher was 'not all that powerful'.[50]

Thatcher's seeming lack of power emboldened her critics to strike a note of caution in a public way. Norman St John Stevas, the former Arts Minister who had been sacked only two months previously, claimed, as centrists always do, that the Conservatives 'could not win the next election without a modification of policies'. St John Stevas, a cultured, flamboyant figure, predicted 'a change in the autumn'.[51] Meanwhile Peter Walker, one of the three 'wets' in the Cabinet who had met for breakfast on the day of the budget, openly challenged the Prime Minister, more than a week and a half after the budget had been delivered. On 23 March, he addressed the Tory Reform Group, a body of Conservatives who stressed the one-nation, more conciliatory traditions within the party. Expressing 'his determination to re-establish the Conservative Party in the middle ground of British politics', Walker emphasised that it was 'essential that the Government faced up to the mounting problems of unemployment'.[52]

Thatcher, of course, was an expert at fighting fire with fire. At the conference of the Conservative Central Council, a group of the party faithful held in Cardiff, the Prime Minister communed with her core supporters in the City Hall. The City Hall had been commissioned in 1897, the year of Queen Victoria's Diamond Jubilee, and opened in October 1906. The Italianate, robustly built structure, with its marble statues representing fallen, ancient Welsh heroes and kings, seemed an appropriate setting for Thatcher's display of resolve. The 500 at the two-day meeting were the 'super-faithful', the 'chairmen of all the local parties and their agents and women's group chairmen'. For these people, Thatcher was still their 'lode star'. While MPs at the end of March were still 'muttering about the possibility of her having to go', the party 'super-faithful', the grassroots support, remained 'rock solid'.[53] The activists were impressed by Thatcher's 'guts and determination'. She was not only full of determination and vigour, she seemed physically uplifted and full of energy. 'Her eyes glittered straight into camera, in the way she has when she is determined to get her message across to the wider television audience.'[54]

It was entirely expected that Thatcher should resort to her preacher instincts in her final rousing peroration. Earlier in her homily, she had railed, as was her wont, against inflation, which 'never tires', which 'works while we rest' and 'eats away while we argue'. She described inflation as like 'the ivy on the tree' which destroyed the 'thing on which it feeds'. She left her most extravagant rhetoric to the end. In words which, consciously or unconsciously, echoed Martin Luther's purported statement to the Diet of Worms in 1521, 'Here I stand, I can do no other,' Thatcher gave some indication of the lonely path she felt bound to tread. 'This is the road I am resolved to follow. This is the path I must go.' In language of even greater scriptural authority, Thatcher said, 'I ask all who have the spirit – the bold, the steadfast and the young in heart – to stand and join with me as we go forward. For there is no other company in which I would travel.'[55] It did not take a theologian to note the biblical, and strictly nonconformist, imagery and language of her final entreaty. This appeal to the road which must be travelled, the image of the solitary wayfarer gathering committed followers along the way, was, in unadulterated form, the language of English nonconformism, the imagery of the Wesleys and John Bunyan.

The dogged appeal to inner conviction was what had helped win Thatcher the leadership of her party in the first place. It was this quality which had been a hallmark of her leadership, which would define that leadership up until its last moment. There was naturally a sense of old-fashioned chivalry, some might even call it sexism, surrounding responses to Thatcher among her political colleagues on the government benches in the House of Commons. Only a couple of days after the budget, 100 Conservative MPs had already signed a Commons motion congratulating the Chancellor on 'a bold package of measures designed to stimulate investment in small and medium-sized businesses'. These MPs included senior figures from the backbenchers' 1922 Committee such as Edward du Cann, its slick Chairman, Sir John Eden, a former government minister under Ted Heath and nephew of the former Conservative Prime Minister, and Maurice Macmillan, a Cabinet minister under Ted Heath, who was the son of Harold Macmillan. That the political heirs of Macmillan and Eden supported Thatcher in this crisis was an indication that the difference between 'wets' and 'drys', old Tory patricians and Thatcherite radicals, was not clear-cut.[56] Macmillan and Eden had been Conservative Prime Ministers of the old school; they had fought in the First World War, having been educated at Eton and Oxford. Thatcher was a different political creature, but she did command support from many of the Tory pragmatists who valued loyalty but also were eager for change.

In the City, Michael Richardson, a celebrated deal-maker with impeccable establishment credentials, and a senior banker at Cazenove and then a director at Rothschilds, urged Thatcher's team to take 'no notice of the silly noises in the press'. The view of Richardson and some of his friends in the more traditional recesses of the City was that had the budget not been 'as tough' as it was, the government would have been heading for 'early disaster'.[57] Richardson, who later made a lot of money for Rothschilds when that bank led many of the privatisations under Thatcher's government, was not a member of the Prime Minister's most intimate circle, but he was a keen supporter who benefited from his closeness to Thatcher and her ideals.

Thatcher's leadership style clearly fostered inner circles and secret cabals of loyalists, from which many felt themselves excluded. There is a sense in which all political leaders form close groups whom they rely upon for support and encouragement. For Thatcher, this tendency almost became a principle in itself. Jim Prior spoke with an air of surprise and bitterness about her intimates. 'Even before 1981 she had one small group who met her for breakfast and which was kept very hush-hush.' This, in Prior's ironic phrase, was a 'cosy arrangement', which was 'later superseded by her close relationship with Cecil Parkinson'. The little group, in which Thatcher confided, included Norman Tebbit and Nigel Lawson, both of whom were not at this stage even in the Cabinet, but it was entirely in Thatcher's character to cultivate junior ministers, with whom she often felt greater affinity, instead of more senior members of her government.[58] Lawson himself admitted that Thatcher frequently asked him 'to see her about something that had cropped up' which was 'distinctly unusual for a Minister who was not even in the Cabinet'.[59]

Despite the support from Thatcher's close-knit followers, the wider public reception of the budget was not encouraging. A Gallup poll, reported in the *Daily Telegraph* on 19 March, looked into public reactions and concluded that the 1981 budget was the 'most unpopular for 30 years'. The poll found that only 24 per cent of the electorate thought that Sir Geoffrey Howe was doing 'a good job as Chancellor'. The previous all-time low figure in response to the same question had been in 1961, when Selwyn Lloyd had held the office. Now 61 per cent of the electorate thought that Howe was doing 'a bad job', a higher figure than the previous record on that measure, which had been held by Denis Healey in the aftermath of his 1977 budget. Only 22 per cent thought the budget was 'fair'; 73 per cent felt the budget was 'unfair'. By contrast, Selwyn Lloyd's budget of 1961, which had attained the previous lowest score on 'fairness', had been judged 'fair' by 33 per cent of the electorate.

The budget entered Thatcherite mythology, not least because it fostered an image which Thatcher had of herself, and which observant commentators had also noticed. 'Mrs Thatcher is emerging from her second year of office as one of the most extraordinary leaders in modern politics,' asserted the *Economist* on 21 March 1981. This was a highly unusual thing to say of a prime minister who had spent less than two years in the job. The image of the leader carrying on with her programme no matter what the circumstances, regardless of public opinion, was beginning to form in the minds of many commentators. 'Her country is in deep recession. Her Cabinet is not so much divided as bewildered. Her once adoring backbenchers are either mutinous or glum.' Yet none of these things seemed to deter her.

Reliant on a small cadre of intimate advisers and devoted followers, Thatcher seemed to be genuinely oblivious to public opinion. It is important to remember that this judgement was not something arrived at, with the confidence of hindsight, after her successive election victories. It was something which was picked up at the time, when it seemed unlikely that she would survive even a single term as Prime Minister. Thatcher had been 'speaking out against almost every traditional Tory interest', continued the *Economist* editorial of 21 March, 'private industry, the City, the counties, the universities, the senior civil service, the defence establishment'. This may have been an exaggeration, but the sentiment captured the general mood of widespread opposition, among traditional Tories, to Thatcherite radicalism. 'Yet she seems impervious to it all.' Compared to her contemporaries on the world stage, Thatcher appeared sublimely self-confident. 'There is none of the inelegant scrabbling for friends of a President Carter or the Olympian retreat of a Giscard d'Estaing.'

To the more faint-hearted among her supporters, Thatcher seemed 'intent only on the senseless self-sacrifice of Tennyson's Light Brigade heroes'. 'And they can only plead: "But Madam, cavalry do not charge guns."' It was interesting to observe that those very qualities which now alienated many were the traits which had won her support in the first place. 'The overriding weakness of Mrs Thatcher's critics is that charging guns was precisely what they selected her to do.' There had never been any subterfuge or dissimulation about the Thatcher project. As was clear to an anonymous journalist, writing in the *Economist* towards the end of March 1981, the 'government was elected in 1979 above all else to roll back the frontiers of the public sector, to leave resources free for private-sector expansion. The key to this strategy lay in reducing public spending and borrowing, to bring down taxes and interest rates.' The beauty of it all was that Thatcher, in her guileless way, had made no attempt really to disguise what she was about.

The seeming severity of the 1981 budget was a direct consequence of Thatcher's perception that she had failed, or was failing, in her own terms. The capitulation to the miners in February had instilled within her a determination to succeed and to be resolute. This was clear to people at the time. The budget was 'a necessary political act, coming after the concessions to the car, steel and coal industries last winter'.[60] In a sense the budget was a form of redemption for Thatcher, still guilt-ridden about the earlier weaknesses she had shown. Such resolve did not mean she was not pragmatic. The budget, doctrinaire though it seemed to many, was an atonement for earlier pragmatic compromises she had already made.

The budget revealed many striking aspects of Thatcher's leadership. None was more paradoxical than her seeming ability to be the opposition to her own government. It was almost as though she was an 'opponent in office'. 'Mrs Thatcher was made leader of the Tory Party in opposition to the policies of Mr Edward Heath. She was then elected prime minister in opposition to the tired corporatism of the Wilson/Callaghan Labour party.' Opposition was 'in her blood'. The natural result of all this 'opposition' was an 'aggression' that had 'always been part of her political appeal, even in government'.

Unlike her more emollient predecessors among Tory Prime Ministers, Thatcher had 'resolutely' stuck to her opposition habits as Prime Minister. While Macmillan had taken with aplomb and style to what he called the 'Rolls-Royce of Number 10', Thatcher had proved herself a more volatile and unpredictable driver. 'She wrenches the steering wheel from side to side, trying to drive single-handedly a machine that wants to go the other way.' Thatcher in this pose was accused of 'neither listening nor leaning on the help of others'. This was not quite true, since she had that well-entrenched cabal of confidants, but from the point of view of the establishment, the party grandees and senior civil servants within the machinery of government, it seemed like a fair characterisation. The path upon which she had set herself suggested a remarkable degree of self-confidence. 'Her self-assurance even in defeat remains a considerable political asset.' This was undoubtedly true. As those words were being written for the *Economist* editorial, the fate of Thatcher and her Chancellor, Sir Geoffrey Howe, remained uncertain. Howe's critics were 'once again demanding his – and even the prime minister's – removal'.[61] The future seemed doubtful.

Civil War on the Left

Thursday 26 March 1981 – At 9 a.m. the whole of the world's press, it seemed, were gathered at the Connaught Rooms in Holborn, a district of central London. The rooms were decked out in pastel shades and stylish, if neutral, furniture. This press conference was filled by journalists, wide-eyed with anticipation. Shirley Williams, a former Labour politician, had just arrived. 'Just as we had been promised: history in the making. Before our very eyes a press conference involving Mrs Shirley Williams started only two minutes late.'[1] Shirley Williams was known for her lack of punctuality.

Opening speeches at this historic press conference were specially manufactured for a TV age. The speeches were 'short, pleasant and platitudinous'.[2] Designed by professionals, and executed with commendable precision, the launch of the SDP on 26 March was an undoubted success. The SDP, or the Social Democratic Party to give its full name, was a creation of the charged days of 1981. To many of its founders, the press conference that marked the launch of the party was a 'brilliant success, planned and stage-managed with great energy'.[3] More than 500 of the world's press were present. The main commercial television news outlet, ITN, devoted all but two minutes of its twenty-five-minute news programme at one o'clock to the launch of this new party. At the end of a frenetic day, Mike Thomas, the thirty-six-year-old former Labour MP for Newcastle East, who had been in charge both of the communications and of the party's launch, estimated that the SDP had attracted more than £15 million of free publicity.[4]

The 26 March press conference was a triumphantly successful media event. The new party had, rather unconventionally, four leaders, who all shared the limelight. Alongside Shirley Williams, there was Bill Rodgers, a thoughtful former Labour minister who was probably the least well known of the three. The two others, prominent though they were, were despised by many of their former colleagues in the Labour party which they had so recently left. David Owen was, in the eyes of many, the spoilt darling of the Labour party, Foreign Secretary at thirty-eight, who had ruthlessly betrayed the party which had given him the glittering prizes of high ministerial office at an age at which many ambitious people are entering the House of Commons for the first time.

Roy Jenkins by 1981 was a politician whose best days, it must be admitted, were well behind him. He had returned from Brussels, where he had served as a successful European Commissioner of the European Economic Community (EEC), to a Britain which was far removed from the civilised atmosphere of consensus politics that had prevailed throughout his career. An effective though controversial Labour Home Secretary, and then Chancellor of the Exchequer, under Harold Wilson, Jenkins was a respected figure. He was famous, even admired, as much for his fun-loving lifestyle, his literary flair and his appreciation of the finer things in life, claret and long lunches, as for his actual political achievements, though these were considerable. He was probably the best known of the four, because of his long standing in the public eye, having been an MP as early as 1948. He was also the most politically distinguished of the Gang of Four, having held two of the senior offices in Westminster politics.

Williams was, however, the best liked. She was earnest and passionate. Many people thought she was unlucky to lose her Hertford and Stevenage seat in the House of Commons in the May 1979 general election. She was also more left wing than the others, advocating the abolition of private schools, while Jenkins and Owen stressed even at the otherwise harmonious launch of the party that they did not think it was right to 'forbid private education by law'.[5] On this issue, Williams was 'outnumbered three to one in the Gang of Four in her belief that private education should be abolished'.[6] With her slightly dishevelled hair and her good nature, Williams seemed to many the conscience of the new party; she certainly exuded more keenly than anyone the ideal-ism and aspiration of their new approach.

Jenkins saw himself as a philosopher, or at least as a thinker, who always sought abstract justifications for the creation of the Social Democratic party. He was by nature an establishment figure, whose love of the good life had infuriated his more sober-minded colleagues within the Labour party. 'He liked good wine, good food, good talk, good books and fiercely competitive croquet – and he did not care who knew it.'[7] In his imagination, the SDP would be a civilised, rather anodyne centre-left party which would avoid the hard dogmas of Mrs Thatcher and the rigid doctrines of the quasi-Marxist left within the Labour party. At the press conference on 26 March, Jenkins placed the Social Democrats at the centre of British politics; the new party 'did not agree with the government's approach to the economy, but neither did it believe in an irresponsible approach to public finance'.[8]

In Jenkins's view, British politics during his absence at the European Commission between 1977 and 1981 had become polarised and lacked the sophistication on which he prided himself. Soon after arriving in Brussels in January 1977, he had told his aide and ally David Marquand that he 'dreamed of the House of Commons every night'.[9] Speaking of his mental anguish in the 1979 BBC Dimbleby Lecture, Jenkins appealed idealistically to a 'radical centre' which would save Britain from the 'sterilities of left and right'.[10] The speech made a significant impact.

Although the creation of the SDP was often presented as a split on the left, the figure of Margaret Thatcher loomed impressively behind the newly created party. At the press conference of 26 March, Shirley Williams had spoken of the significance of the new party which for 'the first time in Britain since the war' would break 'from the major interest groups'. Jenkins had spoken just as grandiosely about the launch of the party being 'the biggest break in the pattern of British politics for at least 60 years and two generations'. The founding fathers of this new political enterprise were not just offering 'another party, another player in the old party game'. They wanted to 'get away from the politics of outdated dogmatism and class confrontation'.[11] Jenkins famously said that he hoped to 'break the mould' of British politics.

The mould, however, had already been broken by Thatcher herself. According to *Claret and Chips*, a history of the founding of the Social Democratic party published in 1982, only a year after its launch, it was Thatcher who had shifted the argument. 'From the start it became a cliché that the party was "breaking the mould of British politics".'[12] The origin of this phrase is obscure, but Roy Jenkins had used it in 'a speech in the early 1970s'. The SDP liked the phrase so much that the press release issued on the morning of the party's launch claimed that 'the mould of British politics has visibly cracked'.[13] Yet the 'essential break in the mould of recent British politics was not made by the SDP, but by Mrs Thatcher'. The 'shape of post-war British politics', so it seemed to the journalist Hugh Stephenson, author of *Claret and Chips*, had been 'a continuous search by both the main political parties for a broad consensus and enough support in the middle ground to ensure electoral victories'. Thatcher had, of course, overturned these old certainties. The 1979 general election had 'presented the electorate with a novel situation'. James Callaghan, the incumbent Prime Minister, had 'offered himself as a Baldwin-like leader'. The impression Callaghan attempted to promote was that, 'so long as the government was in his hands, nothing much would change and no dangerous experiments would be tried'.[14]

Thatcher had memorably declared, barely three months before the May 1979 election itself, 'I'm not a consensus politician, or a pragmatic politician. I am a conviction politician'. To Hugh Stephenson, the implication of the Thatcher remark was clear. She had come to the view that 'successive British governments (including those of which she had been a member) were bankrupt'. In presenting herself in this way, she had chosen 'deliberately to flout the conventions of the post-war two-party system'. She appreciated that she was taking a 'substantial risk in thus breaking out of the conventional mould'. This was 'a risk that she took willingly'.

It became customary to believe that Thatcher had started out as Prime Minister as a moderate, even emollient figure, and became more radical as she grew in confidence during her premiership. This picture is largely false. Contemporary accounts repeatedly say, even in that first term, how different she was, how radical her utterances were, and how upsetting much of her quasi-revolutionary fervour was to various elements of the political establishment on both the left and the right. The birth of the SDP was evidence of this disquiet. The Social Democrats not only despaired of the left turn which their old colleagues within the Labour party had taken, but they put themselves forward as a humane alternative to the rigidities of Thatcherism.

For her part, Thatcher was somewhat bemused by the SDP. She liked definition, clarity and sharp dividing lines. For her, the SDP was another piece of obfuscation which would simply cloud political debate. Asked by the *South Wales Echo* about the 'huge popularity' of the SDP in the polls, Thatcher somewhat dogmatically asserted, as politicians often do, that the 'only poll that really matters is a General Election'. She also expressed her confusion about precisely what it was that the SDP stood for. 'It is hard for me, just as it is for the ordinary voter, to criticise in detail a Political Party that does not have a defined set of policies.' In so far as they had a record, Thatcher felt confident to lump them with the socialists she so clearly felt she understood and whom she enjoyed fighting. On their record, the SDP were a 'group of Socialist dissenters, who have acquiesced in the past in policies of extravagance and nationalisation'.

It was interesting that Thatcher put the SDP members' purported support for 'nationalisation' on the charge sheet she had mentally prepared for them. In her interview with the South Wales paper at the end of March 1981, she resolutely blamed 'nationalisation', the state control of industry, for the economic and employment woes of South Wales, before dismissing the Social Democrats as just another kind of socialist. 'People in South Wales are only too aware of how nationalisation has failed to sustain jobs and the creation of wealth.' More emphatically, she stated, 'No, I cannot believe that the answer to our problems lies either in the creeping Socialism of the Social Democrats – or in the extreme Socialism which is now official Labour policy.'[15]

The phrase 'creeping socialism' revealed Thatcher's contempt for the SDP. For her, honesty and clarity of political views were a mark of sincerity. To her, the Social Democrats were essentially socialists who simply did not have the courage of their convictions. For Thatcherites, the Social Democrats were woolly, imprecise, idealistic and wholly naive about the reality of modern politics; for their supporters, social democracy offered a third way, between Thatcherism and the left-wing Labour party. The mutual incomprehension that existed between Thatcher and her supporters on the one hand and the founders of the new party on the other was revealed fully at a lunch hosted by Rupert Murdoch, the media baron and recent acquirer of *The Times* newspaper, on Friday 20 March 1981, just six days before the launch of the SDP.

Murdoch had acquired *The Times* and *Sunday Times* in January 1981, having already bought the *Sun* in the early 1970s. Thatcher was an appealing character to the Australian newspaperman. She had challenged orthodoxies and fought entrenched interests. This was very much how Murdoch saw his own approach. He had let it be known to his friends and acolytes in journalism that the SDP's 'whole operation' was a 'lot of crap'. In the general discussion, Jenkins launched an attack on Thatcher's government. Murdoch sat quietly, seemingly unimpressed. 'All four of them' were 'very buoyant', although Rodgers, in line with his less well-established public image, seemed 'less so than the others'. Shirley Williams and David Owen insisted to Murdoch that they were not centrists. They were 'democratic socialists', they protested. There was clearly a tension in what they said. They favoured a wealth tax, while Jenkins, a genuine man of the centre, who even entitled his auto-biography *A Life at the Centre*, argued against such a tax. Williams stressed the appeal of the new party to the young, the under-forties, tired of the old politics. Murdoch sat silently, then interjected, 'You sound exactly like the Callaghan government in your general line.'

The SDP founders did not see themselves in this way. The lunch with Murdoch was a fiasco. The press mogul merely observed afterwards that his main impression of the lunch was 'of four people who hated each other's guts'.[16] This was probably a little wide of the mark, but there were tensions which would later spill over into quasi-feuds and seemingly irrecoverable breaches of friendship and trust. Meanwhile, the SDP founders saw themselves almost as evangelical figures, preach-ing a gospel of hope to a distracted and bitterly divided land. After the press conference of 26 March, which lasted an hour, the four figures each went their separate ways to win new converts and relay their message of inspiration across Britain, as each of them initially headed for Edinburgh, Cardiff, Southampton and Norwich to conduct press conferences at lunchtime. These four cities were followed by Birmingham, Manchester, Plymouth and Leeds, while Bob Maclennan, another former Labour minister and founder member of the SDP, held a press conference in Aberdeen, to stress the SDP's geographical reach across the nations of the United Kingdom.

Nobody could deny the slickness of the operation. The SDP had hired Dick Negus, of Negus & Negus, a top graphic designer who, in his career, would work for the Royal Opera House, the National Theatre and British Airways. Negus had attended Battersea Grammar School before ending his education ahead of his sixteenth birthday in 1943. He was a believer in the SDP's cause. His red, white and blue design replaced the monochrome conformity of the older parties; it attracted comment and considerable praise. Mike Thomas, the ex-Labour MP who had also defected to the Social Democrats, was a former public schoolboy who had entered the communications industry. Thomas and Negus represented the chic, modern world of high technology and communications which the SDP seemed to embody.[17] The party's modern credentials were underlined by a press announcement that the new party would register its membership nationally on a computer.[18]

The origins of the party were undoubtedly rooted in the Labour movement, and in the Labour party's response to the decisive electoral defeat of May 1979. The struggle within Labour between the right of the party, represented by former Cabinet ministers like Denis Healey, and the left, who could be said to be led by Michael Foot and, even more flamboyantly, by Tony Benn, burst into public view during 1980. The Labour leadership battle of that year, designed to resolve the tensions within the party, if anything made the situation worse. The party's internal wrangling had come to a head at a meeting in Bishop's Stortford in June. The meeting had been dominated by the unions, which used their influence to pass a resolution that future leadership elections in the Labour party would be conducted using an electoral college, split between unions, constituency parties and MPs. Until that point the party leadership had been chosen by sitting Labour MPs.

When James Callaghan finally stood down as Labour leader in October 1980, the succession had become an issue of 'huge importance'. There was much initial speculation about what Michael Foot's intentions were. Foot's ambitions for the leadership were obscure, to say the least. It is alleged that union leaders such as Clive Jenkins, a colourful personality who sported custom-made shirts, and Foot's wife, Jill, had urged him to stand. Foot's main opponent was the abrasive Denis Healey, another brilliant Oxford graduate from the 1930s. Healey was widely expected to win the leadership, but Foot had buttressed his candidacy by effective House of Commons performances. He had also succeeded in attracting the whole of the left and many in the centre of the party who saw him as a greater unifying force than Healey. To 'general astonishment', Foot succeeded on the second ballot, with 139 votes to Healey's 129.[19] This election earned its own footnote in history as the last time the Labour party leadership was decided exclusively by a vote of its MPs.

The frustrations felt by many on the right of the Labour party in the eighteen months after the May 1979 election were really the driving force behind the creation of the SDP in the spring of 1981. Foot's election had been a watershed for the right. Described as the 'first time since [George] Lansbury [in 1932] that a man clearly identified with the left had been elected leader', Foot's election caused some consternation on the right of the party, the ministerial people, the pragmatists who dominate most political parties when those parties are in power.[20] It was debatable whether Foot was any more associated with the left than Harold Wilson himself had been in 1964, but the perception that he was a man of the left was current, and perception can often be reality in politics.

Even before Foot's election as Labour leader in November 1980, the right represented by Shirley Williams and her colleagues David Owen and Bill Rodgers had expressed unease and public dissatisfaction with the direction of the party. The Gang of Three, as they were already called as early as the summer of 1980, had written a 3,000-word 'open letter' to members of the Labour party in the summer preceding the excitement of the Labour leadership election. Published in the *Guardian*, the house journal of the left, on 1 August, the letter read like a cry of despair. Its authors described the Labour as 'facing the gravest crisis in its history'. They attacked the left of the party, perhaps typified in their minds by Tony Benn. They denounced 'the willingness of some leading members of the party to flirt with extremists who openly regard democracy as a sham'.

The letter's apocalyptic tone was designed to stir the faithful and commit Labour to the true path of democracy and 'internationalism' which the far left of the party appeared to threaten. The letter also hinted darkly that a new party might have to be created if the confrontation between the moderates and extreme left ended badly for the Gang. 'If the Labour party abandons its democratic and internationalist principles, the argument may grow for a new democratic Socialist Party to establish itself as a party of conscience and reform committed to those principles.' Nobody could deny the idealism, even the passion, of the letter's signatories. Along with a deep mistrust of the extreme elements of the left, they nursed a bitter contempt for Thatcher's government: 'We are not prepared to abandon Britain to divisive and often cruel Tory policies because electors do not have an opportunity to vote for an acceptable Socialist alternative to the Conservative government.'

The 1979 election, in the view of the Gang of Three, had not only been a 'major blow' for the Labour party, it had also been a 'serious blow' for the nation, because 'Mrs Thatcher's government, in pursuing its inflexible monetarist doctrines, is driving unemployment to intolerable levels and laying waste large areas of the economy.' Yet the extreme left's policies were even worse, because they represented a threat to democracy itself. The left were bent on committing the Labour party 'to inflexible policies based on bureaucratic centralism and state control'. The Gang of Three, against what they perceived to be an onslaught from the left, remained committed to the 'success of the mixed economy' (an economy combining elements of state control with private ownership), to a 'truly international socialism', and they were proud of their 'unshakeable commitment to representative democracy'.[21]

It was rousing stuff; hundreds of letters 'poured in from all over the country, many from Labour supporters'. Williams remembered how overwhelmingly the letters shared the consternation of the Gang of Three about 'what was happening to their Party'. With characteristic candour she confessed that a few of the letters were 'scathing' – 'our departure would be good riddance'.[22] In his diaries Benn himself described the 1 August letter as 'disgraceful'.[23] The letter did little to deter the MPs who voted for Michael Foot that November, or even to temper the left-wing firebrands who excited audiences at the Labour conference in Blackpool that September. Williams herself had a testy conference, particularly as she saw Tony Benn, one of the great orators of his generation, rouse the conference hall with a classic repudiation of the Callaghan government. It seemed that the letter, which had been earnestly published in August, had fallen largely on deaf ears.

At that 1980 conference, Williams listened to an 'amazing speech' by Tony Benn, a 'rave about what the left would do with power when it got it'. Benn, in his impassioned way, offered a shopping list of all the things he believed a genuinely left-wing British government could achieve. 'His list included the extension of public ownership to all the country's major companies.' This referred to what Aneurin Bevan, another towering orator of the left, had called 'the commanding heights of the economy'. Benn insisted on the 'control of capital movements, withdrawal from the European Common Market, and the abolition of the House of Lords'.

Williams could not match the fervour and popularity of Tony Benn in full cry. She was due to give a speech to the Campaign for Labour Victory that very evening, in the Spanish Hall at Blackpool's conference. The Spanish Hall was a large venue, which could accommodate up to 600 people. It was situated in the Winter Gardens, which was a late Victorian conception full of various halls and theatres. The atmosphere in Blackpool was 'not just electric, it was incendiary'. Williams remembered, 'I had to fight my way through crowds of delegates, some intoxicated by Tony's vision, to get to the hall.' People shouted at her, one or two even spat, while others, keeping their voices down, were more quietly encouraging.

This battle between Williams and Benn was a characteristically British affair, with both protagonists having graduated from Oxford and coming from the well-heeled and politically well-connected upper-middle class. For both Benn and Williams, perhaps each to their own embarrassment, had been educated at famous, even elitist London educational establishments before they had ever got to Oxford. For Benn at Westminster School and Williams at St Paul's School for Girls, going to Oxford was a matter of course; there would simply never have been any question of them going anywhere else. They both represented patrician privilege, enshrined at the top of the Labour party, even though, by the end of 1980, they were political enemies. 'I hadn't written down what I was going to say, but I was buoyed up by a ferocious indignation,' recalled Williams. 'I wonder why Tony was so unambitious?' she asked in her speech. 'After all it took God only six days to make the world.' She did not record how the conference hall reacted to her attempt at light-hearted banter. She did remember that the entire conference was bitterly split, so a joke at Tony Benn's expense was probably not the best way to endear oneself to an audience half of whom were probably his supporters.[24]

After the tumults of September's conference, Foot's election 'horrified the Labour right'. Williams felt genuine anguish at the difficult choices she was forced to make. 'I was torn apart by having to choose between betraying my principles and betraying my friends.' To leave a political party in which one has spent nearly thirty years as activist, candidate and Member of Parliament was a wrenching process. 'For me, leaving the Labour Party was like pulling out my own teeth, one by one. There was my former constituency party, many of whose members were friends, bonded by long chilly nights of canvassing.' Any party activist would recognise Williams's description of the joys and agonies of 'celebrating victories' and 'mourning defeats'.[25]

The fight within the Labour party around the end of 1980 would culminate at the Wembley conference on 24 January 1981, where the exact composition and weight of the party's electoral college for choosing the next leader and deputy leader of the party were decided. For Tony Benn, the Wembley conference was a triumph. An 'historic day', the 'product of ten years' work', he called it.[26] The special conference had, 'after an exhaustive ballot', agreed to an electoral college divided '40% to the trade unions' and '30% to the Parliamentary Labour party (PLP)', with the constituency parties making up the rest. The right had been soundly defeated. Benn and his friends had effectively driven the right of the Labour party from the field and looked set to dominate that party for the immediate future.

For Benn himself the end of 1980 and the beginning of 1981 marked his 'apogee'. Williams remembered him at the Blackpool conference being 'the hero of the left with an appeal that went beyond their relatively small numbers'. Although he turned fifty-five in 1980, Benn retained a boyish enthusiasm for politics, as well as an engaging oratorical style. His platform manner was hectoring, but sometimes playfully irreverent. He struck poses which in turn delighted his followers, while infuriating his opponents within the Labour party. For people outside the party, particularly for Thatcher's adherents, Benn represented the unacceptable face of British socialism. He was the embodiment of the 'loony left' that would be mocked as the 1980s wore on. To many outside the Labour party, he was merely a figure of fun, a pantomime character with no real depth. To those, like the Gang of Three, who were desperately trying to make Labour a party of government once again, his childishness was infuriating.

For the Labour right who stayed within the party, this was a desperate time. After Benn's Blackpool speech, Roy Hattersley, a senior figure on the right of the party, felt a certain despair. Nothing seemed to go well for Labour. The Blackpool conference, in Hattersley's view, had been 'part tragedy, but mostly farce'.[27] Healey, Hattersley remembered, was the ultimate 'self-destructive candidate who seemed to be driven by an irresistible desire to offend potential supporters'. Michael Foot, however, was a disaster as far as Hattersley was concerned. 'I always felt like a passenger in an aeroplane which was being flown by an unqualified pilot.' Hattersley and others on the Labour right put up with this situation. For the founders of the SDP, the situation was intolerable.

Benn's antics and those of his acolytes continued to infuriate the Labour right. Williams resented 'being ridiculed and abused at National Executive meetings' by Dennis Skinner, the so-called Beast of Bolsover, the parliamentary constituency for which he sat. The hapless Michael Foot sat above all this turmoil not really knowing what to do. He had not engineered this division within the party and, by the time he took over the Labour leadership, the split had already begun to grow. His literary predilections had always marked him out as a thinker, a man of ideas rather than action, and he was probably the very worst leader Labour could have elected at such a divisive time. 'I have no doubt that he preferred literature to leadership' was Hattersley's withering verdict.[28] Foot bewailed the lost opportunity all the bitterness and conflict of 1981 represented for the Labour movement: '1981 could and should have been the year in which the Labour movement applied all its energies' to 'destroy the Tory Government'. Instead, Labour had, in his sad recollection, 'turned it into a period of futility and shame'.[29] Foot used his considerable literary powers to describe the chaos which he could do nothing to avert.

The Gang of Three, by contrast, firmly believed in leadership. They had already made tentative approaches to Roy Jenkins, their 'King over the water' in Brussels. The Gang of Three travelled to the Oxfordshire village of East Hendred, where Jenkins resided, to have lunch with the great man on 28 November 1980. Well known for her independent flair and reluctance to defer to anybody on account of rank, Shirley Williams slightly resented this act of homage. She felt like the 'veteran of long and bitter wars who sees the general arrive for a flying visit'. Williams and many of her friends on the right of the Labour party 'bore scars of the last four years', and Roy 'didn't'.

As a consequence of this lunch, the media renamed the group, including Roy Jenkins, the Gang of Four. Williams recognised the contradictions between Roy and herself. She knew what she wanted. She was convinced that the new party should be 'democratic but also socialist, committed to greater equality, redistribution of income and wealth, comprehensive schools and the National Health Service'. Williams wasn't convinced that 'Roy shared all those objectives'. Roy was a grandee, a sixty-year-old veteran with a distinguished career behind him. His love of elegant living was well known, and Williams did not want her new party 'to be fashioned by someone, however distinguished, who had not been part of our struggle'. In short, Jenkins did not have the scars from fighting the Bennites and their friends on the extreme left of the Labour party. Williams did, however, recognise that Jenkins, as far as the media was concerned at least, had 'a gravitas, a reputation as an experienced statesman', that the nascent SDP badly needed 'to lend weight to our fragile enterprise'.[30]

A day after the special conference at Wembley, on Sunday 25 January, the Gang of Four made a statement outside David Owen's house in Limehouse, in the East End of London, announcing the formation of a Council for Social Democracy. Owen's house was situated in Narrow Street, opposite the Brightlingsea Buildings where Clement Attlee had lived when he worked as a social worker in the East End before the First World War.[31] The Limehouse Declaration was aggressive and reflected the divisive atmosphere which accompanied its birth. It denounced the 'calamitous outcome' of the previous day's Labour party conference at Wembley. The 'Conference disaster' was the 'culmination of a long process by which the Labour Party has moved steadily away from its roots in the people of this country and its commitment to parliamentary government'.[32]

The Gang of Four had been agonising all winter over the precise nature of their relationship with the Labour party and the need to establish a new party. The Limehouse Declaration was a rather ungracious notice of farewell, some might suggest, to the party in whose bosom they had nurtured their political careers. Owen, the youngest and most nakedly ambitious of the Gang, had made the adoption of the electoral college to choose Labour's leader the main stumbling block to his continuation as a Labour Member of Parliament. In a letter written to a Labour activist, dating from October 1980, he had stated that electoral colleges for him were 'the most serious challenge of all', as they represented 'a real attack on the whole concept of Parliamentary democracy'. What irked him was the idea that a future Labour prime minister could 'be chosen by a combination of unrepresentative trade union block votes and unrepresentative constituency delegates'.

Owen had asserted, back in October, that the Labour right would do 'everything in our power' to prevent the adoption of electoral colleges. While he pledged never to 'become a Liberal, or join a rootless Centre Party that means abandoning my socialist convictions', he was not afraid of splitting the party. 'We are hoping people will join the Campaign for Labour Victory to help us mobilise support before January to avoid the grave danger of the Party splitting.'[33] The dilemma faced by the SDP founders was clear to many activists. The risk, of course, was that the SDP would split the left generally and leave the field open to the Conservatives. As one Labour activist wrote to Bill Rodgers, just a week before the Limehouse Declaration towards the end of January 1981, there 'are many active Labour members in the centre/centre-left of the party that would see any move away as being totally defeatist and something that is likely to keep the Tories in for many years'.[34] It is interesting that the Liberals, with only eleven seats in the House of Commons, were not viewed in any way as a credible third force.

John Parker, the veteran Labour MP for Dagenham, now Father of the House of Commons (the MP who had been in the House for the longest time), begged Bill Rodgers to stay in the party in a letter written on 20 January, five days before the Limehouse Declaration. 'May I as an old friend express the hope that you will not leave the Labour Party.' A seventy-four-year-old who had been first elected in 1935, Parker made use of his experience in an attempt to dissuade Rodgers from leaving Labour. 'As an MP for 46 years I do not believe that any breakaway lasts more than a few years.' Presciently, he observed that a breakaway party 'ruins the careers of those involved', while perhaps even more acutely he noted that a 'Socialist Party – Right or Left – has no chance of making good without the backing of the trade unions'.[35]

Other Labour MPs who were ideologically sympathetic to the Gang of Four were less emollient in their attempts to prevent the creation of the new party. The technocratic Jeremy Bray, MP for Motherwell, an economist who boasted a double first in Mathematics from Cambridge but 'had difficulty in communicating with lesser minds', was highly personal and aggressive in a letter he addressed to 'Bill and Shirley', also dated 20 January. 'The Seventies were not bad years for you,' he archly observed. 'You all arrived in the Cabinet. You had your opportunities. You became accustomed to being noticed, flattered,' but those years were 'bad years for the country and for many people'.[36] Marcia Falkender, who had been Harold Wilson's secretary, conceded that Bray was brilliant, but dismissed him as resembling 'every mad professor of comic fiction'.[37]

Bray made a charge against Williams and Rodgers which would often be made during the life of the SDP. The SDP founders were careerists: when 'within the Party the frustrations began to boil over, and the smooth progression of careers, of outlook, of ideas which fitted you so comfortably began to be challenged, you found it unsettling,' he said tauntingly. As an attempt to win over experienced politicians on the brink of leaving their party for another, Bray's sardonic letter was utterly useless. It expressed the frustration and sense of betrayal that many Labour MPs felt at the impending creation of the SDP. Bray's most cutting remarks were reserved for Shirley Williams. She was 'always worried, always conscious stricken [sic]', without ever 'actually resigning or even standing very firm'. It was Rodgers, Bray reminded her, who had called her 'Rubber Knees'.[38]

The SDP would not be discouraged by these letters, even though all the Gang of Four, with the possible exception of Roy Jenkins, who had been above the political fray in Brussels, felt the pain of separating from former colleagues. As Bill Rodgers, speaking to a meeting of his Stockton North activists, declared on 1 March, 'This is a painful occasion and a highly personal one.' He had made 'the break with sadness', after being a member of the Labour party for thirty-five years. Like nearly every defector in history, Rodgers claimed that he had not left the party, but rather the party had left him. The Labour party had 'lost touch with its values and drawn away from the voters it should seek to serve'. David Owen remained on affable terms with Jim Callaghan, the Labour Prime Minister who had promoted him at such a young age to the high office of Secretary of State for Foreign Affairs. As late as 20 February 1981, Callaghan thanked Owen for an Ackermann print he had received and claimed that he and his wife Audrey were 'delighted with it'. Callaghan added that the gift would be 'a treasured possession' and would remind him 'of the days when we worked together'. A genial and friendly figure who revelled in his 'Sunny Jim' image, Callaghan did not like confrontation. He wrote to Owen, 'I want to see you all come back in due course.'

These placatory words would not persuade them. For weeks, the SDP were the hottest political show on the road. There had been a great deal of speculation about the aims and ambitions of the new party between the Limehouse Declaration and the official launch of the party on 26 March. Media pundits, the public, Westminster at large, all were enthralled by their media skills, by the modernity and even by the touch of glamour the SDP seemed to inject into British public life. Thousands of ordinary people had nodded emphatically at the very last line of the Limehouse Declaration which stated, 'we believe that the need for a realignment of British politics must now be faced'.[39] Indeed, in the first week after the Declaration, 8,000 messages of support came in. Another 15,000 messages would be received in the ensuing weeks.[40] The launch of the party itself in March added to the media frenzy and the sense that British politics was entering a brave new world of limit-less possibilities and much needed renewal. In the first half of 1981 the claim that 'the leader of the SDP would be the next Prime Minister became a serious possibility'. There was a feeling of novelty and excite-ment about the whole enterprise. Rather vaguely it was alleged that perhaps 'as many as half of the first wave of SDP activists were people who had never been involved in party politics before'.[41]

One contingent of excited supporters sent encouragement from across the Atlantic. 'We are writing to applaud your courageous decision to relinquish the party whip,' wrote Tim Hough to David Owen at the end of March. Hough was a Cambridge law graduate who had ended up at Harvard Business School. Now at the ripe old age of twenty-three, he wrote with enthusiasm about how he and a 'consortium of British students here at Harvard Business School' had 'diligently followed the welcome birth of the "new" party'. He would later join McKinsey on graduating from Harvard Business School in 1982 before pursuing a highly successful career in the 1980s in private equity and business in Hong Kong and South Africa. Back in 1981, however, he was a political idealist, yearning to 'end British Yo-Yo politics and our consequent national decline'. With the confidence learnt at one of the world's most prestigious business schools, Hough claimed that he and his friends possessed 'considerable experience in strategic consulting'. Offering his services, he assured Owen that he and his fellow supporters at Harvard Business School did not want the SDP to fail 'through lack of political conviction or effective professional management'.[42]

Hough need not have bothered. The SDP were not lacking in media consultants, advertising men and public relations experts, ever willing to support their new party. The SDP had been born out of a need to present a credible alternative to Mrs Thatcher's government, which many elements on the left believed represented the gravest threat to their world view since the Second World War. It was interesting to observe how both the SDP and the Bennites believed that they, and not the other gang, offered the most powerful opposition to Thatcher, and that it was an opposition of which the Thatcherite Tories were frightened, and which they took seriously. 'The Tories are running scared of "the Limehouse Left" as Mrs Thatcher dubbed the Council for Social Democracy,' the nascent Social Democrats declared in an open letter to members in March 1981. 'They know it represents a far more serious challenge than the old Labour Party with its creaking organisation . . . saddled with the frightening image of the Bennite left. The Tories know who their real enemies are.'[43]

Tony Benn made much the same claim. In his analysis, it was his brand of unadulterated socialism that the Tories really feared. In his diary entry for 8 October 1980, still fresh from his oratorical triumph at the Labour conference in Blackpool, he was exultant, floating high on the belief that his ideas represented the true threat to the governing Tories. 'The fact is that last week at Blackpool we really pulverised the Tories by the strength and force of alternative policy.' Benn would always believe that it was his strain within the Labour party which really terrified the Tories, not the soft-left version peddled by the Gang of Four and their misguided cronies. 'Nobody is going to tell me that Mrs Thatcher is frightened of Shirley Williams or Bill Rodgers or Jim Callaghan, or Denis Healey or Peter Shore. But they [sic] are transfixed by the thought that there might be a radical Labour Government.'

Thatcher remained the key player, the one protagonist who at once attracted attention and inspired fear among her opponents. It was her perceived harshness and single-mindedness which had given the SDP its opening. The SDP and 'its phenomenal early success' were 'created by other parties'. 'Mrs Thatcher, Sir Geoffrey Howe, Mr Foot and Mr Benn were the effective recruiting sergeants for the SDP,' according to Hugh Stephenson.[44] The early days of the party were successful and full of hope. By the time the party was launched at the end of March, it already had fourteen MPs (thirteen defectors from Labour and one Tory), which immediately made it the third largest group in the House of Commons. 'The wave of enthusiasm and support from the general public after 26 March far exceeded the expectations of even the most optimistic of those involved.'[45] Letters received by the Gang of Four and the founding officials of the party from activists, councillors and members of the public were encouraging.

One letter addressed to Alec McGivan, the twenty-seven-year old National Organiser of the SDP, came from a newly recruited SDP activist, Brian McGillan, in North Shields in England's North-east, a traditional Labour stronghold. The letter, dated 12 March, was representative of many sent from throughout Britain. 'For the past two weeks I have been canvassing for support in my own area and the response has been magnificent. People are crying for change and a move away from the two-party system.' Another letter, despatched the day before came from Bexleyheath in Kent, a more Tory-leaning part of the country. 'For thirty years, namely from 1944–1974, I was a member of the Labour Party,' wrote Alastair Reid, a Labour candidate at two general elections. 'I have been waiting for the formation of "a centre party". The polarisation of British politics made me very weary indeed.'[46] Confidence in the future seemed boundless, as David Owen wrote to a Mrs Janet Knowles on 31 March, five days after the launch of the party, 'Together [with the Liberals] I believe we can break the two party system stranglehold, and even form the next Government in 1984.'[47]

Even voices from the usually staid *Economist*, swept up by the excitement of the SDP launch, rapidly wrote off the Tories' chances in an article entitled 'Born to Lead', published on 28 March, a mere two days after the spectacular SDP launch. 'With modern Toryism entering what seems like a doomed phase', the Social Democrats' aim should be to 'displace Labour as the major party of the Left' and present 'a more credible and independent anti-Conservative force than the present Labour party'.[48]

The polls showed the SDP as potentially carrying all before it, and sweeping away the old two-party system. Its breakthrough somehow seemed inevitable, as a Gallup poll for the *Daily Telegraph* on 13 April showed the new party on 33 per cent, ahead of the governing Conservatives on 30 per cent and just behind Labour on 34 per cent.[49] By April, the SDP's continuing success started to cause alarm among the more established politicians. Michael Foot, steeped in the literature of the eighteenth century, compared its rise to the South Sea Bubble. Speaking at the annual meeting of his Ebbw Vale constituency on 10 April, he described the SDP launch as a 'shabby public relations exercise without parallel in British politics'. He developed the theme by referring to the 'most infamous City fraud in English history'.

The South Sea Bubble had seen money raised for schemes the purpose of which was 'hereafter to be revealed'. 'The purpose of the Social Democratic Bubble', Foot claimed, 'is hereafter to be revealed.' He then levelled a charge often made against the Social Democrats, that they were simply a media operation dominated by public opinion pollsters: their purpose would only be revealed 'once they've collected your cash, once they've made a deal with David Steel [the Liberal leader], once they've discovered what policy will prove most popular with the public opinion pollsters'.[50] The accusation that they were a vague media-driven, synthetic organisation was something which the SDP could never quite shake off.

Yet nobody could deny the confidence and gusto with which the leaders of the SDP had set about their task of refashioning British politics. David Owen, the youngest and arguably most photogenic of the Gang of Four, almost became a fashionable political icon. In an article for the tabloid magazine *NOW!*, published with exquisite timing a couple of days before the 26 March launch, Owen gave a characteristically forceful account of his philosophy in which he argued that the Social Democrats 'must never be seen as the soggy centre' if they were to succeed. He painted a picture of Britain as it would become in 1983–4, a picture of 'Orwellian' grimness, because for obvious reasons Orwell's novel *1984* haunted the public imagination in early-1980s Britain. By the next general election, 'unemployment will be savagely high, our economic growth rate abysmally low and our public services deteriorating fast'.

This gloomy prognosis of Britain's future invited the SDP to enter as shining knights to save the country. 'In such a climate the public

will want a Government that is decisive and direct.' Owen had the
grace to acknowledge that this was a strength possessed by Margaret
Thatcher. It was this 'element of Mrs Thatcher's character which is now
her only appeal and is the main reason why she should never be under-
estimated'. But Owen believed that the politics of the 1980s required
'involvement and persuasion as well as courage and decisiveness'.[51]
Owen, still only forty-two, was often dismissed as a vain, lightweight
figure with no intellectual depth, and certainly without the hinterland
of a Michael Foot or Roy Jenkins, both of whom had established themselves as accomplished political historians as early as the 1950s. Yet,
despite being a less self-consciously literary figure, Owen could write
clearly and effectively. He also had a certain intellectual clarity, which
perhaps derived from his training in medicine and the sciences.

Owen saw the future clearly and he believed that Labour, as it was
currently constituted, was an inadequate alternative. 'It was very clear
after the January 1981 Conference that without creating a new party,
there would not be a left of centre government capable within the foreseeable future of reversing our nation's relative economic decline.' Many
people, even among those who stayed within the Labour party, would
have shared this opinion; and many more believed Owen's essential
message as the 1980s turned into the 1990s. Owen would be hailed
by some on the left as a prophet who foresaw many of the developments Labour needed to embrace in order to become electable. For
him, Labour's failure was not to keep in step with centre-left parties in
Europe. 'Alone of Western European socialist parties, the British Labour
Party continues to follow a centralist bureaucratic Marxist analysis.'[52]

Despite the SDP rejection of Labour, Thatcher remained Prime Minister,
and the main target of the ire and passion of the Social Democrats. As
is often the case, it is the political enemies and opponents who fully
appreciate the qualities of the protagonist with whom they struggle to
compete. Owen acknowledged Thatcher's directness and decisiveness,

perhaps in the belief that he shared some of these qualities himself. Jenkins also admired Margaret Thatcher's courage but asked at what cost such courage was shown. At a speech given at the end of May, Jenkins noted that the 'casualties' of Thatcherism had been 'immense'. 'Jobs, industry, social cohesion have suffered,' he said. 'Taxation has increased, public borrowing has increased,' yet 'Mrs Thatcher as a general has maintained her courage.' Such courage, in Roy Jenkins's view, suggested a slight detachment from reality. Thatcher displayed her courage 'only at the price of detaching her gaze from the reality of the battle'.[53]

The Social Democrats, above all else, saw themselves as pragmatic realists, unshackled by ideology or what they would have called rigid dogmatism. In many ways they were ahead of their time. They presented themselves as a modern force, trying to offer a voice of sanity in a highly polarised world. Of course, for people like Margaret Thatcher, polarisation, opposition, conflict, were all things to be embraced, even celebrated. For Thatcher, truth and falsehood were binary propositions, opposing and mutually exclusive ideas. The Social Democrats, in complete contrast to her, were happy with compromise and a lack of clearly defined edges. 'The Conservative and Labour Party leadership are locked together like Siamese twins,' proclaimed David Owen grandly to a group of Social Democrat students at Liverpool University at the end of April.

Owen presented a compelling picture of SDP unity and hope against the divided traditional parties, Conservative and Labour, which had dominated British politics for fifty years. Conservative MPs lived 'either in fear or hope that the Cabinet "wets"' would revolt. Labour were riven by their own internal disputes, between right and left, and in the midst of their own bruising deputy-leadership election fought between Denis Healey and the increasingly maniacal Tony Benn. 'Is it any wonder that the public now sees the Social Democratic Party as the true Opposition and future government of the country?' Owen asked the Liverpool students.

Owen made the case, which has often been made since, that it was only the lack of a decent opposition that kept Margaret Thatcher on her path of reducing spending in the teeth of a recession. 'In any normal circumstances a government as incompetent and as insensitive as this one, would have been forced to change its policies either by its own Party or the Opposition.' Yet, at the same time, it seemed unlikely that anyone would force Thatcher to reverse her general direction. 'The sad fact is that the Prime Minister's dogmatic and doctrinaire leadership continues unchecked,' while the Labour party's equally 'dogmatic and doctrinaire policies' were scarcely more appealing.[54]

The appeal of the Social Democrats was simple enough. It all seemed so neat and logical. Owen, in his forensic, scientific manner, once again put it in simple terms. 'The message of the Social Democrats is to marry three essential political attributes.' Owen believed in uniting the 'tradition of social concern of the Labour Party with the traditional realism of the Conservative Party', while tying this combination to a programme of decentralised government.[55] Ironically, Owen's logical and scientific mentality was often depicted as being unfeeling and inhuman, which was very similar to the accusations made against Margaret Thatcher. Shirley Williams represented a softer, gentler side to the movement. She championed such progressive issues as 'Third World Development', at a time when few in the mainstream of politics seemed interested in such issues. Williams was in the eyes of her detractors the typical 'bleeding heart' liberal. 'The Social Democrats have deliberately decided to make Britain's responsibility to the Third World a central issue of policy.' In a bold association of ideas, Williams argued that support for the development of 'the Third World countries' was not an act of charity, but 'an obligation'. In the same way that 'the welfare state evolved far beyond the Victorian tradition of charity towards the poor'.[56]

Williams showed a human side to being a politician which she cleverly used against the seemingly harsh Mrs Thatcher. Speaking out against unemployment in April, she portrayed a Prime Minister who was stern, dogmatic and unfeeling. 'The Prime Minister rebukes us for our idleness, rebukes other countries for their doubts, rebukes her ministers for wetness, rebukes everyone but herself.' She added, 'As the dole queues of the despairing grow longer shouldn't we repeat Cromwell's cry to the Long Parliament, "Bethink you that you may be mistaken."'[57] All through the first few months of the SDP's life, the Gang of Four used their individual skills to criticise the government and the opposition Labour party. It was, initially at least, an effective team effort.

In an interview for the BBC's *Listener* magazine, Owen explained why the SDP held to a 'collective' leadership of four, rather than adopting the more conventional idea of having a single leader: 'I'm sometimes perhaps a bit too tough,' while 'Roy brings great experience as a former Chancellor.' Shirley Williams had 'marvellous empathy and ability', while Bill Rodgers, who was something of a silent man to the public, had 'deep roots in the North of England, in industrial England'. The novel idea of having a group of leaders, rather than one figure who claimed absolute authority, proved effective in the short run, even if tensions among the leadership group might emerge from time to time.

One area in which tension did emerge was in the selection of candidates for by-elections. Two of the Gang of Four were already Members of Parliament. Bill Rodgers and David Owen had both been elected as Labour MPs in the 1979 general election. By the conventions of the House of Commons, an MP who 'crossed the floor' did not have to stand down as an MP, thereby creating a by-election. MPs who resigned from the House, of course, triggered the holding of a by-election. It became an accepted proposition that the SDP would have to try their strength in a real election contest. The party had not contested the May 1981 local elections, mainly because it did not have the resources to do this effectively.[58] The two members of the Gang of Four who were not MPs were believed to be anxious to get elected to the Commons.

Luckily for the SDP, in the last week of May, the Labour MP for Warrington in Lancashire, Sir Thomas Williams, decided to retire from

politics, in order to become a circuit judge. Williams had been a practising barrister throughout his parliamentary career, which had begun
as long ago as 1949, when he had been elected for Hammersmith South
in London. After losing his seat in 1959, he had resumed his career by
getting elected in a parliamentary by-election in Warrington in 1961.
By resigning his parliamentary seat, the sixty-four-year-old precipitated
one of the most famous by-elections of the modern era.

The parliamentary constituency of Warrington was a solid, working-
class Labour seat. It presented something of a challenge to the SDP, but
it was felt that the party, given all the early enthusiasm surrounding its
launch, should contest the seat. As far as Shirley Williams remembered,
by the beginning of June the SDP 'was slipping from the heights of
enthusiasm reached during the launch' of the party at the end of March.
'There was talk of us being a flash in the pan.' It was necessary for the
SDP to prove their critics wrong and win a seat in a by-election, or at
least get a decent result. 'It was critical to the Party's fortunes to do well
in Warrington.' The date of the by-election had been set for 16 July.

Shirley Williams was invited to stand. In many ways the seat suited
her well. Warrington may have been a 'solid Labour seat', but it had a
strong Catholic tradition and was a cohesive community. In Williams's
own opinion, if 'ever a constituency was made for me, this was it'.
However, she balked at the challenge of fighting the seat. She lamented
the fact that after her divorce from the eminent moral philosopher
Bernard Williams in 1974, she had become a single mother with 'no
substantial financial resources'. She refused the nomination to contest
the seat on behalf of the Social Democrats and, in her own words, her
'reputation for boldness, acquired in the long fight within the Labour
Party, never wholly recovered'. She regarded this missed chance as
'probably the single biggest mistake' of her political life.[59]

It fell to Roy Jenkins to fly the flag for the SDP at the Warrington
by-election. By contrast, he seized 'with both hands' the opportunity
that Williams had let pass. Jenkins had a lot to lose, not least his role

as an elder statesman. Now, as the SDP candidate for Warrington, he was returning to the grass roots, to local politics with its attendant inconveniences and uncertainties. For a man used to lunching at the best restaurants in London and Brussels, for a member of the Garrick Club and Brooks's, engaging with local activists on Warrington High Street was not perhaps the most appealing prospect. But Jenkins was determined to 'throw everything he had' into the fight.[60] As many pointed out, he had a 'notoriously sybaritic image and lack of any recent contact with the British working class'. He had even spent much of the first week of June in Lausanne by the shores of Lake Leman, attending an international monetary conference; and he had enjoyed the last week in May in the Tuscan city of Lucca. But now, on 8 June, he announced his intention to fight the by-election. He was adopted as the SDP candidate by local party members and, now aged sixty, he threw himself into one of the most intense and public election campaigns.[61]

For six weeks the Warrington by-election absorbed the media's attention. Volunteers for the SDP flooded into the town and caught the spirit of the campaign. Jenkins, who had never been the most approachable of politicians, worked the streets and addressed spontaneous meetings on street corners. The by-election in fact seemed to galvanise the whole of the Social Democratic party. It also gave the party a chance to rehearse and hone its message, contrasting its youthful energy and idealism with the two older, more staid and less inviting traditional parties.

On the Monday before the Thursday of the by-election, David Owen appealed to the Warrington voter in an article written for the *Daily Express*. 'The Warrington voter has an historic opportunity to start the process of political change in Britain.' He reiterated his 'plague on both your houses' theme, which seemed to be the best card in the SDP hand. 'The British people do not want the extreme Left. Nor do they want the extreme Right. The present-day Conservative Party of Mrs Thatcher,

Sir Keith Joseph and Stan Sorrell [the Conservative candidate in the Warrington by-election] has little in common with the Conservative Party of Winston Churchill, Anthony Eden, Harold Macmillan or Ted Heath.' These Tory Prime Ministers 'would never have endorsed the present Government's insensitivity to rising unemployment'.[62]

Thatcher herself had written a rather dry letter, dated 9 July, the previous Thursday and a full week before the election, to the forlorn candidate Stan Sorrell, who never really stood a chance. She repeated her familiar message: 'we are beginning to succeed in our battle to get control of inflation'; 'British industry is becoming increasingly efficient and competitive.' As if to humanise her message, she added, 'I recognise and care deeply about the loss of jobs which we all know has come about through a variety of causes – not least of which has been the world recession.' The letter was a characteristic statement of Thatcher's short, succinct and defiant style. 'Our task is a great one,' she concluded, but 'I want to reassure you and the people of Warrington that we intend to see it through to success. I know I can depend on you to put our case with conviction and vigour.'[63]

Thatcher's fine words of purpose and defiance did not, in the case of the Warrington by-election, presage any great performance from the Conservatives. Sorrell barely got 7 per cent of the vote, in an election which saw the Conservative vote share decrease by more than 20 per cent. For Jenkins the election was a triumph, as he got within 1,800 votes of the Labour candidate, winning more than 42 per cent of the vote. The *Guardian* described his result as 'one of the most stupendous achievements by any party in any by-election in postwar history'.[64] For a new party 'to come into an election and take 42% of the vote, as Mr Jenkins did last night, is unprecedented'. Jenkins, a man not noted for his modesty, was equally impressed by his own performance. In a somewhat petty jibe, he congratulated Doug Hoyle, the victorious Labour candidate, not for winning but for 'achieving the lowest Labour share of the vote in the Warrington constituency for fifty years'. To the tumultuous applause of his supporters, he described the result as 'my first defeat in thirty years in politics' and 'by far the greatest victory that I have participated in'.[65]

The campaign had been a success for the SDP. The party had used Warrington as a good test case. By July, David Owen was being hailed by *Company* magazine as 'the handsomest man in British politics – not a difficult achievement you might think when you look round the House of Commons'.[66] Roy Jenkins was being talked of as a future prime minister. Of course the current Prime Minister was still, in the summer of 1981, in place. The rise of the SDP had been a challenge which, as usual, she met with unflinching, some might say rigid, determination. At the beginning of the Warrington campaign, in a speech at the Adelphi Hotel in Liverpool, Jenkins had offered a rare psychological insight into Margaret Thatcher. He pointed to the strain of religiosity, of determined self-righteousness, which her opponents found so infuriating.

'Some leading members of this government invite applause for "sticking to their guns". But those guns are often trained on our own people. The Government have retreated into a psychological bunker, where each fall in production, each good company driven bankrupt . . . is brushed off as a victory for the "strategy",' Jenkins said. He then made an explicit reference to religion. 'Some of the sterner religions teach that a mortification of the spirit may be achieved through a mortification of the flesh. But the management of the economy is a practical matter, not a religious one.'[67] Thatcher had pretty much said the opposite. Economics was a 'moral' issue for her, as she kept repeating throughout 1981 and beyond.

4

Death in Ireland

Tuesday 5 May 1981 – The floor of the House of Commons was unusually agitated. Prime Minister's Question Time was an exciting affair. The Leader of the Opposition, Michael Foot, seemed solemn and struck a note of grave concern. 'The whole country's affairs have been darkened by the events that have taken place in Northern Ireland.' Foot once again affirmed that 'matters in Northern Ireland, as elsewhere in the country, should be settled democratically, and not at the point of a gun'.

While the House of Commons was debating the death of a Provisional IRA hunger striker, British tabloids were full of the story of the 'Yorkshire Ripper', Peter Sutcliffe, who had been charged with murdering thirteen women and attempting to murder seven others.[1] The *Daily Mail* reported the Ripper's bloodlust under the headline, 'My mission to kill'.[2]

On the floor of the House of Commons, Thatcher was her usual assertive self. 'What has been said in the House today' showed MPs' 'determination to stamp out terrorism'. The House had been surprised by the death of Bobby Sands, a twenty-seven-year-old Republican activist, who had been elected as an MP barely a month before. There was a degree of consensus about the need to show solidarity against terrorism and violence, although one or two opposition MPs adopted a different tone. Patrick Duffy, a Labour MP with ministerial experience, questioned the whole basis of the consensus. There had always been 'too much "me too-ism" in the House of Commons on the subject'.

Was the Prime Minister aware of the 'widespread impression overseas' that the death of Bobby Sands was due 'to the right honourable Lady's intransigence?'[3]

'Intransigence' was a word frequently used to describe Thatcher throughout 1981, especially when talking about the Northern Ireland hunger strikes, during which ten Republican prisoners would eventually starve themselves to death. She was clearly focused and determined in her dealings with terrorists. This was borne out by the next exchange between Duffy and the Prime Minister. Duffy asked a slightly startled Thatcher whether she was 'further aware that by appearing hard and unfeeling' she had shown her government's 'moral bankruptcy' and the 'colossal and criminal incompetence of Conservative Governments at all times in their dealings on Ireland'. Thatcher responded with exactly the same words she had used in her earlier response to Foot; her government would continue in its effort 'to stamp out terrorism'. Sands was 'a convicted criminal'. He had chosen 'to take his own life'. This was a choice which 'his organisation did not allow many of its victims'.[4]

Sands had died a little after one o'clock that morning.[5] An Irish romantic with some literary flair, he had lived most of his adult life in prison. Born in March 1954 in a northern suburb of Belfast, he had received a five-year sentence in April 1973 for possession of four handguns. He was sent to Long Kesh prison, which was renamed the Maze in 1976. The Maze was organised by paramilitary groups which controlled their own areas within the prison. It was here that Sands received whatever political education he ever had, a mixture of traditional Republicanism and revolutionary theories then fashionable in much of the developing and post-colonial world. He showed intelligence and ability and became 'officer commanding' of the paramilitary units in the prison. He took a leading role in organising instruction to other inmates in 'political education and Irish language classes'.[6]

Despite some violent connections, Sands seemed to his family like an otherwise normal young man with an extraordinary commitment to

Irish freedom. His sister Marcella, shortly after his death, remembered that Bobby had learnt to speak the Irish language in prison. 'He had his radio and guitar, and he played traditional Irish music.' The family later denied that he had any time for women, though there was a report that he had married a 'Belfast woman' while in prison and that he had separated from her, and she was said to be living with their son in England.[7] Sands was released, after serving three years of his sentence. Within six months, however, he was involved in an IRA attempt to bomb a furniture showroom in south-west Belfast. This attempt was foiled by the Royal Ulster Constabulary (RUC). This time Sands was sentenced to fourteen years and in September 1977 he was sent back to Long Kesh (as Republicans continued to call it). In the period between his two sentences, special-category status for supposed political offences had been abolished. All new paramilitary offenders, along with Sands, were put into the new accommodation, known as the H Blocks.

Sands spent much of his time, along with other IRA prisoners, campaigning to have their special-category status restored. The tragedy for Sands was that his coming of age coincided with the 'Troubles', an intense period of sectarian violence which erupted throughout Northern Ireland. In Marcella Sands's recollection, Bobby's childhood had been normal, as the family had lived in Rathcoole, a large Protestant suburb of Belfast. 'We always had Protestant friends,' Marcella claimed. 'We were a normal happy family.' It was in June 1972, when he left school at eighteen, that the Troubles, and Sands's own involvement in often violent Republicanism, began.

For Bobby's father John, his son's death, after a hunger strike lasting sixty-six days, seemed inexplicable. 'I was a war veteran of the British Navy at Anzio and the South Pacific,' he proudly told a reporter. Now an embittered fifty-eight-year-old, he added that the 'freedom I fought for didn't help us'.[8] For his family, the death of Bobby Sands represented the wider tragedy of Ireland. He was a young man like many others, Marcella implied, who had had ordinary ambitions before being absorbed by a political struggle. 'He had his plans for the future. He wanted to be teaching children Irish.'

Of course, Sands was anything but normal. He had died after being on hunger strike and, for those sixty-six days, had survived on nothing but water and salt. Among other demands, he wanted Republican prisoners to have the 'right to wear civilian clothing, dispensation from prison work and permission to associate freely in their compounds'. He began his hunger strike on 1 March. On the first examination, his weight was 10st 1lb. After forty days, on 9 April, he weighed 7st 13½lb, having lost more than two stone or 29½ pounds.

Sands's death on 5 May became a global media event. In the ensuing days, there were 'cameramen who swarmed into the City from almost every corner of the world'. For a brief moment, Belfast became the centre of the world, as journalists, particularly from the United States, descended upon the capital of the province of Northern Ireland. 'Where is the Christian quarter?' was one particularly stupid question. The journalists were especially excited about the prospect of reporting on violent confrontations between Republican youths and the British Army. Journalists had been 'frustrated to the point of panic about the difficulty of getting anybody to throw a bottle or tip over a bus' in time for their deadlines.[9]

The international impact of Bobby Sands's death was no doubt accentuated by his election as a Member of Parliament less than a month before. Sands had been largely unknown 'to all but a tiny handful of Americans of Irish descent' until his election to the British parliament.[10] As an MP, Sands had acquired a status which made it difficult for his death to be dismissed as that of just another Irish Republican. His hunger strike, particularly in its last concluding phase, posed a unique challenge to Margaret Thatcher and her government. For the IRA and Sands himself, Mrs Thatcher was their 'foremost adversary'.[11]

The democratic process on which Sands and his fellow Republicans embarked was a masterstroke for the Republican movement. The circumstances surrounding the Fermanagh and South Tyrone by-election were not initially that unusual. The death of Frank McGuire, the Irish Republican, in March 1981 created a vacancy. The seat was a highly polarised, marginal seat with balanced populations of Catholic Nationalists and Protestant Unionists. There was believed to be a 'small Nationalist majority' in the constituency, and the nomination of Bobby Sands as a candidate 'introduced', in the measured words of Humphrey Atkins, the emollient Secretary of State for Northern Ireland, 'a new dimension into the situation'. Sands described himself as 'anti-H block/ Armagh political prisoner'.[12] Armagh was the only women's prison in Northern Ireland, where some inmates went on hunger strike in sympathy with their male counterparts at the Maze.

The only other candidate was Harry West, a traditional Ulster Unionist from Fermanagh. West was sixty-four and had been leader of the Ulster Unionist party from 1974 to 1979. He had held the Fermanagh and South Tyrone seat in Westminster for ten months in 1974. He was very much a tough, uncompromising figure in the tradition of Ulster Unionist politicians. He was the son of a farmer and had attended Portora Royal School, a bastion of the Protestant Unionist establishment, where such diverse figures as Oscar Wilde, Samuel Beckett and Henry Francis Lyte, author of the Anglican hymn 'Abide with Me', had been educated. West had, in his turn, become a governor of the school, in which capacity he once tried to arrange for the dismissal of a history teacher who had been so bold as to teach his pupils about the Easter Rising.[13] Very much a figure of the Protestant establishment in Northern Ireland, he was about as different a candidate from Bobby Sands as anybody could be.

The battle between West and Sands had a significance which has now been obscured. The Fermanagh and South Tyrone seat had been represented by some of the most blue-blooded representatives of the old Anglo-Irish and British aristocracy. This had been the case when the Unionists won the seat. In recent times, Lord Robert Grosvenor, later 5th Duke of Westminster, who represented the seat from 1955 till 1964, and his cousin, the Marquess of Hamilton, later 5th Duke of Abercorn, sat for the seat as Ulster Unionist MPs. The Marquess of Hamilton had been defeated by the Republican Frank McManus in the 1970 general election. The point of all this background was that Fermanagh and South Tyrone had for a while been an electoral battleground between two sharply contending visions of Northern Ireland's future.

Though not as socially elevated as Lord Robert Grosvenor or the Marquess of Hamilton, Harry West was firmly within the Unionist tradition, a 'bluff, affable and well-built' man with experience of politics both at Stormont, where the Northern Irish government had been located, and at Westminster.[14] Sands was not politically experienced. He was a young Catholic who had not been educated to any particularly high level, but he had literary ambitions as shown in some of the poetry he wrote. In his diary and other writings he defined his political beliefs in terms of the anti-colonial struggle and the radical left. 'I am a political prisoner because I am a casualty of a perennial war that is being fought between the oppressed Irish people and an alien, oppressive, unwanted regime that refuses to withdraw from our land.' Sands revealed his 'utter disgust and anger' at the 'Reagan/Thatcher plot'. He believed that these two conservative figures intended to 'counteract Russian expansionism with imperialist expansionism, to protect their vital interests they say'.[15]

Sands may have been politically naive, but the Thatcher government, in the form of Humphrey Atkins, took his potential election to the House of Commons very seriously. Atkins hoped that there would be 'sufficient Catholic/Nationalist abstentions' to make sure that Sands was not elected. Sands's binary, simplistic view of the nature of the Irish problem showed exactly the kind of reductionism that many of Thatcher's opponents accused her of. The campaign in the by-election was a strange affair. Bobby Sands, one of the two candidates, remained a prisoner on hunger strike, yet his status as a prisoner did not in any way compromise the legality of his candidature in a parliamentary election. Some people expressed surprise at this. In the 1955 general election two Republican prisoners, Mitchell and Clarke, had stood for and won seats, but these men had been unseated as 'convicted felons'. Subsequently, more than a decade later, the Criminal Law Act of 1967 had abolished the concept of a 'felon'. In 1981, as far as Humphrey Atkins understood the situation, it was a quirk of the law that the only criminal conviction which 'now disqualifies a person from running for Parliament is treason'.[16]

Atkins was a tall, charming former naval officer, with a debonair manner acquired from his background and education. Rather unconventionally, his father had been a British colonist in Kenya, where he had been gored by a rhinoceros when young Humphrey was only three years old. First elected to the House of Commons for the south London seat of Mitcham and Morden, he was returned for the Spelthorne constituency in 1970, which he described, with admirable feeling, as 'a most socially agreeable place'.[17] His charm was what made him appeal to Margaret Thatcher who, it was alleged, had a weakness for tall, dashing men. As a former Chief Whip, Atkins was a man of compromises and deals. He was not of the stamp of a Thatcher or a Bobby Sands. In general, his natural preference was to avoid confrontation. His old-fashioned courtesy, some people said, was a little affected and 'his somewhat overpowering sense of good manners cut little ice in the rough and tumble of Ulster politics'.[18]

Atkins's correspondence with Thatcher in April displayed a tendency to fuss and worry which Thatcher no doubt found slightly trying. He worried about the implications of Bobby Sands winning the Fermanagh by-election, while relaying the 'strong view of the Chief Constable' of the RUC that the British government 'should not embroil itself in the Fermanagh campaign in any way'. Atkins still believed, only six days before the by-election, that 'the best weapons against Sands' were the redoubtable figure of Harry West, the Unionist candidate, and the 'non-violent Catholic community themselves'. There still existed the belief in British official circles that Sands would somehow be defeated, but adequate provision was being made in case he was victorious. Atkins pointed out to Thatcher that there was no 'legal requirement' to allow Sands to attend Westminster or even take the oath of allegiance.[19]

Polling day in the Fermanagh and South Tyrone by-election on 9 April was unsurprisingly beset by controversy. There were allegations of soldiers voting more than once and, naturally enough, there was tight security in place to protect ballot boxes. After the polling stations had closed at 10 p.m., ballot boxes were flown by military helicopter to the official centre in Enniskillen, where the count would take place. Election observers on both sides expected a high turnout which they believed would favour Sands, although even on polling day Harry West still appeared to be the favourite. There was a highly irregular and 'unprecedented' intervention from the Labour shadow spokesman for Northern Ireland, Don Concannon, when he insisted that a 'vote for Sands' would be a vote of approval for the perpetrators of the 'murder of Lord Mountbatten and all the other senseless murders' that had taken place in Northern Ireland since the Troubles began in 1969.[20]

The result of the by-election was described as a 'serious blow' to the British government's security strategy in Northern Ireland. The whole basis of the strategy had been to 'criminalise' the IRA and those elements of the Republican movement which favoured violent means to secure their goals. The government had hoped that Sands's 'criminal' background would have alienated enough Nationalist support for him to be defeated in the Fermanagh and South Tyrone poll. Sands, however, won the election by a narrow but decisive margin, ending up ahead by 1,446 votes with 30,492 votes against Harry West's 29,046.

The result was a triumph for the Republicans and the IRA. Sands's supporters gleefully pointed out that his total of 30,000 votes was 10,000 more than the number of votes Margaret Thatcher had won in her own constituency in Finchley in 1979. Sands himself was believed to have heard the election result on radio in the prison hospital at the Maze. His election agent, Owen Carron, gave the traditional but highly emotional speech of thanks on behalf of the imprisoned and ever weakening Sands. Carron roused the Republicans present at the College of Further Education in Enniskillen with a speech that they all wanted to hear. He accused the British government of having 'done their best' to ensure a Unionist victory. He further added that the people of Fermanagh had 'voted against Unionism, voted against the H block', and that it was time that 'Britain did what she should always do – get out of Ireland'. West, the defeated Unionist candidate, could only describe the result as a 'sorry sight'.[21]

The prospect of having an elected MP starve himself to death was undoubtedly an embarrassment for the government. The British embassy in Washington became wary of the possible impact of Sands's election on public opinion in the United States. The British Ambassador to Washington, Nicko Henderson, pointed out that the 'election of Sands' would 'obviously be heavily exploited by NORAID [the Irish Northern Aid Committee – a body which raised money for the IRA in the US]', as well as by pro-IRA commentators in the United States. The weekend after Sands's election, Bernadette McAliskey, a Republican activist and former Sinn Fein MP in the Westminster parliament, arrived in New York to take part in television programmes and push the Republican message across the American media.

British officials in Washington believed that 'little or nothing' could be done to 'counter this effort in pro-IRA circles'.[22] Sands's election victory also 'demolished' one of the central arguments that the British government had employed, that 'the vast majority' of people in Northern Ireland 'Catholic as well as Protestant' were hostile to terrorism. It had always been a contention of successive British governments that the IRA did not 'enjoy numerically significant popular support'. Sands's victory sadly 'reflected an essentially sectarian voting pattern'. West had 'delivered' the Protestant vote. There had been no mainstream Catholic candidate, and, in the absence of one, Catholic voters had overwhelmingly backed Sands, even though his criminal past was well known, as were his IRA connections.

The British official class, embarrassed by Sands's victory, now looked for ways to disqualify or disbar him from the House of Commons. Atkins had already written on 8 April, the day before the by-election, to Francis Pym, the Leader of the House of Commons, suggesting understandably that it seemed 'beyond doubt that the Commons should not and would not countenance having a terrorist as a member'. Atkins believed that there 'would be a wide-spread view at Westminster that Sands should be expelled'. Atkins had assured Pym, a landowner and ex-cavalry officer, that he would not at the moment judge Sands's election 'to be a likely outcome', although it was a 'contingency for which we need to be prepared in advance'.

Atkins lacked a sense of proportion. The 'sooner Sands is expelled the better', he noted. He was quite prepared to organise a motion to expel Sands which could be 'moved at any time after the writ of election is returned', meaning that Atkins wished the House of Commons to vote to expel Sands almost immediately after he had been elected. 'I will be ready to ensure that, in the event of Sands being elected, the writ reaches Westminster at the earliest possible opportunity which in practice would be Monday 13th April.' This would allow time to vote to expel Sands before the House rose for the Easter Recess on 16 April.[23]

Atkins's letter of 8 April to Francis Pym showed how desperate he was to expel Sands and to reduce the government's humiliation at the hands of the IRA and the wider Republican movement. He was always perhaps more hysterical about the threat posed by Sands than any of his other ministerial colleagues. He felt that, as long as Sands was an MP, even though he was barred from taking his seat, he would have 'enhanced opportunity of embarrassing the Northern Ireland prison authorities'. He could then, Atkins feared, use his status to promote his 'main campaign to get convicted terrorists treated as "political prisoners" rather than simply criminals'.[24]

Pym had a different view. Early in the week following Sands's electoral triumph, he reported to the Cabinet the 'view of political leaders at Westminster that they should not try to expel Mr Sands'. After his election, a section of the British press seemed more reconciled to the idea of a compromise. Owen Carron, Bobby Sands's indefatigable election agent, held a press conference at the House of Commons on Tuesday 14 April, five days after the by-election. He said 'he was hopeful that talks could be arranged' between Sands and the British government. The next day the *Guardian* felt that Sands's new status as an elected representative made the case for a compromise more compelling. 'Mr Sands is on hunger strike for the right to be treated as a political prisoner.' The main consequences of being granted this status would be the 'freedom to wear his own clothes and abstain from prison clothes'. The seemingly trivial nature of these demands, according to the *Guardian*, 'should be capable of accommodation now that Mr Sands has won the election'.[25]

Thatcher remained slightly aloof from the technicalities of keeping Sands out of the House of Commons, but her public utterances were tough and uncompromising. April 1981 saw her travelling to the Gulf States as part of a mission to promote trade in the Middle East, as well as to cultivate key strategic and diplomatic relationships. While she was in the Gulf, telegrams from the Foreign Office in London, which had been briefed by the Northern Ireland Office in Belfast, were being regularly sent to her team. In a telegram to Abu Dhabi on 21 April, the Northern Ireland Office provided an assessment of the situation, pointing out once again that the focus of dissent had been 'supplied by Sands' election'. Now an elected Member of Parliament, Sands had become 'a folk hero'. The situation was made worse by the fact that schools were now on holiday, while the 'rioting in the last week' had included 'the first use of petrol bombs in Londonderry'.

The gloomy forecast from British officials in Northern Ireland was that there would continue to be 'trouble in Londonderry' until Sands 'either dies or comes off his hunger strike'. Meanwhile the officials were relieved that, 'apart from minor hooliganism', the trouble had not yet affected other parts of Northern Ireland. For her part, Thatcher used a press conference held during her visit to the Gulf to give what was probably her most defiant and unequivocal statement on the whole issue of the hunger strikes. At Riyadh, the capital of Saudi Arabia, answering a relatively bland question relating to the potential visit to Sands by three MPs from the Republic of Ireland, Thatcher simply asserted her much trumpeted line once again. 'There is no question of political status for someone serving a sentence for crime.' This was a bold statement. Her next remark deserves to be remembered as one of the most characteristically Thatcherite statements: 'Crime is crime is crime. It is not political, it is crime.'[26]

It was this kind of dogmatic certainty which infuriated opponents and delighted her ardent followers who, like many people in different contexts, loved certainty and direction in their political leaders. Later in the press conference, when asked about the possibility of any concessions at all to the prisoners, Thatcher simply reiterated, 'No, no concessions, no possible concessions on political status.' It was a rhetorical quirk of Thatcher's to repeat a formula of words, rather like a small child reciting a catechism. 'No, no, no' with its attendant variations was a common pattern of speech for her, most famously many years later, on 30 October 1990, when she responded to suggestions that the powers of European institutions might be increased.[27]

The 'no, no, no' aspect of her personality – repeating her favourite formulas, as though they were some incantatory prayer – was a feature of Thatcher's public utterances throughout 1981, but in no circumstances was this cry more repeated than on the issue of Northern Ireland. Thatcher refused to meet the Irish MPs who had proposed to visit Bobby Sands in his bed in the prison hospital. Relying once more on her penchant for legalism and the slightly priggish tone she adopted sometimes, she said, 'It is not my practice to meet MPs of other countries about a UK citizen resident in the UK.'[28] Thatcher could project a sense of power, of sureness of view, and she could provide inspiration, but emotional sensitivity, at least in public, was something she struggled to convey. It was in this field that the hunger strikes were so successful for the Republican cause, 'recruiting a lot of young people into the IRA'.[29]

The visit of three MPs from the Republic of Ireland was again a minor provocation to Thatcher since, like any sovereign government, the British government resented any interference in a domestic matter by politicians from foreign countries. The three Irish MPs, or TDs as they are more properly styled, sought to come to Ireland just after Easter, which fell in 1981 on the weekend of 17–19 April. Easter, mainly because of its obvious Christian symbolism and the legacy of the Easter 1916 Rising against British rule, was an 'emotive' time in the Irish calendar.[30] There was no doubt that the three Irish TDs, all noted Republicans, were seeking to increase their profiles ahead of a possible general election in the Republic later in the summer. 'We are surely beginning to see', an official in Atkins's office wrote to Nicholas Sanders who worked in the Prime Minister's private office, the 'run-up to a parliamentary election in the south'. It was, after all, Easter, 'traditionally the time for expressions, verbal and physical, of Republican sentiment in Ireland north and south'.[31]

The three TDs, Sile de Valera, granddaughter of the first President of the Republic, Éamon de Valera, Neil Blaney and John O'Connell, were all Members of the European Parliament. Two of the three were members of Fianna Fáil, the staunchly Republican party, while O'Connell was a member of the Irish Labour party. Atkins, in his conciliatory way, had been amenable to the idea that these three MPs should visit the prisoners. The Irish TDs arguably did not achieve much. They requested a 'confidential meeting in London' which was denied.

Thatcher and her government were in an awkward position, between two mutually implacably hostile forces, that of Unionism represented, at its most belligerent, by the Reverend Ian Paisley, and that of Nationalism, represented by Sands, the IRA and the other Republicans. Earlier in the spring, towards the end of March, Margaret Thatcher had been subjected to forcefully worded letters sent by Paisley in his own large and uncontrolled handwriting to the Prime Minister. Thatcher had visited the province on 5–6 March, just before the budget. On this occasion Paisley had written, 'You have come to Northern Ireland to deceive the people.' This, he believed, was part of a wider conspiracy, on the part of Margaret Thatcher and the Irish Taoiseach, or Prime Minister, Charles Haughey, to 'sell out' the Unionist population in the province. 'Hundreds of law-abiding citizens were not permitted under your orders to make a protest against your treachery in Dublin.'

Paisley objected to Thatcher having any dealings at all with Haughey, 'the son of an IRA man from Swatragh and himself an alleged gun runner', in Paisley's disdainful words.[32] Although most of the media attention was firmly focused on the fate of Sands, during much of April and March many hardline Unionists, whipped up by Ian Paisley's powerful rhetoric, were equally vocal and potentially violent. The moderate Unionists were of 'virtually no help'. Their main party the UUP, or Ulster Unionist party, was, in the words of a British government official in Northern Ireland at the beginning of April, 'divided' and lacking in 'firm leadership'.

Although the Ulster Unionists had managed to get their man adopted as the official Unionist candidate in the Fermanagh and South Tyrone by-election, Paisley could mobilise public opinion on the ground. 'Dr Paisley', by April, was clearly bent on continuing his 'campaign against the Government'. 'What tricks he has still got up his sleeve we do not yet know,' British government officials said, but the Northern Ireland Office was obviously planning how it would deal 'with possible Paisley moves which threaten law and order'.[33] Thatcher's visit on 5 and 6 March had been well timed in meeting the 'immediate purpose' of conveying 'reassurance to the Protestant/Unionist population and taking some of the wind from Dr Paisley's sails'.

Paisley's rallies had enjoyed some support. About 15,000 of his followers had gathered at Stormont, the old seat of the Northern Ireland government, on 28 March to protest against any deals Thatcher was alleged to be making with the Republic of Ireland. This number was only half of the 30,000 Paisley had hoped for. 'Meanwhile Paisley's antics continue against the background of the continuing hunger strike at the Maze Prison,' was the somewhat exasperated remark from the bureaucrats at the Northern Ireland Office. In the midst of all the pathos and excitement surrounding the circumstances of Bobby Sands's death, it was easy to forget that the Ian Paisley 'bandwagon' was something with which Thatcher and her government were forced to contend.[34] Yet at the beginning of April, the Unionist 'bandwagon' had not been 'brought to a halt', and the British government would 'need to continue to make reassuring noises to the Unionist community as Paisley tries to accelerate his campaign'.[35]

In the midst of this political whirlwind, Charles Haughey, the crafty and venal Irish Prime Minister, was another factor that Thatcher had to take into account. Haughey lurked in the background during the hunger strikes, particularly in the final stages of Bobby Sands's death. There were rumours, just before Easter, that Sands's family would 'ask Mr Haughey to intercede with the Prime Minister'.[36] Haughey, while trying to portray himself as a disciplined and hardline Republican, was not averse to the finer things in life, and was a well-known practitioner of flattery and compromise. His principal concern was that violence in Northern Ireland might 'spill over into the Republic'.

For Haughey, like nearly everyone else connected with the politics of Northern Ireland, matters 'had taken a turn for the worse because of the election of Sands to Parliament'. Writing on 22 April, Dermot Nally, a Haughey ally and fixer, told Downing Street that the Taoiseach was 'under pressure to do something', because of the intervention of the three Irish TDs and Members of the European Parliament, who were now posing as intermediaries in the hunger-strike dispute. Haughey offered the possibility that two European Commissioners for Human Rights, appointed by the Council of Europe, could be persuaded to visit the Maze 'privately', whatever that meant, 'to see what improvements in the prison administration' had been carried out.[37]

Haughey got his wish. The European Commissioners met British officials at the Foreign Office and the Northern Ireland Office on the evening of 24 April. The British civil servants made it clear to the Commissioners that they did not want Gerry Adams, the young Sinn Fein leader, to be present at the meeting between them and Sands at the Maze. The Commissioners dutifully told their official hosts that 'it was their normal practice only to see the complainant with the complainant's lawyer'. Haughey's suggestion that European Commissioners should be involved had received some support, as it appeared, from none other than Marcella Sands, Bobby's sister. She had applied to the Commission 'under Article 25 of the European Convention on Human Rights'. Whether this application really came from Marcella or not, it described her 'brother' as 'a victim of a violation of the convention by the British Government'.

The application stated correctly enough that Sands's 'state of health' was such that he was 'unable himself to make an application directly'. It also argued that the conditions of his imprisonment, in contravention of Article 10 of the Convention, meant that Sands was unable to give expression to the opinions of his constituents, 'despite the fact that he is a democratically elected Member of the British Parliament'. The application denounced 'the inflexible approach of the state authorities'. It was ironic that the team around Sands set so much store on his having been elected as a 'Member of the British Parliament', when Republicans denied that parliament's jurisdiction over Northern Ireland.[38]

Marcella Sands's application, dated 24 April, clearly envisaged the European Commissioners of Human Rights playing some role in the Sands affair. Yet, when they reached the Maze prison on Saturday 25 April, they learnt that Mr Sands himself 'did not wish to associate himself with the application'. Sands, however, did express a 'willingness to see the delegation in the presence of three persons named by him'. This was, of course, precisely what the British government did not want to happen. It came as no surprise that after 'further consultation' the delegation reached the conclusion that 'in these circumstances it was not possible to see and confer with Mr Sands and no meeting took place'.[39]

The merry-go-round with the European Commissioners was exactly the kind of official exercise which Thatcher hated. The Republicans themselves thought better of calling in European Human Rights Commissioners. They turned sharply against the involvement of those well-meaning but ultimately ineffectual bureaucrats and on 25 April issued a statement from the Maze prison, allegedly made by members of Bobby Sands's family. The four Republican prisoners were on hunger strike, it was asserted, on behalf of their '440 comrades here in the H blocks and Armagh'. The statement claimed that the European Commissioners' intervention had been 'divisive' and had 'helped Government attempts to confuse the issue'.

Marcella Sands had made the application in 'good faith' but had been 'misled by Mr Haughey into believing that the Commission would deliver on the political prisoners' demands'. This clearly was not going to happen. Sands, or rather the people around him, accused Haughey of using the Commission's intervention for his own ends, as 'a vehicle for getting the British Government off the hook'.[40]

Behind the very human tragedy of Bobby Sands and his anxious family, there was a wide range of political actors seeking to exploit the tragic story of one individual for their own ends. The Northern Ireland Office in Belfast was convinced that Gerry Adams had been responsible for the press statements which suggested that Marcella Sands 'didn't request at any time for the commission to investigate the demands of the protesting prisoners in H Block and Armagh'. This was clearly an attempt to rewrite history. It made sense to blame Charles Haughey.

At this moment in his career, Haughey had been Taoiseach for barely eighteen months. Although he liked to portray himself as a man of the people, Haughey enjoyed an 'extraordinarily lavish lifestyle', which was funded by obscure sources. He owned a Georgian mansion on a 280-acre estate, just a few miles from the working-class constituency, in north Dublin, where he had a devoted following. He posed as an Anglophobe, which he was by birth and conviction, yet he cultivated all the tastes and mannerisms of the Anglo-Irish gentry. He prided himself on his collection, and knowledge, of antique furniture, fine art, horses and wines.[41] Like many radical politicians who mellow with age, he could play the old tunes of anti-British rhetoric, and he certainly had credentials as a Republican. Yet, in his love of money and conspicuous consumption, he had outgrown the narrow and dour Republicanism of his youth.

In the issue of the hunger strikes, Haughey was caught between trying to burnish his Republican credentials and trying to behave like a responsible head of government in an Ireland which had only recently, in 1973, joined the European Economic Community. Sands and his associates had expected that Haughey would be 'compelled to support their demands publicly', but this was something that the Taoiseach refused to do. Privately he expressed sympathy for the cause of the hunger strikers. 'What can I do?' he plaintively asked a sister of one prisoner. Publicly, he said and did nothing and, even more clandestinely, suggested to the British government that he was really on their side.[42] Haughey was also said to put special trust in a 'unique relationship' with Margaret Thatcher.[43]

In the last days of Sands's life, a battle was being fought between the IRA and the Irish government in Dublin over the hunger strikers' legacy. Atkins felt this when he spoke to Thatcher in a telephone call which took place on the evening of Saturday 25 April: 'The truth is that there is a great struggle going on between the Dublin Government on the one hand and the IRA on the other as to the control of all this.'[44]

The immense celebrity of Bobby Sands ensured that many highly placed people, at home and abroad, felt obliged to give their opinions and attempted to intervene. Naturally enough, senior churchmen of the Catholic Church were prompt to come forward to act as intermediaries between the prisoners and a government, led by Thatcher, which was increasingly being seen as intransigent. On 27 April, Cardinal Tomas O'Fiaich sent a telegram to Margaret Thatcher, appealing to her and her Cabinet 'to implement proposals on prison dress and work'. Telegrams were received from Catholic prelates from even further afield. The Cardinal Archbishop of Los Angeles, Tim Manning, in a telegram dated 25 April, urged the Prime Minister to reach an accommodation in his capacity as the 'Irish-born Cardinal Archbishop of Los Angeles with its nine million people'. Terence Cooke, the Catholic Archbishop of New York, also added his weight to the dispute.

On 29 April, Humphrey Atkins met Father Magee, the personal envoy of the Pope, to discuss his meeting with Sands. Magee told Atkins that Sands was 'surprisingly well' and that Sands had asked him to 'thank the Pope for sending a representative'. In response to Father Magee's plea to end the hunger strike, Sands responded, 'Do not ask me that.' Magee explained that his entreaty was a 'personal plea from the Pope', to which Sands simply replied that the Pope would 'understand that the people of Northern Ireland' were a 'downtrodden people'. It was clear to all that Sands was approaching what, in the eyes of many of his allies, was a martyr's fate.[45]

On 29 April, the Socialist Group of the European Parliament, through the offices of the UK Representative in Brussels, requested the British government's 'immediate intervention in the Northern Ireland Crisis'. This group, presumably trying to appeal to their domestic electorates, suggested that the government send a 'representative to talk with Sands in an effort to break the deadlock'. Finally, in a phrase which probably did not inspire Thatcher's cooperation, they concluded, 'The Socialist Group urges you to act.' Once again, Thatcher politely but firmly rejected their demand.[46]

For Thatcher, the situation of the hunger strikers was straightforward. They were criminals, violent thugs who had contravened the rule of law. To many in Northern Ireland and in the wider world, they were victims of colonial oppression. This feeling was expressed even more acutely in the immediate aftermath of Sands's death on 5 May. It was the reaction in the United States which, naturally enough, caused the Thatcher government most concern. Margaret Thatcher told Charles Haughey at one stage that 'she was less concerned about the situation in Dublin than about that in North America'.[47] Opinion in the United States was polarised as the drama of Bobby Sands's final days unfolded. In the days before Sands died, 'in New York and other large cities where the Irish once held sway' small rallies and demonstrations had taken place, usually in front of British consulates or the local offices of British Airways.

Demonstrations also took place further afield. From Delhi, it was reported that the 'extensive and critical Indian press coverage' of Sands's death had been accompanied by an altercation in the Upper House of Parliament between members of the Congress party and members of the opposition who had insisted on standing for a minute's silence in 'honour' of Sands. There were rumours of demonstrations being planned outside the mission in Delhi, though the High Commissioner had so far, on 7 May, not reported any further developments.[48] The mood in the capitals of Western Europe, however, was more supportive of the British government's stance. From Bonn, the West German capital, on 6 May it was reported that the mood was conciliatory towards the British government. 'Comment shows widespread understanding of HMG's position,' the telegram from Bonn noted. There were 'passing remarks of respect' for the 'courage and willpower' that Sands had shown. Yet there was recognition that 'if Britain had made concessions' enormous pressure would have been placed on governments 'in Germany, Italy, France or Spain to make similar concessions to terrorists there'. The respectable *Die Welt* paper sternly acknowledged that to make 'these criminals political prisoners would be to justify murder and terrorism'.[49]

Of all the foreign interventions, perhaps the most extraordinary was one made by a group nicknamed 'the four horsemen' by British government officials. This group of four senior US politicians, each boasting some Irish descent, intruded on the scene of Anglo-Irish relations and sought to make political capital at home. Senator Edward Kennedy was the well-known son of Joseph Kennedy, and younger brother of the Democratic party icons, President John F. Kennedy and Senator Robert Kennedy; Hugh Carey was the Governor of New York, the grandson of Irish immigrants; while Tip O'Neill was the well-known Speaker of the House of Representatives, a 'gregarious and irrepressibly liberal Bostonian' with a 'bulbous nose' and 'a mop of white hair'.[50] Daniel Moynihan, in contrast, was a donnish figure, a Senator from New York State, who had been a respected sociologist.

The 'four horsemen' had large numbers of Irish Americans in their constituencies in the United States. All based in the north-east or New York, they had urged Irish-Americans to stop sending money to arm the IRA. Moynihan had described the terror group privately as 'a bunch of murderous thugs'.[51] Yet, in the aftermath of the death of Bobby Sands, their critical gaze was cast upon Margaret Thatcher and her government. Senator Kennedy issued a press statement on 5 May, the very day of Bobby Sands's death, in which he 'urged' the 'British Government, which has clear responsibility for prison administration in Northern Ireland', to act 'on an urgent basis to end its policy of inflexibility, and to implement reasonable reforms capable of achieving a humanitarian settlement of the hunger strikes, so that the tragedy of Bobby Sands is not repeated'.[52]

Kennedy, a large, flamboyant and bruising character who spoke with a thick Boston brogue, was described as a 'Rabelaisian figure in the Senate and in life'.[53] He was a forceful character even if he was a little verbose in his speaking and writing style. Though it was not right to 'yield to terrorism', it was also wrong to 'yield to impulses of intransigence'. Through the dense fog of Kennedy's overblown rhetoric, a clear picture of how Thatcher and her government were viewed can be discerned. 'Intransigence' and 'inflexibility' were words frequently employed to describe Mrs Thatcher's attitude towards the hunger strikers. Hugh Carey, the Governor of New York, made much the same point, writing somewhat bizarrely to Lord Carrington, the Foreign Secretary, urging him to use his 'stature' and 'influence' in Cabinet to 'halt this widening tragedy'.

The presumption of these US politicians who, because of their family links to Ireland, felt a moral authority in this subject must have been irksome to Thatcher. Their message to the Prime Minister included a condemnation of violence which threatened to be 'very unpopular' with the Irish American community who were 'exerting enormous pressure'.[54]

Domestic feeling in Massachusetts, the home state of Senator Kennedy and Speaker O'Neill, was expressed by a highly unusual intervention from the office of the Assistant Majority Leader in the Massachusetts House of Representatives, who appealed directly to 'Prime Minister Thatcher'. From the elegant and imposing neo-classical edifice of the State House in Boston, Marie Howe urged Thatcher 'in the name of common decency to be flexible in your position with the prisoners in British occupied Ireland'. Once again, the question of Thatcher's 'inflexibility' dominated the minds of certain foreign politicians. 'The entire world is well aware', the state Congresswoman wrote, 'of the intransigent position of your Government regarding this deplorable situation.' The Massachusetts legislature passed a bald resolution condemning 'the Government of Prime Minister Margaret

Thatcher for its insensitivity to the value of human life and the real issues of Ireland's divisive struggle, and wholeheartedly supports the ultimate objectives of the IRA'.[55]

Despite the posturing and the big words and speeches, there was a real sense in which Thatcher had to deal with a potential public relations fiasco for her government on the international stage. She was concerned that the 'message' of her government on this particular issue was not getting out to British missions across the world. The telegram from Delhi on 7 May gave her especial concern, as the team of British diplomats in that capital had suggested that 'it would be helpful to have further guidance' and particularly 'to know the precise charges on which Sands was convicted and the form of trial he underwent'. Such a request displayed a fundamental ignorance about the situation in Northern Ireland. Thatcher was rather disappointed. 'The Prime Minister has been under the impression that all our missions overseas were being kept fully in the picture about the developing situation in Northern Ireland.' She found it 'surprising' that 'so important a mission as Delhi should lack background of the kind referred to'.

Behind the well-scripted formal language used in diplomatic correspondence, it was not difficult to sense the frustration that Thatcher often felt at having to justify herself to a world which, in her view, had only a rudimentary understanding of the issues at stake. Governor Carey of New York wanted to come to the United Kingdom to meet the Prime Minister personally. This was clearly 'to enhance his own political standing rather than to have a reasoned discussion on Northern Ireland', as far as the British embassy in Washington was concerned.[56] He was obviously rebuffed.

Meanwhile Thatcher was forced to hold conversations in her private rooms in the House of Commons with various key figures such as John Hume, a moderate Catholic Republican from the non-violent SDLP (Social Democratic and Labour party), James Molyneaux, the leader of the Ulster Unionists, and Michael Foot. In his meeting with Thatcher

on the evening of Thursday 14 May, Foot suggested that he was 'looking for concessions' which would enable the hunger strikers 'to call it
off', or, failing that, 'put the onus for the continuation of the present
situation on them'. This, according to the Downing Street account
of the conversation, was what 'Mr Hume had been saying'. Thatcher
turned indignantly on Foot, saying that she was 'amazed' by what he
had to say. She then confronted him with a barrage of legalism. The
report 'made by the European Commission on Human Rights last year
had been implemented in full'; there was 'now a thoroughly liberal
regime being applied in modern prisons'. Foot was thinking in terms
of politics and public mood; Thatcher was, as ever, comfortable with a
legalistic, even scientific, justification for her policy.

To Mrs Thatcher's way of thinking, Michael Foot 'was giving notice
that he was a push-over'.[57] It was only natural, in the sensitive politics of Northern Ireland, that the Reverend Ian Paisley should have
complained that he had not been given due respect by the Prime
Minister. In a telegram sent on the morning of Thatcher's meeting with
Michael Foot, Paisley complained bitterly of the shocking treatment he
had received. 'This morning I was advised by your office that you were
willing to see me but only for fifteen minutes.' This was outrageous in
light of the fact that 'you are reported to have given Mr Hume, who is
not even a Member of Parliament, some 60–90 minutes to put the case
of the IRA murderers'. This, Paisley believed was a 'calculated insult' to
a man who wished 'to make representations on behalf of the law abid-
ing Protestant community'. He flatly refused to take up the offer of 'a
fifteen minute meeting'.[58] It was this level of intransigence which made
Paisley, like Thatcher, such a formidable force.

In the meantime, on 14 May, the very day on which she would see
the Leader of the Opposition, Thatcher had sent a strongly worded
response to the 'four horsemen'. 'I welcome your clear restatement of
your unequivocal condemnation of all violence in Northern Ireland.'
But on the question of her inflexibility, she relied on the strict letter of

the law to exculpate herself. 'You question a "posture of inflexibility" that must lead inevitably to more violence and death in Northern Ireland. But that is *not* [emphasis in original] the government's posture.'

Employing her favourite means of defending herself by going on the offensive, Thatcher pointed out that 'HM Government has in fact acted with great flexibility. We have offered a series of improvements in conditions to all prisoners, most of which the protesters have rejected.' Rather disingenuously, she pointed to the fact that her government had, in her words, 'facilitated visits to the hunger strikers by the European Commission of Human Rights', which of course had not been her idea, but rather Charles Haughey's, if anyone's. Rather like a school-child rattling off her times table, she then listed the other people or bodies who had been allowed to visit the hunger strikers: members of the Dublin parliament, the representative of the official opposition in the United Kingdom and the 'personal representative of the Pope', for good measure. 'None of these actions has had any effect upon the prisoners whose sole purpose is to establish a political justification' for what Thatcher described as 'their appalling record of murder and violence' which, moreover, 'deserve the same total condemnation in Northern Ireland as they would in the United States'.[59]

Thatcher developed what can only be described as an obsession with justifying her government in the United States. Her officials were even anxious by the third week of May to find out what the policy in the United States was regarding the clothing prisoners were allowed to wear during their incarceration. It 'would be helpful to know whether convicted prisoners in the United States were allowed to wear their own clothing'.[60] Her concern with US public opinion was understandable, since the recently elected US President, Ronald Reagan, was arguably one of the few international politicians to be wholly supportive of her general political point of view.

Although it has now emerged that Thatcher was perhaps not as rigid in her dealings with the IRA as her public pose would suggest, the Prime Minister's mental world of simple binary opposites could easily cope with the hunger strikes. The hunger strikers were evildoers who had, as she told the US politicians, a clear record 'of murder and violence'. It was that unbending sense of moral rectitude which carried Thatcher through the crisis arising from Bobby Sands's death. Publicly, the image of a Prime Minister resolutely uncompromising in her dealings with terrorists conformed to her 'Iron Lady' image. Privately, there is evidence that later, in July 1981, after four of the ten hunger strikers had died, she did in reality authorise 'a communication with the IRA leadership through an intermediary, Brendan Duffy'. But, if this was the case, she probably convinced herself that she had not embarked on such a course. Her overtures, it would appear, were in any case rejected by an IRA leadership which, it has been argued, may have prolonged the hunger strike 'unnecessarily in order to extract maximum political benefit' from the pathos surrounding it.[61]

These subjects, even after the passing of a generation, remain controversial. What was palpable and defiantly unequivocal was the strength of Margaret Thatcher's rhetoric, her own sense of moral conviction, of righteous indignation and resolve. As she told the 'four horsemen', after assuring them of her government's 'flexibility', her government was 'not prepared to surrender control of the prisons'. She was 'not prepared to be coerced by protest action, in whatever form, into changes for which there is no justification on humanitarian grounds'.[62]

As May proceeded, and the initial sense of outrage surrounding Sands's death had diminished, Thatcher began to feel more self-assured. In the course of that month, she addressed several conferences of well-wishers, and it was at these gatherings and public events that she put her case most forcefully. The Conservative Women's Conference held on 20 May at Methodist Central Hall was one such event. Here Thatcher once again expressed her devotion to the cause of freedom, and her determination to withstand terror and intimidation: 'Terrorism can only be beaten if terrorists know they can never win.' Once again, her tendency to seek to defend her position by using abstract ideas like 'freedom' and 'democracy' came to the fore. She never shrank from using these big and often problematic concepts to defend her positions. 'In a democracy our determination to defeat the terrorists is based on our commitment to freedom,' she thundered.

Her remarks at the Conservative Women's Conference were a vintage expression of her whole philosophy of government. She stressed that there was a 'desire for harmony' in Britain, but she took the unfashionable view that the ability of governments directly to foster harmony was limited. Harmony 'can't be handed down from above'. She believed in the necessity of some kind of political conflict, a battle of ideas. This, of course, was very different from the vision offered by the Social Democrats and their allies. 'Those who pretend that' harmony can be handed down from above 'are either offering policies with which no one could quarrel – which are no policies at all – or are moving towards coercion'. For Thatcher, some kind of battle of ideas was essential to politics. 'It's the nature of free men to hold differing opinions . . . True harmony is the outcome of co-operation freely given. It cannot be imposed, though Government must create the conditions that make it possible.'[63]

Thatcher, in this communion with her faithful flock, resorted to the catechisms of her youth. She finished her rousing address with short, staccato proverbial utterances: 'It takes struggles in life to make strength. It takes fights for principles to make fortitude. It takes crises to give courage,' just as it took 'singleness of purpose to reach an objective'. Finally, she roused her audience with a pledge of ultimate success. 'We have the strength. We have the fortitude. We have the courage. And we shall reach our objective.' It seems unclear to which persons exactly the 'we' referred to. She would later get into considerable trouble when she uttered the phrase 'We have become a grandmother' on the birth of her first grandchild, Michael, in 1989.[64] Yet she used the pronoun 'we' constantly, especially when she was at her most belligerent.

Thatcher was very good, as politicians often are, at exculpating herself and her government from any responsibility in the creation of domestic problems. She was always prone to find wider patterns, and point to an international dimension, to difficulties experienced at home. It is not 'just in Northern Ireland', she told the delegates of the Conservative women, 'that the terrorist casts his cruel shadow. The international scene is disfigured by violence. The attacks on President Reagan and the Pope [these had taken place on 30 March and 13 May respectively]; terrorism outrages in Spain, Italy and Germany. The world is daily assaulted by those who seek to impose their views upon us through violence and fear.' Thatcher made the same point in an address to the Scottish Conservative conference in Perth on 8 May, three days after the death of Bobby Sands. 'It is no comfort to us to know that a similar challenge is being mounted in other European countries. In Germany, France, Italy and Spain groups whose only mandate is their fanaticism, backed by bullet and bomb, have been seeking to displace the ballot box as the means by which civilised communities resolved their differences.'[65]

On 24 May, a Sunday, Thatcher gave an address at the reopening of John Wesley's House on City Road in the Square Mile of the City of London, the capital's financial district. She was fulfilling a pledge to attend the opening of the House given to the Speaker of the House of Commons, George Thomas, himself a committed Welsh Methodist, in January. Her diary secretary, Caroline Stephens, had tried in vain to dissuade Thatcher from attending this commemoration, since she felt the Prime Minister deserved a rest from her frequent diary commitments. This event, however, was something which Margaret Thatcher felt compelled to attend and participate in. 'I want to say what a great honour and privilege it for me', she said, 'to re-open the house where John Wesley lived, and for us all to be here.'

Thatcher went on to discourse on the biblical text which had been chosen when Wesley died: 'Know ye not that there is a friend and a great man for us this day in Israel?' Thatcher unconsciously reworded the reference. The actual biblical text, from 2 Samuel 3:38, reads, 'Know ye not that there is a prince and a great man fallen this day in Israel?' If she had felt unsure of it she could easily have got a civil servant to give the exact reference, word perfect. The fact that she often misquoted the King James version showed that she felt so familiar with it that she had no need to check the wording. It could be said that few misquoted the King James Bible more frequently than Margaret Thatcher.

She referred in this homiletic speech to John Wesley's mother: 'you would know her as a lady with an iron will'. It was clear that John Wesley was an intensely personal hero of hers. 'He preached 40,000 sermons – a bit daunting, isn't it? . . . He crossed the Irish Channel fifty times. He wrote over four hundred books. When he was eighty-one, in this house, he was complaining that he could write no more than fifteen hours a day. When he was eighty-six he was found bitterly complaining that he hadn't the strength to preach more than two sermons a day.' She alluded gently to Wesley's Lincolnshire roots, without labouring the point by mentioning that Lincolnshire was also the county of her birth. 'What more can one say about this astonishing man? The son of a Lincolnshire vicar.'

The Wesley brothers, both John and Charles, were, for Thatcher, a pair of perfect heroes. 'People often say today: "What can one person do amongst so many? What can one person do?" You hear the cry so often, but you never heard that from John Wesley. You never heard it from Charles. They were sure one man and a faith could change the world . . . and they did.' In summing up the credo and inspiration of the Wesleys, Thatcher was no doubt talking about the sources of her own drive and determination. 'How often do you say, as I say quite often, to someone whom you know: "You can't do better than your best?" But faith and an inspirational brilliance do enable us to do just that: better than our best, and it enabled John and Charles Wesley to do better than their best.' Through these brothers, the band of Methodists 'began to circle the world and bring about a great influence among the peoples of the world'. Above all, the Wesleys had 'that faith within'. It was this which 'enabled them to speak and to convey the truth to their generation'.[66]

Fortified by this 'inner faith', Thatcher felt empowered to deal with terrorists. At the end of the month, on Thursday 28 May, four days after the rousing address to the Methodists at City Hall, Thatcher addressed an audience at Stormont in Northern Ireland. She turned accusations of her own intransigence and inflexibility on their head. It was the Provisional IRA which had remained 'inflexible and intransigent in the face of all that we have done'. Her government would 'staunchly uphold the law and ensure that it is applied equally and fairly'. Once again, in a remarkable way, she stressed the limitations of government, suggesting that her administration 'cannot bring peace and tranquillity. These things are not in our gift.' She stressed individual responsibility for bringing about peace. 'The necessary will, desire and understand-ing' to bring about peace 'can only come from the hearts and minds of men and women here in the Province'. This was a message of Protestant individualism, the lessons, once again, of Bunyan and John Wesley. 'No Government can make people thoughtful and considerate towards one and other [sic].'[67]

After the lunchtime speech, Thatcher gave extensive interviews to ITN, Ulster TV and other local news stations, voicing her firmly held convictions about Northern Ireland and the hunger strikes. The theme in these interviews was much the same: 'you can't compromise with violence, ever. You have to beat it.' Since the death of Bobby Sands, barely three weeks previously, twenty people had died in the province through violence. Thatcher praised the security forces – 'both the Army and the Police' – for 'impartially upholding the law'. When charged with being 'inflexible', Thatcher found a new way to defend herself. 'In upholding the rule of law, in defending people impartially, in standing out against violence, I am inflexible,' she said to the ITN reporter. She rebutted the charge entirely in her interview with Ulster TV: 'Inflexible,

inflexible, how totally and utterly wrong. Do you know the Maze is one of the most humanitarian prisons in the world.' In her scientific and methodical way, Thatcher boasted of how she had 'enquired after the regimes practised in prisons in the United States and in Europe'. To RTE Belfast: 'I am not being inflexible. The people who are being inflexible and intransigent are the people in charge of the hunger strike in the Maze.' She now had her lines sharpened and ready.[68]

The hunger strikes had threatened to be an international public relations disaster for Thatcher. It was such a problem that John J. Louis, the US Ambassador to the United Kingdom, offered to help. In a letter to Thatcher dated 29 June, he wrote, 'I hope you will forgive my gratuitous suggestions to you concerning possible methods for explaining the Northern Ireland situation more effectively to the citizens of the United States. I suggested the idea of employing a New York public relations and advertising firm only because I have spent part of my life in that business, and because I know that the *best* of these firms can do much to help in this area.'[69] Louis was a dignified and quiet man, 'more of a traditional business conservative than an ideologue of the Reagan Revolution'. He had inherited a fortune and had pursued a successful career in advertising and marketing, before becoming US Ambassador to the Court of St James's in March 1981.

To Thatcher, public relations were important, but moral certainty and conviction were of greater weight. As the hunger strikes rumbled on and petered out in the course of 1981, it was her own sense of moral rectitude which sustained her. The outcome for Haughey had been damaging. His Fianna Fáil party had been 'hurt by the H-Block issue' in the general election in June in the Republic of Ireland. In imitation of Sands's own electoral triumph, nine constituencies saw H Block candidates put up, and Haughey was 'taunted by supporters of the H-Block candidates' wherever he went.[70] His party 'lost ground' during the campaign, and the H Block issue, in the words of his biographer, 'probably made the difference that led to Haughey's defeat in his bid for re-election as Taoiseach' in that June election.[71] Thatcher had potentially another three years before she would be forced to face her own electoral trial. She welcomed such election contests as the ultimate expression of democracy and of freedom which, according to her own lights, she had defended so valiantly against the men of violence in Ireland.

Riots

Monday 13 July 1981 – The Prime Minister was in Liverpool for a series of back-to-back meetings. She looked agitated and concerned, but she was in a mood for listening. The first meeting was scheduled for 9.30 a.m. at police headquarters. Thatcher met Kenneth Oxford, the Chief Constable of Merseyside, together with the Deputy Chief Constable and other senior officers of the force. Oxford was clear about what he wanted. People 'charged with offences arising from the disturbances should be dealt with quickly by the courts'. The Chief Constable believed that 'Short sharp sentences would have a considerable deterrent effect.'[1]

The Chief Constable of Merseyside and his force had been stretched the week before by urban riots which had ripped through Toxteth, a district of urban Liverpool, through Moss Side in Manchester and through Southall in west London. The Southall disturbances had been aggravated by the clash 'between white skinheads and Asian youths'.[2] During the confrontation on 3 July in Southall, Thatcher remembered the police becoming 'the main victims, attacked with petrol bombs, bricks and anything else to hand'. Thatcher, whose authoritarian instincts were well known, remembered with horror how the 'mob' had 'even turned on firemen and ambulancemen'.

In Toxteth police intercepted a motorcyclist on Selborne Street. A crowd of young people quickly gathered, as people jostled and abuse was hurled. Amid the tension, a violent scuffle ensued which saw three policeman injured and the arrest of a young black man, Leroy Cooper, a twenty-year-old photography student. Leroy had been attending a youth club near Selborne Street and, as reports of the interception filtered through, he and his friends 'went up to see what was going on'. He arrived at the scene and the police said 'it was nothing to do with' any of the gathering crowd. In the violence that followed, Leroy Cooper was identified as the chief culprit. He was charged with assaulting three police officers. In the trial that followed, he pleaded guilty because he 'didn't want a sentence of three to five years'. He always protested his innocence. 'The idea that I had allegedly battered and maimed three police officers was ridiculous.'[3]

The significance of the incident that took place on 3 July 1981 in Toxteth went beyond the fate of Leroy Cooper, who was in prison for six weeks on remand following his arrest. The incident sparked a wave of disturbances that evolved into full-blown riots, 'with pitched battles between police officers and youths throwing petrol bombs and paving stones'.[4] The explosion of violence witnessed by Toxteth on the weekend of 4–5 July did not emerge overnight, but rather was the result of simmering resentment and tensions over many months. The Merseyside force of the time had a 'particularly bad reputation in the area for stopping and searching black youths'. Officers were frequently accused of planting drugs on youths in a practice known locally as 'agriculture' or 'going farming'.

One community worker in the area remembered the background to the Toxteth riots of 1981. 'There were a lot of incidents of harassment, drug planting, people being criminalised for trivial reasons, heavy-handed policing and the final spark was the heavy-handed arrest' of Leroy Cooper.[5] More relevantly, in the redoubtable figure of Kenneth Oxford, the Merseyside Police had a chief constable of 'the old school' who 'maintained a starkly traditional view of police work and its management'. His management style was 'feudal', while his personality was 'authoritarian'. He was often accused of arrogance in his personal dealings with colleagues. 'If I am arrogant,' he pompously remarked, 'then the spice of arrogance is a necessary constituent of command.'[6]

Against this background, youths in Toxteth were ready for a violent expression of their discontent. Once unleashed, 'the ferocity of the disturbances overwhelmed the authorities'. In addition to attacks on supermarkets, the firebombing of a bank and numerous other businesses, the rioters succeeded in achieving the 'total destruction' of the Liverpool Racquet Club, which had opened on Upper Parliament Street in 1877.[7] Wally Brown, a prominent community leader, who acted as a negotiator and intermediary at the time of the riots, vividly remembered the burning of the Rialto, a complex of buildings around an old ballroom. 'It had a cupola roof which must have been made of copper and was glowing.' The police now resorted to using tear gas amid the disorder.[8]

The first wave of rioting in Toxteth lasted for nine days and spread throughout Liverpool. Police reinforcements had to be summoned from as far away as 'Cumbria, the West Midlands and even Devon' in a bid to restore some degree of order to a distracted and tumultuous city. After the first week of the riots, the Merseyside Chief Constable, the self-assured Mr Oxford, made a careful tabulation of the damage that had been wrought: 468 police officers had been injured, 500 people had been arrested and at least seventy buildings had been demolished. Oxford refused to seek sociological or economic causes for the riots. In his view, the devastation had been the work of 'thieves and vagabonds' who needed no excuse for their violent and destructive acts.[9]

Thatcher no doubt shared Kenneth Oxford's uncomplicated views. She instinctively sided with the police and the forces of 'law and order', in that familiar phrase which was never far from her lips. On Wednesday 8 July, the Prime Minister used a party political broadcast to talk directly about the riots. The broadcast had been scheduled long before Toxteth had burst into flames. She opened with the candid admission that she had 'expected tonight to talk wholly about unemployment but events in Liverpool have changed that'. To many on the left, however, and certainly to the Social Democrats, the two issues, the scale and nature of unemployment and the phenomenon of urban riots, were linked. To Margaret Thatcher, they were separate and unrelated.

'What happened there', the Prime Minister remarked in a visibly pained way, 'horrified us all.' She continued, 'A thousand policemen embattled in one of our great cities. Two-hundred injured,' before adding sharply that 'Nothing can justify, nothing can excuse and no-one can condone the appalling violence we've all seen on television.' Once again, it was the nature of individual personal morality, and not government policy, which was to blame: 'Government and Parliament can make the law. Police and courts can uphold the law, but a free society will only survive if we, its citizens, obey the law and teach our children to do so.' Her stark message was one which put the blame for the riots squarely on the shoulders of the rioters and not on the police, and still less on society.

The dispute over the cause of the riots revealed a faultline in British politics. To the left, the SDP and the 'wets', inner-city riots were a direct consequence of Thatcher's divisive economic policies. This idea was popularly aired by the SDP leaders in their bid to distinguish their own caring realism from Thatcherite dogma and hard-heartedness. 'With unemployment rising steadily over 20 years our inner city problems have grown apace as have racial and social tensions and Brixton, Toxteth and Moss Side only underline the deterioration,' wrote David Owen that summer.[10] To Thatcher and the right, including many in the police forces in the country, the riots were a simple 'law and order' issue. To Thatcher in particular, there was the moral element: the notion of moral depravity and moral health, underpinned by the even more basic concepts of good and evil.

It was clear to writers at the time that there was an equivalence, in Thatcher's mind, between the rioters in urban districts on the mainland and the violent IRA, and their hunger-strike associates, in Northern Ireland. Throughout July 1981, Thatcher's 'general tone remained strict'. Her message on the riots 'was strongly reminiscent of years of official comment on Northern Ireland'. Her response to riots in London, Manchester and Liverpool was what the British government had been saying about the Irish Troubles for years. She had rehearsed those lines well. The riots were 'a law and order issue'. Most on the left thought that fixing economic and social policy would lead to more harmonious community relations. Thatcher put it the other way round. 'Until law and order and public confidence have been restored,' she told the House of Commons on 16 July, 'we cannot set about improving the economic or social conditions of this country.'[11]

Publicly, on the floor of the House of Commons and in the media, Thatcher did not deviate from her official line: the rioters were morally culpable, ill-disciplined malefactors who were bent on causing trouble. Even *The Times*, recently acquired by Rupert Murdoch, and no mouthpiece for the bleeding-heart left, felt that Thatcher's 8 July broadcast – her 'nothing can justify, nothing can excuse' pronouncement – had been slightly misjudged. 'She failed to raise the tone of her remarks to the level of events.' *The Times* seemed to share an establishment view that some kind of knowledge of society itself was needed to understand the riots. 'Not for the first time she was unable to strike the right note when a broad sense of social understanding was required.'[12]

Like every Prime Minister, Thatcher was beset by various pressures and conflicting impulses in the wider public. There were elements on the left who bewailed her tough and 'divisive' policies, while the populist media on the right, including occasionally *The Times*, saw a broader left-wing conspiracy to overthrow, or at least destabilise, British society. According to two left-leaning journalists, Martin Kettle and Lucy Hodges, the 'search for reds under the beds went on all summer'. The *Daily Mail* warned, in the context of the riots, of 'masked motorcyclists' who were reportedly cruising round stirring up dissent and violence. Ronald Butt, a *Times* columnist, blamed the 'wide range of race relations bodies'. There were, according to Butt, the 'most reputable' ones which nevertheless went on about the disadvantages of the 'immigrants', but there were also 'much less respectable bodies which peddle black hatred for white society'.

The Times also revealed that in the Moss Side disturbances in Manchester, which took place in the same week that Toxteth flared up, members of the Revolutionary Communist Tendency were 'present during the riot'. Several newspapers fastened on the role of a member of the Militant Tendency in the Labour party, Clare Doyle, who worked in Brixton and had addressed a meeting in Toxteth.[13] Doyle, a thirty-six-year-old teacher and self-described 'socialist agitator', was referred to as 'Red Clare' by some of the tabloids. Her fleeting visit to Liverpool to speak at a meeting was used to depict her as an incendiarist.[14]

Against this background of a much less multiculturally sensitive Britain than would be the case in subsequent decades, the Prime Minister's publicly expressed instincts were broadly supported, particularly by the police. Ordinary police officers wrote to the *Police Review*, where they clearly stated their views on the riots. 'I fully accept that deprivation, inner-city decay and various other equally colourful phrases are relevant,' wrote Sergeant Alan Barron from London, 'but let us not forget that violence and damage perpetrated in the majority of cases is pure and wanton with no racial or political connotation.' The Chief Constable of Leicestershire, Alan Goodson, bluntly denied any racial content in the riots. He blamed gangs bent on criminality and depravity. 'They [the rioters] were hell bent on damaging windows and in some cases stealing.' In 'no sense was it a race riot'. In Nottinghamshire the Chief Constable Charles McLachlan said much the same thing: 'This wasn't racial, it was pure hooliganism.'[15]

Publicly, Thatcher derided the notion that any of the havoc had been caused by social deprivation or unemployment. At Prime Minister's Question Time on 9 July, she poured scorn on the suggestion that unemployment had been a cause of the public disturbances. 'In the area where violence and rioting had occurred, a good deal of it has been carried out by children of school age, some of them between nine and sixteen. That was nothing whatever to do with the dole queue.' A week later, once again before MPs, she blamed the social legislation of the 1960s, promoted by Roy Jenkins as Home Secretary between 1964 and 1967, for much of the disorder Britain was now experiencing. It was the week of the Warrington by-election, which Roy Jenkins was fighting on behalf of the SDP. Thatcher told the House of Commons, 'Mr Jenkins' saying that a permissive society is a civilized society is something that most of us would totally reject.' This view was shared by MPs across the House of Commons. James Wellbeloved, a former Labour member who had defected to the SDP, believed that the riots had been 'the penalty for a decade or more of undermining and subverting respect for decent authority'.[16]

Privately, as her trip to Liverpool demonstrated, she displayed a more conciliatory mood, trying to show people that she wanted to learn and was prepared to listen. From 9.30 in the morning till 2 p.m. on Monday 13 July, Thatcher held meetings with the police, community leaders, councillors and senior churchmen, from both Protestant and Catholic denominations. She wanted to learn more about the situation in Toxteth, and she seemed amenable to altering slightly some of her more trenchant views. For a leader with such a firm set of convictions, who rarely seemed not to know her own mind, this series of meetings with such a wide range of people was unusual.

Her second meeting of the morning was with a group of councillors who sat on Liverpool City Council, as well as some from the Merseyside County Council. The Prime Minister began the meeting, which started at 10.50, with an express wish to 'make it clear that it was essential that everybody gave the police their support'. This was characteristically bold and somewhat insensitive since, for many in the community, the police were the main source of the problem. Support for the police was essential, according to Thatcher, because 'society could not carry on if law and order were not upheld'.[17] The councillors promoted a different agenda entirely. Against Thatcher's view that the riots were a symptom of disorder and permissiveness, the local politicians stressed unemployment, the very cause which she had dismissed the previous Thursday in the House of Commons.

For the councillors 'unemployment was a major factor in the present unrest in Liverpool'. They then did something which comes naturally to local politicians engaging with officials from central government. They asked for more money. 'The Government should now consider giving aid primarily to generate more jobs in the worst hit areas.' According to the councillors, the unemployed, 'without hope of jobs in the foreseeable future', felt that they 'were being written off by the rest of society'. The reaction of the young was not against the police 'as such', but because they were the 'nearest embodiment of authority'. As far as the sensitive issue of race was concerned, the councillors underplayed that factor in the ongoing disturbances. 'There was friction occasionally between white and black', there was also a 'tension between the old immigrants whose forebears had arrived two or three generations ago, and new immigrants'.

Thatcher seemed to be in a more conciliatory mood at the next meeting which took place with 'Liverpool Community Leaders' in the Town Hall a little past noon. The Town Hall, a proud symbol of Liverpool's commercial traditions completed in 1754, is an impressive neo-classical building with an imposing façade of pillars and a dome. It was ironic that the Prime Minister's meeting with community leaders should have taken place in a building which, according to one historian, explicitly celebrated 'Liverpool's proud history of human trafficking and colonial trade'.[18] Probably unconscious of the significance of her surroundings, the Prime Minister was in her most humble mood. She hoped that the community leaders would 'tell her frankly what they thought about the present situation in Liverpool. She had come to listen.'

Wally Brown, the thirty-five-year-old Toxteth youth leader and engineering apprentice, won respect in the city for his role as a 'mediator' during the disturbances. Brown told Thatcher that 'he and his colleagues were a cross section of the people involved in and with Toxteth'. They wanted to make it clear that the riot was not the work of 'outside agitators'. Rather, 'it was the gut reaction of the local people to many things'. Brown was also insistent that he did not think yet another inquiry into the causes of violence was necessary. For him, there were two obvious issues – policing and unemployment.

'First and foremost,' according to Brown, 'there was the question of policing.' This had been the 'main trigger' for the disturbances and rioting that had swept through the city. It had to be tackled 'urgently'. Kenneth Oxford and his 'old school' policing methods were criticised. The community leaders felt that Oxford 'believed in slapping people down and keeping them down'.[19] Brown, perhaps not surprisingly, held that the second major issue was 'unemployment and social conditions'. The solution to this, he inevitably suggested, would be more resources 'in order to provide more jobs, more education and more leisure opportunities'.

Thatcher was honest with the community leaders. She told them unequivocally that she disagreed with much that had been said, but she recognised the 'genuineness' of their views. She was particularly concerned about what Wally Brown had told her about the police. She observed that his views 'contrasted sharply' with what the Southall community leaders, in London, had told her the previous Friday. The people she met from Southall had 'not complained at all about the police'. They had 'regarded them as their friends'. It was relevant, though this was not explicitly stated in the notes of the meeting, that the Southall community leaders were of Asian origin and represented the opinions of shopkeepers, as well as those of the youth. The case in Toxteth was different, as the Afro-Caribbean community felt more alienated from authority.

Thatcher claimed plausibly that she was 'not concerned about the colour of people's skin, but she was concerned about crime'. In her uncomplicated view, the police were there 'to prevent crime, and when it was committed, to hand offenders over to the courts to be dealt with'. She condemned anyone, 'whatever his colour, who attacked the police'. She further added that she had not heard 'a word' from Kenneth Oxford against the local community. Thatcher finished her meeting with the community leaders at 1 p.m., and it was entirely in character that she met a delegation of senior figures from the clergy of Liverpool immediately afterwards. Her work habits were notoriously stringent, and it was typical that she chose to press on, regardless of time. The Roman Catholic Archbishop of Liverpool, Derek Worlock, and the Anglican Bishop of Warrington, Michael Henshall, were then introduced to her.

Thatcher told the churchmen, first of all, that she had just spent an hour with the community leaders and she had been 'amazed at their hatred for the police'. The bishops, particularly Archbishop Worlock, were keen to stress the issue of racial tension and the 'silent colour bar', which they felt prevailed in the city. This was remarkable because Wally Brown and the community leaders had specifically downplayed the issue.

The terms in which Worlock spoke seemed old-fashioned, even in 1981. He observed that there was 'no coloured barrister at the Liverpool Bar'. There were 'only 8 coloured policemen in the Merseyside force'. Worlock spoke naively about race relations, suggesting that 'one did not find coloured assistants in the shops in the way one did in London'. The word 'coloured' was a throwback to the 1950s. He believed in greater engagement, though he did not ask for any more money. The Archbishop did ask 'whether it would be possible for a Minister to be made responsible for taking a direct interest in Merseyside'. The Prime Minister thanked the clergymen for meeting her. Worlock was not a supporter of Thatcher, being 'sharply critical' of her 'individualist ethos'.[20] She, in her turn, reiterated her views about the limitations of government. 'Many of today's problems had been identified 15 years ago,' she said. 'We had thought then that if people were given homes and good schooling, this would give them the basis they needed for a satisfactory life.' It now seemed that 'this approach had not been wholly right. We should have to think again.'[21]

In subsequent years, Thatcher would imply that her attitudes had not changed. She rejected sociological explanations and, to her way of thinking, complicated notions of racial injustice or more general deprivation. 'I had been told that some of the young people involved got into trouble through boredom and not having enough to do.' Their scruffy houses undermined this assessment, however. 'But you had only to look at the grounds around those houses with the grass untended, some of it almost waist high, and the litter, to see that this was a false analysis.' The parlous state of the neighbourhood showed that the young 'had plenty of constructive things to do if they wanted'. Thatcher, on her visit, ended up asking herself, 'how people could live in such circumstances without trying to clear up the mess and improve their surroundings'.[22] In her memoirs she stuck to the generally authoritarian prescriptions and analyses of what, to many on the left, were more complex problems.

Thatcher associated violence and disorder with moral weakness and depravity or 'ill-discipline'. Her approach to social questions, based as it was on notions of a highly personal morality, was characterised as essentially Victorian, but this fails to appreciate the extent to which Thatcher's 'Victorian values' were simply an expression of the Protestant individualism which she had learnt at her father's knee, and which went back to Bunyan's *The Pilgrim's Progress*, published in 1678, and further back to Martin Luther. Indeed, years later, a left-wing sociologist would write that perhaps 'no one in recent times has used the legacy of the Puritans – their spirit of Protestant individualism – to greater effect than Margaret Thatcher', who cast herself as 'the solitary pilgrim of Protestant England's first tale, *Pilgrim's Progress*'.[23]

Yet coupled with this strain of individual responsibility was a respect for authority which seemed more totalitarian. 'Authority of all kinds – in

Thatcher's birthplace,
Grantham. The shop was
owned by her father, Alfred
Roberts, a Methodist lay
preacher. It would come to
be a symbol of Thatcher's
economic and political values.

Margaret Thatcher
washing up in 1974,
the year before she
became leader of the
Conservative party.

The winter of discontent, 1979. The economic crisis gave Thatcher a clear path to power.

Margaret Thatcher, newly elected in 1979, with husband Denis, who did not share his wife's enthusiasm for Methodism.

Alan Walters arriving in Downing Street for his first day as Mrs Thatcher's adviser in January 1981.

Chancellor Geoffrey Howe presents his famous 'no-hope Budget', March 1981.

Prominent Labour leaders at the party conference, September 1981. To many reformers, these figures represented the unchanging traditional face of the Labour party at a time of crisis.

Social Democratic Party leaders, Roy Jenkins, David Owen, William Rodgers and Shirley Williams take part in a press conference to launch the SDP at the Connaught Rooms in London on 26 March 1981. The logo and marketing were regarded as highly effective, even if some questioned the party's intellectual coherence.

Veteran Labour leader Michael Foot addressing a crowd at The Miners' Gala in Cardiff, July 1981. Foot was an accomplished orator who relished public meetings.

Tony Benn, 1981. Benn also enjoyed open air meetings. He became steadily more left wing as he grew older or, as Harold Wilson uncharitably maintained, 'he immatured with age'.

IRA members in combat jackets, masks and berets at the burial of IRA hunger striker, Bobby Sands MP, in Belfast, May 1981. Thatcher was consistently criticised for being 'intransigent' during the course of the hunger strikes.

Bobby Sands's death became a powerful symbol of defiance against Margaret Thatcher's leadership.

Police dog handlers on Atlantic Road on the second day of riots in Brixton, South London, 13 April 1981.

Policeman stands on guard after a night of rioting in Toxteth, Liverpool, July 1981. Images of urban violence were a powerful weapon against Mrs Thatcher's style of government. The political left, as well as elements within her own party, criticised the social effects of Thatcher's policies. She saw the disturbances merely as evidence of the breakdown of law and order.

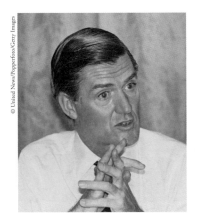

Conservative party politician, Cecil Parkinson. The son of a Lancashire railwayman who went on to represent Cambridge University in athletics, Parkinson was the archetypal thrusting meritocrat promoted by Thatcher.

Norman Tebbit, pictured at a London press conference soon after his appointment to Cabinet in September 1981. Tebbit, like Parkinson, was educated at a state grammar school. The rise of Tebbit and Parkinson sealed the political demise of the 'Wets'.

British Prime Minister Margaret Thatcher waves at the end of the Tory party conference at Blackpool, October 1981. She had reasserted her control of the party, but still struggled in the opinion polls.

the home, the school, the churches and the state – had been in decline for most of the post-war years.' This fact alone, it would seem, explained the 'rise in football hooliganism, race riots and delinquency over that period'.[24] It was a striking feature of Thatcher's intellectual make-up, some might even say that it was part of her genius, that she could join a strong sense of individualism, with its Protestant underpinnings and capitalist assumptions, to a strong authoritarian desire for discipline, conformity and order.

The Toxteth riots had followed riots in Brixton which had taken place three months earlier. The outbreak of the Brixton riots in April 1981 had been a shock to the political establishment, still reeling from the dramatic and adverse circumstances of Thatcher's budget only one month before. Brixton in April had turned out to be a mere prelude to a hot, confrontational summer. In all these riots, visual images helped define a moment of national shame, as was felt at the time. 'Unprecedented images of police in familiar helmets crouching behind unfamiliar riot shields, illuminated by the glare of burning buildings' were shown in newspapers around the world.[25]

Brixton, perhaps even more than Toxteth, took place against a background of racial tension and deprivation and provided a more searching test for community relations. The immediate background to the Brixton riots was remarkably similar to the Toxteth disturbances in the summer. On the afternoon of Friday 10 April, a police patrol in Brixton helped a young black man who had been stabbed in the back. An ambulance was called and police were bandaging the youth in the car when another group attacked it.

This incident started a build-up of police strength and increasing tension which led to an explosion on Saturday afternoon, after another 'black youth was arrested outside a minicab office'.[26] The police had used the incident on Friday as an excuse to increase patrols in the area around Railton Road through the night and into the morning. The issue of police harassment was more particular to Brixton than to Toxteth. Liverpool, unlike parts of south London, was distinguished by the fact that it had been home to a multicultural population for a few generations. As the future Minister for Merseyside, Michael Heseltine, would later point out, 'Toxteth differs from most other areas of immigration in that the black population there is in considerable measure made up of people whose ancestors first came to Liverpool in the nineteenth century.'

People tended to exaggerate the extent to which Liverpool had been a 'multicultural' city as far back as the nineteenth century, but it was certainly true that the nature of the Afro-Caribbean population in Brixton was different from that in Liverpool. The tension between the police and the local communities had been particularly acute in south London as a consequence of specific local circumstances. In March 1981, thousands of young black men and women had marched to central London from the south-eastern suburb of New Cross. They were protesting about what they regarded as white apathy over the fate of thirteen young West Indians who had perished in a fire at Deptford two months earlier. The march was 'militant'. It was called the Black People's Day of Action, with 20,000 demonstrators 'marching from Deptford to Hyde Park'.[27]

The New Cross fire, which had occurred on the evening of Saturday 17 January, had started with an explosion that turned what had been a relatively innocent sixteenth-birthday party into an inferno of smoke and fire. The cause of the fire was never fully ascertained, though there were suspicions of a deliberate act, and some witnesses claimed to see 'a white man who pulled up at the house in an Austin Princess and slung a Molotov cocktail into the party'.[28] The New Cross fire had come at the end of a decade of social upheaval, in which, for the first time, angry black youths had demonstrated against the injustices they experienced on a daily basis. One notable incident had been the 'battle royale' against the police at the Notting Hill Carnival in 1976.[29] Urban violence of a racial dimension had been a feature of British life in the decade preceding 1981.

It was felt that the response to the Black People's Day of Action had been severe. During the demonstration, which took place on Monday 2 March, a 'busy working day', and which lasted eight hours, 'windows in Fleet Street were smashed, a newspaper stall overturned and jeweller's shop looted'.[30] The reaction of tabloid newspapers to this march was felt to be disproportionate and prejudiced. The *Daily Express* ran the headline 'Rampage of Mob', while the *Sun* made a reference to the race of the participants in the demonstration which was, even at the time, regarded as inflammatory. 'The Day the Blacks Ran Riot in London', the headline declared.[31] Against this tense background, the police only a few weeks later launched Operation Swamp, whose purpose was to clear Brixton of troublemakers. It was described by a subsequent study as 'another street sweep involving 150 local officers in plain clothes'. The operation produced 1,000 stops and 150 arrests in the first ten days of April.[32]

More generally, many youths felt harassed by the notorious 'sus' law, which gave the police great powers to arrest and even intimidate young, generally black, men. The offence which the 'sus' law covered was defined by section 4 of the Vagrancy Act which had been passed by parliament as long ago as 1824. This allowed the police to arrest a person for 'loitering with intent to commit an arrestable offence'.[33] Since it talked of 'intent', it was very difficult to define, and it constituted in effect a 'thought crime', since no other crime had to be committed and 'there was no need for a victim, no need for any witnesses beyond two police officers'. This particular offence could be tried only in the magistrates' court and there was no right to trial by jury. Within London, use of the 'sus' law was concentrated in four boroughs around central London: Westminster, largely in the West End, Kensington and Chelsea, Camden and Lambeth. It was, for whatever reason, little used in other areas. Arrests of black men accounted 'for 44 per cent of London's "sus" arrests in 1978 and 40 per cent in 1979'.[34]

On 11 April, 'Bloody Saturday' as it was referred to by *Time* magazine, 'all hell seemed to break loose. Rocks, bricks and Molotov
cocktails began to fly' in Brixton.[35] The first petrol bombs set fire to
police and private cars in Railton and Leeson Roads. The fire brigade
were summoned to the area to deal with petrol-bomb attacks but
were unable to get through because their vehicles were 'stoned'. The
Windsor Castle, a pub on Leeson Road, was completely destroyed by
9.30 p.m. Another pub, the George, was petrol-bombed. Towards the
end of the day, the police began to regain control of the area, but the
fire brigade were unable to 'resume normal duty' till nine o'clock on
Sunday morning. Throughout that Saturday night, fourteen properties
were destroyed or damaged by fire.

In Brixton, there was a widespread feeling that the behaviour of the
police was the principal cause of the riots. One local man, the director
of a West Indian club, said that some kind of trouble had 'been coming
a long time'. Interestingly this man did not think the riots had been
'a setback for race relations in this area'. 'A lot of us have been saying
this would happen for years and no one has been paying attention' was
his rather disengaged remark.[36] The Brixton riots of April 1981 can be
understood only within this context of police activity and a feeling that
injustice was being meted out to an oppressed minority. The impact of
Brixton was felt in the changes to policing practice and the eventual
repeal of the 'sus' law in July 1981, when the Criminal Attempts Act
1981 abolished the offence of 'loitering with intent' which had been
enshrined in the old Vagrancy Act.[37]

Thatcher's immediate response to the Brixton riots was her constant
refrain all summer: 'nothing could justify violence' and 'unemployment
had nothing to do with the riots'. On the Monday immediately following 'Bloody Saturday' she appeared on the ITN news in an interview
filmed at 10 Downing Street, conducted by Alastair Burnet. He asked
whether she accepted that there was 'deep disaffection among many
black young people, especially towards the police'. Thatcher accepted

that there was 'probably deep disaffection among the problems', but she was adamant that, 'whatever the problems, nothing, but nothing, justifies what happened on Saturday and Sunday nights'. She saw the violence, once again in the broadest, almost abstract terms, as anti-democratic. 'It is totally and utterly wrong as all the ways of protest and demonstration and democratic methods we have that anyone should attempt to take it out on the police or the citizens of the area [sic].' Overturning cars, 'looting properties' and 'throwing bombs and missiles at the police' were unacceptable. She could not condemn such violence too strongly.

When asked whether she thought that 'high unemployment' was a primary cause of the Brixton riots, Thatcher flatly said, 'No I don't somehow think that is the primary cause. After all we had much higher unemployment in the 1930s but we didn't get this behaviour in any way.'[38] This line of argument was a precursor to the famous, some might say notorious, Norman Tebbit speech, when he recounted to the Conservative party conference in October 1981 how he 'grew up in the '30s with an unemployed father. He didn't riot; he got on his bike and looked for work and he kept looking 'til he found it'.[39]

Tebbit, the ultra-Thatcherite loyalist, was simply echoing what his boss had been saying for most of that tumultuous year. When asked by Burnet what could be done to alleviate 'high unemployment among young blacks, bad housing, bad environment', Thatcher said there were schemes available but that there had been 'an unusually large number of school leavers'. She once more questioned the whole premise of government pouring in money as an effective solution. 'But, you know, money has been poured into Lambeth . . . There is a lot of money, I think it's something like £40 million going on housing there this year.' This convinced her that 'it would be a mistake to think that money can solve the problems'. In a phrase which pithily summed up her attitude to government and human behaviour, she said, 'Money can't buy either trust or racial harmony. We have to try to go about it in a different way.'[40]

Despite publicly denying that unemployment had anything to do with the riots, the shocking developments in Brixton did prompt some quick actions from the Prime Minister. On the morning of Monday 13 April, she 'discussed the weekend's events in Brixton' with the Home Secretary and a couple of other senior ministers, including the Chief Whip, Michael Jopling. They all agreed that 'there would have to be an inquiry into what had happened at Brixton'. It was decided that the inquiry would be carried out by Lord Scarman. 'He should sit alone, and ideally he should conduct the inquiry in private,' although the evidence presented to him might need to be published when the inquiry had been completed. The remit for Scarman's report was wide, considering the Prime Minister's publicly stated, narrowly focused explanation of the cause of the disorder. Scarman would be asked to 'inquire urgently into the serious disorder in Brixton on 10–12 April and to report, with the power to make recommendations'.[41]

Scarman himself was a mild-mannered judge who had been very much a pillar of the liberal establishment. Born in 1911, he was approaching seventy when he was asked to produce a report into the Brixton riots. It has long been customary in the British political establishment, whenever a scandal or serious disturbance occurs, to establish an inquiry, invariably chaired by a senior, respectable judge of advanced years and solid reputation. Scarman was ideally suited to this role. He was educated at Radley, a solid English public school, and at Oxford, where he won a double first in Classics, or 'Greats', as the degree is more familiarly known. His judgments were generally on the liberal side of any question, and it was rumoured that he had been the favoured appointment of Willie Whitelaw, Thatcher's patrician and rather 'wet' Home Secretary, rather than the Prime Minister herself.

Scarman also had form as a figure on whom the establishment relied for producing fair, balanced inquiries whenever anything went wrong. 'When central government needed a judicial inquiry into a matter of public concern, it was repeatedly to Scarman that it turned.' He had presided over inquiries into the 1969 disturbances in Northern Ireland, as well the inquiry into the Red Lion Square disturbances, where a demonstration by the far-right National Front had led to a fatality. Scarman had also chaired the inquiry into the Grunwick trade union dispute which took place in 1977. In a typically British fashion, there could hardly have been a greater contrast between the black youths who felt victimised by the police and the 'white middle-class judge, whose cadaverous face and stooping shoulders suggested, correctly, a life spent mostly with volumes of the classics and English statute law'.⁴²

The contrast between Scarman's world view and that of Margaret Thatcher was scarcely less pronounced. Scarman described himself as a 'schoolboy Liberal' and the conclusions of his report pointed to factors in the cause of the riots which Thatcher always flatly denied. In his report, he stressed the 'deprived' nature of the Brixton area and, although he praised the police for their conduct on the night of the riots, he acknowledged that 'racial disadvantage' was 'a fact of current British life'. He addressed the two issues which Wally Brown had observed in Toxteth. Scarman called for 'government action to tackle the dispro-portionately high level of unemployment among young black men'. He also called for 'a new emphasis on community policing to restore trust between the black community and the police'. The policing was often 'immature and racially prejudiced', he concluded, but he fell short of describing the police as 'institutionally racist'. In an establishment way, he maintained that the 'racists in the Metropolitan Police represented only a few "bad apples" in the barrel'.⁴³

It is unlikely that Thatcher, given her authoritarian views and her steadfast, almost blindly loyal support of the police, would have placed much weight on the Scarman report. She was going through the motions, yielding to an establishment consensus view, which she did not share. She never believed that social causes could explain, still less justify, acts of violence. In July, in the aftermath of Toxteth, her concern was very much with bringing 'rioters to justice quickly' and 'reviv[ing] the Riot Act in some way'. It looked to many on the left 'as though she was dragging a reluctant William Whitelaw behind her'.[44]

In the debate on the civil disturbances that took place in early July, the patrician Whitelaw acknowledged the 'great skill' with which police had 'handled the riots', but he also mentioned the need for 'the community's support in sharing in the task of establishing a peaceful and orderly society'. He spoke of 'the necessary policy of continuing to develop closer and increasingly sensitive relations between the police and local community'. He did not see this as in any way compromising the requirement for 'firm police measures to put down violence when it occurs'. This was a nuanced picture, and a far cry from the more clear-cut, quasi-biblical certainties of the Prime Minister. Yet, Thatcher would probably have argued, nuance in itself was not going to inspire or reassure the victims of civil disorder. It was not going to make people feel safer at night.

In the course of the same debate, which took place on 16 July, Enoch Powell, now the Ulster Unionist MP for South Down, spoke with his customary intensity about 'the local concentration of New Commonwealth population' and about the prospect of future conflict as immigrant populations increased. 'The Government have a duty frankly to tell the people of London and of the other cities what after all an ex-Home Secretary some 15 years ago told the House of Lords – that one-third of the population of our great cities would, before the end of the century, be coloured. Let the Government say what they believe, what their advice is, what their information is, about the future composition of the population of the metropolis and of those other cities.' Powell believed that there should be a debate. 'Let people and Government face and debate their future.'[45]

Thatcher carefully avoided stirring the more incendiary passions concerning race. She was too shrewd a politician to speak in the dramatically charged manner of Enoch Powell. Many on the left had never forgiven her for the apocalyptic way in which she had spoken of people's concerns about immigration, when she was Leader of the Opposition in 1978. In a famous interview, given in January of that year to Granada Television's *World in Action*, she referred to a House of Commons committee that had 'looked at' immigration and concluded that 'if we went on as we are then by the end of the century there would be four million people of the new commonwealth or Pakistan here. Now that is an awful lot.' 'New Commonwealth' was a code-word for the non-white Commonwealth, people from former colonies outside the 'old Commonwealth', which consisted of countries like Australia, New Zealand and Canada, where white British people had emigrated. The 'new Commonwealth' was a phrase much used in the 1960s and 1970s to describe the large influx of people who had emigrated to Britain from these countries since the end of the Second World War.

During the interview, Thatcher cleverly referred to other people who 'are really rather afraid that this country might be rather swamped by people with a different culture'.[46] The word 'swamped' inevitably received all the headlines and attention. It was controversial and highly charged. It did not help things that the Brixton police operation had been called Operation Swamp, which was described as 'an extraordinarily inept name to choose', given that its 'political echoes were of the jungle and of Margaret Thatcher's "notorious" pre-election comment about white communities which feared swamping by blacks'.[47] Of course, Thatcher had not been so explicitly racial in her comments. What was also overlooked in the coverage of the interview was the way in which Thatcher tied the 'swamping' to her simple sense of Britain's national story and character. Having used the verb 'swamp', she pointed to Britain's historic mission and accomplishments, 'and, you know', she continued, 'the British character has done so much for democracy, for law and done so much throughout the world that if there is any fear that it might be swamped people are going to react and be rather hostile to those coming in'.

It was again a paradox to some to argue that Britain's success in exporting democracy round the world somehow made people at home more anxious about allowing immigrants into Britain, but such paradoxes sat easily in Thatcher's mind. She had a strong sense of British exceptionalism which a large number of British people shared. She could mix this with a natural suspicion of 'foreigners' whether they came from the continent of Europe or the 'new Commonwealth', and, unlike most of the British establishment, she was not afraid to voice those concerns. She observed that it was a failing of politicians not to address the concerns and fears of ordinary voters. 'I shall not make it [immigration] a major election issue, but I think there is a feeling that the big political parties have not been talking about this and sometimes, you know, we are falsely accused of racial prejudice.' This had the adverse effect that 'we do not talk about it as much as we should'.

Thatcher could be unabashed about her desire 'to keep fundamental British characteristics' which, she added inevitably, 'had done so much for the world'. She did not 'want people to go to extremes' but 'we must be prepared to deal' with those type of issues. 'We are a British nation with British characteristics,' and every country 'can take some small minorities and in many ways they add to the richness and variety of this country', but, crucially, 'The moment the minority threatens to become a big one, people get frightened.' Thatcher finished the interview with a firm piece of pragmatism which, on top of her strong ideological commitments, was also a feature of her leadership. 'We are not in politics to ignore people's worries,' she said: 'we are in politics to deal with them.'[48]

Pragmatism was what characterised Thatcher's view on race relations. She herself was probably right when she said she 'didn't see colour, only crime'. In her slightly naive way, she referred to talking 'with the West Indian dinner ladies' who worked in the canteen at Brixton police station, after disturbances that had occurred again in Brixton in July. The dinner ladies had gone into work 'throughout the disturbances, determined that the police should be supported with proper canteen facilities whenever they needed them at any hour of day or night'. The dinner ladies, Thatcher had no doubt, 'were clearly as disgusted as I was with those who were causing the trouble'.[49] She felt some solidarity with anyone who stood on the side of 'law and order' against the men of violence. She herself had no time for what she no doubt considered 'bleeding heart', 'wishy-washy' exculpations of guilt in issues of morality, in simple cases of right and wrong.

Yet, with regard to the inner cities, she showed some flexibility. In agreeing to appoint Scarman, whom she explicitly mentioned as Willie Whitelaw's recommendation for the role, Thatcher certainly acted contrary to her natural inclinations.[50] Later she acceded, whether consciously or unconsciously we do not know, to Archbishop Worlock's suggestion that there should be a Minister for Merseyside, or some such figure, appointed to supervise the regeneration of Merseyside. This too showed some degree of compromise on her part, as she always stressed the limited role of government in affecting human behaviour. 'Harmony cannot be imposed from above' was a thought to which she gave expression both in the context of Northern Ireland and in connection with race relations in English urban centres. Yet in the appointments of Scarman and Heseltine, in which she acquiesced, she had acted against her instincts.

It was widely known that her instincts on race and nationality were somewhat to the right of the party establishment. As the *Economist* had pointed out in September 1979, Thatcher's views on 'race, hanging, social security' suggested a 'narrower middle-class Toryism than many of her more aristocratic' Cabinet colleagues 'could readily stomach'.[51] On the issue of race she had, certainly in the Granada interview of January 1978, expressed a view of British national identity, and of the problems associated with immigration from the 'new Commonwealth', that no other major politician had publicly aired, with the solitary exception of Enoch Powell, who had been sacked from Ted Heath's shadow Cabinet for his 'Rivers of Blood' speech in 1968.

Michael Heseltine was one such Cabinet colleague who took a more liberal stance on social issues. A self-made millionaire, he had a self-confidence and a charisma which matched that of the Prime Minister. As the son of an Army officer and a product of Shrewsbury, one of Britain's oldest public schools, however, he identified himself much more closely with the old patrician establishment of the party than she did. Heseltine had been President of the Oxford Union about seven years after Thatcher had left Oxford. Thatcher could not have joined the Union even if she had wanted to, since that august establishment did not allow female members until 1963. Heseltine had done National Service with the Welsh Guards, an elite unit within the British Army. His manners and style were of the old guard, the Old Etonians and landowners, who dominated the party, even though many of them would later consider him to be a middle-class arriviste.[52]

Heseltine was appointed Minister for Merseyside and with enthusiasm set about the task of rebuilding confidence and investment in the area. In her memoirs, Thatcher let her bitterness at being deposed as Prime Minister in 1990 cloud her memories of these two instances in which she had not followed her most visceral instincts. She retreated back to her old message about the need to establish 'law and order'. 'Whatever Lord Scarman might recommend . . . – and whatever Michael Heseltine might achieve later by skilful public relations when he had begun to investigate the problems of Merseyside – the immediate requirement was that law and order should be restored.'[53]

Outwardly, Thatcher still talked the language of strong policing, of 'law and order'. She put pressure on her Home Secretary to meet the requirements for, as she herself wrote, 'riot shields, more vehicles, longer truncheons, and sufficient stocks of rubber bullets and water cannon'.[54] She had always fought to increase police pay by more than inflation, even when insisting that, in general, public spending needed to be curtailed. That was her outward position. During the summer of 1981, however, Heseltine drafted a paper which, as he remembered, 'embodied the phrase most frequently heard during the two and a half weeks' he spent in Liverpool. '"It took a riot", they all said, "to bring you here and to make government listen."' His paper, 'It Took a Riot', was never officially published, and it set out a six-part strategy, which included the recommendation to pump 'substantial additional public resources' into Merseyside and 'other hard-pressed urban areas to create jobs on worthwhile schemes'.

As Heseltine remembered, he 'could not persuade Mrs Thatcher to accept all of it', but before the 1981 party conference she did announce that he would stay on as Minister for Merseyside, a job he continued 'for the whole of the next year and a half'.[55] The application of more public money to solve social problems was the very solution Thatcher had repudiated in television interviews and on the floor of the House of Commons. It did not fit her strong 'law and order' narrative, or her more latent and instinctual belief in the primacy of individual responsibility for good and bad moral choices. Yet the influence accorded to Scarman and Heseltine, both male public-school and Oxford-educated members of the liberal establishment she affected to despise, show how readily Thatcher could live with contradictions between her words and her government's actions.

6

'Among Friends'

Thursday 23 July 1981 – Thatcher entered the room to applause. She was about to give the annual Prime Ministerial 'end of term' address to the 1922 Committee, the body of Conservative backbenchers. The mood, in one of the larger committee rooms of the House of Commons, was apprehensive, but the tension was smoothed, to a certain extent, by the Chairman of the '22, Edward Du Cann, who was well known 'for heaping excessive praise on guest speakers'. He did not fail on this occasion. Du Cann was famously charming. When asked what the time was by a colleague, he is reported to have replied, 'What time would you like it to be?' On this occasion, however, even he could not gloss over the worry obviously felt by some backbench Conservative MPs. It would be 'idle to pretend', he is supposed to have remarked, that the '1922 Committee was not deeply anxious about the present state of the economy'.

People later reported that the Prime Minister had been 'startled' by such 'unaccustomed frankness' from a man known for his ingratiating manner. The audience of Conservative MPs was also quite surprised by his frank tone. Thatcher began in an aggressive way, resorting to her usual tactic of employing attack as the best form of defence. Her theme was one of dogged determination which would lead to 'ultimate success'. She referred to the 1979 Conservative manifesto. She had said then that 'the policies being put before the country were not a recipe for an easy life'. Now she argued that 'too much had gone wrong with Britain for it all to be put right in a matter of a few years'. She told the anxious backbenchers that it was no good 'throwing money about, and thus creating a "phoney boom" similar to that generated in 1973'.[1]

Thatcher was always conscious of the failures of the 1970–4 Heath government in which she served as Education Secretary. Memories of the 'phoney boom' of 1973, when the Chancellor, Anthony Barber, stoked the economy with a budget which increased spending and cut taxes, still induced embarrassment in many Conservative MPs. The 'Barber boom' had ended in 'rapidly rising inflation and a record balance of payments deficit'.[2] Thatcher had been elected leader in contrast to all that. 'I don't want to go down that road.' She had a keen sense of her audience and of what they wanted to hear. She admitted, 'amid growls of agreement from the crowded audience', that the government might have been more successful 'if ministers had succeeded in being tougher with public expenditure in the early stages of the government'. She was generally good at sensing backbench opinion, and siding with it, against her more senior associates in government. This was an unusual quality in a prime minister. It was only at the very end of her career at the top of British politics that the ability to look at the government as an outsider, or as a backbencher, eluded her.

In the course of this bravura performance in front of her own back-benchers, she rejected the charge of 'inflexibility over the nationalised industries'. The old charge of 'inflexibility', which had been applied to her especially over Ireland, always somehow clung around Thatcher. She pointed out that her government had 'provided the cash for British Leyland, in the knowledge that the Midlands could not have stood the collapse of its largest car manufacturer'. Thatcher was known not to like supporting 'lame duck' industries, but she was equally good at defending herself against charges she felt were unjustified. She appealed to the Conservative MPs' latent instincts in favour of 'law and order' by emphatically asserting that the government had been 'absolutely right' to provide substantial pay increases for the police and the armed forces: 'they never strike, they never let us down'.

At the end of her justification of her leadership and government, Thatcher made one of her idiosyncratic appeals. According to the newspaper report, she reminded MPs (paraphrasing a verse from the Bible), 'If the trumpet shall sound an uncertain note, who shall gird himself to the battle?' As if to drive home the reference, she pointed out, bluntly and rather crudely, that 'we are all of us, ministers and backbenchers alike, the trumpeters'. To round off the annual summer recess talk with a somewhat mangled quotation from the New Testament was powerful stuff indeed. This was wholly in character. Thatcher's recollection of the text of the King James Version was faulty. The actual text, from 1 Corinthians 14 read, 'For if the trumpet give an uncertain sound, who shall prepare himself to the battle?'

Thatcher's version was more bombastic than the original, the phrase 'who shall prepare himself to the battle?' being altogether more prosaic than 'who shall gird himself to the battle?' She rattled off what she remembered as quotations without using speechwriters or civil servants to check the exact wording of her favourite references. Whatever the exact phrase, battles, of course, were very much part of Thatcher's view of political life. There was 'polite applause' at the end of the Prime Minister's remarks, but what the Conservative MPs made of the biblical reference can only be guessed at.

The context of Thatcher's appeal to New Testament fortitude and her homily about the 'uneasy life' followed a difficult Cabinet meeting that morning of Thursday 23 July. In her own recollection, there were two starkly contrasting visions among the Cabinet of the situation in the country that the government faced. One group of her ministers believed that 'unemployment over three million – the figure now predicted – was politically unacceptable and that higher government spending should be used to accelerate and strengthen economic recovery'. Thatcher's views were 'entirely different'. For her, 'the way to achieve recovery was to ensure that a smaller proportion of the nation's income went to government, freeing resources for the private sector where the majority of people worked'.

Thatcher's recollection was one of her own ideological certainty and a quasi-philosophical battle within her government. This battle 'came to a head', in her view, at 'the Cabinet discussion on Thursday 23 July'. As she remembered, 'before I went down to the Cabinet Room that morning, I had said to Denis that we had not come this far to go back now'. Thatcher felt a sense of foreboding. 'I would not stay as Prime Minister unless we saw the strategy through.'[3] Ian Gilmour had much the same recollection and could scarcely conceal his horror when he heard the plans of Thatcher and her minions, when they 'put forward proposals – almost incredible even for them – to cut public spending by another £5 billion'.[4] Thatcher remembered the ensuing row within Cabinet as 'one of the bitterest arguments on the economy, or any subject' during her premiership.[5]

In Thatcher's mind, the Cabinet meeting of the 23 July was a battle in which the 'wets' 'argued their case with redoubled vigour, strengthened by the lack of any evidence that our policies had turned things round'. At this stage, she was highly conscious of her own potential isolation. All through her leadership, since its earliest days in 1975, she had been conscious of 'insiders and outsiders', 'us and them'. The 'wets' in the Cabinet meeting of 23 July rehearsed all the old arguments that she had heard so many times. They 'argued for extra public spending and borrowing as a better route to recovery than tax cuts'. Even some of her natural allies, 'like John Nott', her hawkish and hitherto rather dry Defence Secretary, 'who had been known for their views on sound finance', attacked the proposals as 'unnecessarily harsh'.

The Prime Minister's 'whole strategy' was under assault. 'It was as if tempers suddenly broke. I too became extremely angry.' What fuelled her anger was, no doubt, her sense of betrayal, the feeling that people were letting her down, and that they lacked the will and resolve she herself possessed. 'I had thought we could rely on these people when the crunch came.' Yet in her hour of need there were still a few brave souls on whom she could depend. These characters, like figures from some kind of latter-day morality tale, were 'as loyal as ever', notably Willie Whitelaw, Keith Joseph and, of course, 'Geoffrey himself who was a tower of strength at this time'. Indeed, as she gratefully remembered, 'it was their loyalty that saw us through'. The insistent words, the 'we' and 'us', which fill her memoirs, once again give an insight into the Manichaean nature of Thatcher's thinking. That is how she saw her team. The enemy was 'they' or 'them'.

For Gilmour, whom no doubt Thatcher regarded as an enemy, 'The Prime Minister found herself virtually isolated' that morning. She was 'alone in a laager with Keith Joseph and the two Treasury ministers, Geoffrey Howe and Leon Brittan'.[6] For Gilmour, writing from his semi-retirement in 1992, it was obvious that after this 'débâcle' Thatcher clearly 'had to change either her policy or her cabinet'. For her, the likes of Gilmour were an obstacle to progress and success. 'I had said at the beginning of the government "give me six strong men and true, and I will get through."' To her regret, 'Very rarely did I have as many as six.' On one point, her later memory coincided with the account of Ian Gilmour: 'when I closed the meeting I knew that there were too many in Cabinet who did not share that view' – the view that the economic strategy should continue. She knew, 'after what had been said it would be difficult for this group of ministers to act as a team again'.[7] There were reports in the press of Cabinet dissent, as well as alternative suggestions for the role of party leader and Prime Minister.[8] Lord Hailsham, the seventy-three-year-old Lord Chancellor, talked darkly of Weimar Germany, where unemployment had given birth to fascism. He also spoke of the Republican party in 1930s America which, he said, had been destroyed by Herbert Hoover's policies for 'thirty years'.[9]

What gave Thatcher strength during this period was not so much the unqualified and unanimous support of members of her Cabinet as staunch support from her kitchen cabinet of independent advisers and mavericks. Two months previously, two economists, Allan Meltzer and Professor Brian Griffiths, had written to the Prime Minister to stiffen her resolve. Meltzer was an American economist with distinctly mone-tarist and free-market views, while Brian Griffiths was a Welsh econo-mist, who had been a lecturer at the London School of Economics and was now Professor of Banking and International Finance at City University in London. 'We have followed the progress of your poli-cies with great interest,' they wrote admiringly. They told the Prime Minister, 'we admire your courage in maintaining a firm stand in the face of opposition from many quarters', but they pointed out that 'hard choices' were 'not being made in budget policy, monetary policy or regulatory policies affecting productivity'.

This was a bold and candid letter. 'We applaud the present initiative to cut public spending in 1982–83 by 5–7% as an indication of the impor-tance you place on controlling the size of the public sector.'[10] What these economists were advertising was that they were technically capable and ideologically committed, and so ready to act as supporters who were not part of any government establishment. They effectively offered them-selves as shock troops to fight battles with ideological enemies as well as to sell policies to the chattering classes, the type of people who read *The Times* or *Daily Telegraph* at their breakfast table. Thatcher could pick up these hints. Griffiths quickly became a confidant and would be appointed head of the Prime Minister's Policy Unit in 1985.

Meanwhile, on the morning of Tuesday 14 July, Griffiths was invited to 10 Downing Street to discuss the public marketing of Thatcher's economic policy in the print media. Alan Walters, Thatcher's own economic adviser, and Ian Gow, her tireless Parliamentary Private Secretary, were also present. The Prime Minister opened the meeting. She complained that 'almost every newspaper, with the notable exception of the *Daily Mail*, was now attacking the Government's economic policies'. In her view, it 'would be highly desirable if Professor Griffiths and other like-minded economists could write letters and articles of rebuttal to the *Times*, the *Guardian* and the *Financial Times*'.

This was a direct appeal for expert advocates to go out and fight for the government's policies. Griffiths was perhaps less belligerent than Thatcher might have hoped. He protested that he had a 'special arrangement' with the *Daily Telegraph* which made it 'difficult for him to write in other newspapers'. He said he would try and get 'some other people' to do that. He mentioned Ralph Harris, Patrick Minford and Alan Budd. The surprisingly emollient Walters said he would also 'follow this up'.[11] The names that Griffiths mentioned would all have been familiar to Thatcher and her close-knit entourage. But what was noticeable about Thatcher, from her days as Leader of the Opposition, was her ability to get ideologically committed people to come together to form a team.

Throughout the Easter and summer of 1981, Thatcher made the usual appearances and speeches at all kinds of events which a prime minister is expected to make. She felt that she was on probation and that she was, ever the grammar-school prize-winning girl, trying to prove herself. She could relax at dinners held by people convinced of her message. She attended, for example, the Ross McWhirter Foundation dinner in the City of London on 7 April, a fact she advertised when asked about her engagements at Prime Minister's Question Time in the House of Commons that day. At these dinners, among the glitter of a grand dining hall, with a largely male audience, usually dressed in black tie, Thatcher could give free rein to her inspiration and her philosophy of government. More revealingly, on the menu cards at such dinners, she would often, in her unmistakable hand, write down notes and random thoughts.

On the cover of the Fourth Ross McWhirter Memorial Dinner menu card, at the bottom of which was an elegant drawing of the Skinners' Hall, the venue of the dinner, Thatcher wrote, 'Disperse the darkness.' It is not clear what this referred to, but it supports the idea that religious imagery was an integral part of her vision, even in the most secular or prosaic of circumstances. The dinner was ostensibly held to award prizes to successful entrants of an essay competition, in which there was a senior category for those aged under twenty-five and a junior category for those aged under nineteen. The respective essay subjects were 'Have the Courts proved the best bulwark of our Freedoms' and 'Should the powers of the Police be increased or diminished?' The essays and the prizewinners have now perhaps fallen into oblivion, but Thatcher's notes on the menu card should be given passing attention. The themes, the words were all subjects on which she had spoken at length many times before.

Paul Johnson, a supporter of Margaret Thatcher after a spell as editor of the left-leaning *New Statesman*, gave the main speech at the dinner on the subject of 'Freedom – the *Moral* Foundation'. Johnson argued for a 'free society' as against a 'compulsory society'. The 'compulsory society' turned 'charity into a nationalised industry' and transformed 'the human impulse into a statutory benefit'.[12] Some of the words on Thatcher's menu card were her personal notes on Johnson's speech; other comments were plainly her own thoughts. Evidently meant for a short speech of her own, the notes were written in a clear hand, with underlinings of all the words she felt were of key importance. 'Ministerial Tea & Sympathy – not enough' was one distinctly Thatcherite phrase; 'among friends' was another.

In a powerful phrase, Johnson observed that there is 'no such thing as a power of attorney over a man's conscience'. Thatcher would have nodded enthusiastically as he added that people 'are answerable as individuals . . . there can be no collective excuses'. In directly quoting Thatcher herself, Johnson was acknowledging the intellectual kinship of those who shared a similar philosophy. 'Margaret Thatcher once said to me: "Why have we allowed the Socialists to claim morality on their side?"' She asked why did people say 'so little about the morality of freedom?'

Thatcher's notes on Johnson's speech proclaimed the belief that a 'free society' was an 'arena for service'. The one characteristic which many had attributed to her, namely courage, she described as 'the ultimate virtue'. Johnson had not mentioned this in his address. Her notes stressed the 'individual conscience', with both words capitalised. Thatcher defined success as being achieved when people 'stopped avoiding a confrontation with reality and decided it couldn't be ignored any longer'. She self-confidently wrote underneath that particular insight: 'in a way I have tried to do the same thing'.[13]

The reflections and spontaneous thoughts aroused in Thatcher by Johnson's speech were along familiar lines. She seemed to favour writing little messages for herself, catchphrases and axioms which earlier generations of Englishmen and women had written diligently into commonplace books, particularly in the seventeenth century. On the menu card Thatcher wrote, 'Don't get pushed into a corner by economists.' The economy was clearly very much in her mind as she sat among like-minded diners in the Skinners' Hall that April evening. 'Economic battle' is another phrase which she scrawled on that occasion.

The Ross McWhirter Foundation dinner was exactly the kind of event at which Thatcher felt at home, 'among friends'. Ross McWhirter himself was the younger of a pair of twins who were known on the political right in the 1960s and 1970s. Ross's elder twin, Norris, was also a prominent activist, and both brothers had thrown themselves into the attempt to stop the spread of comprehensive schools. Ross was assassinated by the IRA outside his home in Enfield, north London, in November 1975 after he had offered a reward of £50,000, which he had campaigned to raise, 'for people who gave information leading to conviction for the IRA terrorist campaign in London that killed fifty-four people'.[14] The twins were perhaps most famous for their contribution to athletics, in which they had both represented Oxford University, and for helping to create *The Guinness Book of Records*.

After Ross's death, Norris took on many of his causes. For him, Ross's death was 'not a bereavement' but rather 'an amputation'. It was Norris who set up the Ross McWhirter Foundation 'to honour those who had fought tyranny – usually communist or left-wing tyranny'.[15] Ross's assassination only six years previously would have been well remembered by nearly every MP. In publicly acknowledging her attendance at the dinner in the Commons that day, she was proudly identifying with the friends of freedom against men of violence, like the IRA.

The Prime Minister's diary was managed by Caroline Stephens, a secretary who was to marry Richard Ryder, later a Conservative MP and Chief Whip. The diary engagements Thatcher chose to accept were indicative of her preferences as there would have been many requests and demands on her time. In May, apart from quasi-obligatory visits to Scotland and Northern Ireland, one of her more bizarre appearances was at the opening of the British Robot Association Conference in Brighton on Monday the 18th. Here she delivered a fairly lengthy speech. It was not the kind of thing that many of her predecessors as Prime Minister would necessarily have felt comfortable doing, but Thatcher prided herself on her scientific background. She was not only the first woman to hold the office of Prime Minister, she was also the first Prime Minister who had a degree in science.

Alongside the certainties of religion, its moral absolutes and clear injunctions, Thatcher loved the 'rule of law'. She loved rules and quite rigid formulas. This frame of mind led her, as a young grammar-school girl, into science, and as a scientist she respected clear empirical evidence, data, rigour and facts. Her identification with science and progress was sometimes obscured in the conflict of 1981, but this positivistic way of thinking was clearly something which provided her with solace. Science, like morality, was another arena of human activity where the lines between right and wrong, truth and error were clearly marked. Science appealed to Thatcher's love of facts and demonstration.

Any speech by a prime minister praising the efficiency of robots would be open to satirical comment. In her love of empirical data, scientific reasoning and provable facts, Thatcher showed herself to be the child of the Victorians her critics always said she was. She expressly invoked

Britain's Victorian past in her address to the British Robot Association: 'What would many Victorians have replied if you had asked them what could be the employment consequences of the replacement of the horse by the internal combustion engine?' To many people, Thatcher's insistence on evidence and facts had an old-fashioned air about it, which was all of a piece with her moralism and 'Victorian values'. In her combative way, she pointed out that the same kind of objections made about robots in 1981 could have been made about the introduction of motor cars. Robots and the internal combustion engine had put men and women out of work. 'Disastrous, they would have said. Look at all the coachmen, saddlers, blacksmiths, and stable boys who'd be put out of jobs.'[16]

Thatcher seemed to be in an unusually jocular mood. She opened her remarks by pointing to man's endeavours throughout 'recorded history' to 'harness nature's energy and nature's raw materials for his own benefit'. In a rare humorous if heavy-handed aside, notable for the people it attacked, Thatcher observed that 'No Union of Prehistoric Stonemasons objected that the coming of the Iron Age would put them out of business.' She continued, as if to emphasise the point, 'We know of no industrial action by the Society of Manual Hauliers when the first wheel came on the market.' Her belief in science and technology, and their benefits, was the crowning feature of her radicalism. 'Until comparatively recently in history no-one questioned that man's use of more, and increasingly complex, machinery was a highly desirable evolution of the relationship between man and his environment.'

Apart from allowing her to affirm her belief in scientific progress, the conference gave Thatcher the opportunity to reel off statistics and facts. 'Now, what I want is, Facts,' said the schoolmaster Thomas Gradgrind, at the beginning of Charles Dickens's novel *Hard Times*. 'Facts alone are wanted in life.'[17] The British Prime Minister would have satisfied Gradgrind's insatiable demand for 'facts'. 'Japan has nearly 6,000 robots and 2.4 per cent unemployment; Germany has 1,250 robots and

4 per cent unemployment; Sweden has 1,200 robots and 2.5 per cent unemployment. We have only 279 robots, and I am sure none of my audience needs reminding of our level of unemployment.'

Robots were Thatcher's notion of a good idea in the workplace. 'Robots actually like monotonous tasks, don't know what danger is, don't have to breathe fresh air, seldom fall ill and never quarrel.' Far from being a threat to employment, robots, like the 'development of the motor car', would open 'new areas of employment'. More importantly, and more revealingly in terms of the light it shed on Thatcher's mentality, robots posed the risk of 'failure to compete', the 'failure which will face those who do not grasp the opportunities offered by robotics'.

Of course, all Prime Ministers and political leaders love to show off their modern, technological credentials, but the zeal which Thatcher demonstrated in this arena, as in other fields, was characteristic. Of her predecessors, Churchill had hazily spoken of the need for science to be harnessed, but his intellectual interests never lay in that line of inquiry. Harold Wilson, an Oxford-trained economist, had also tried to flaunt, largely for political purposes, his own passion for science and the 'white heat' of the 'scientific revolution'.[18] Wilson, a clever and self-consciously meritocratic figure, educated at a Northern grammar school, implicitly contrasted the 'scientific revolution' of his imagined future with the out-of-touch Conservatives, with their grouse moors and their classical education.

In many ways, Thatcher was similar to Harold Wilson. She too had been educated at a grammar school. Like Wilson, she was unafraid to adopt the modern rhetoric of scientific progress, to embrace the world of robots and high technology. Yet Wilson was another PPE (Philosophy, Politics and Economics) graduate, the undergraduate subject in Oxford most favoured by Britain's post-war political elite. By the 1970s, Wilson himself, Ted Heath, Roy Jenkins, Shirley Williams and Tony Benn were all senior politicians who had graduated from Oxford in this subject. Thatcher at least had a degree in a scientific subject. As a chemist, she

had been diligent and methodical even if, as some of her detractors
maintained, she had been a little unimaginative.[19]

A friendly audience was also guaranteed at the dinner held to celebrate
the tenth anniversary of the *Daily Mail*'s conversion into the format
of a tabloid newspaper. This dinner was held at Claridge's Hotel on 1
May 1981. It was a sumptuous affair, at which Thatcher was accompanied by her husband Denis. Once again, Thatcher made notes on the
menu in her fluent, emphatic hand. She wrote words of reassurance
and defiance, 'feel pretty good', 'quietly confident – win through' and,
more blandly, 'really believe in Britain'. She addressed the gathering.
The dinner itself, with a salmon starter course, roast beef followed by
strawberries and cream, was a British affair. Thatcher praised the *Daily
Mail*'s editor David English for his 'decisive and determined leadership'
which had a 'clear idea of where it wants to go and how to get there'.

  More alarmingly for her opponents within and outside the
Conservative party, the Prime Minister gave a glimpse of her own
ambitions for political longevity. She appreciated the parallel David
English had drawn between his own attempts to switch his newspaper
to tabloid format and Thatcher's attempts to run the country. 'David
English sees some similarity between his early struggles to establish the
new *Daily Mail* and the trial of my Government during its first two
years.' English had been a tough editor, a giant of Fleet Street. 'Just as
he kept his nerve, so we shall keep ours – and win through.' Attending
a speech in honour of a national newspaper's tenth anniversary as a
tabloid would not, in ordinary circumstances, be a top priority for a
prime minister. The *Daily Mail*, however, was different. David English
has been described as 'brilliant and ruthless and charming'. His journalists were the highest paid, but they were 'also paid in humiliation
and exclusion if they failed to reach his standards'.

  David English was Thatcher's kind of leader. 'In a competitive world
working in a winning environment makes people happy,' he used to

say. He and Thatcher were 'made for each other'.[20] Both provincial in origin, determined to succeed in London, 'lower-middle class and entrepreneurial in doctrine', the similarities between them were obvious. Thatcher was pleased to compare herself to him. English had been editor of the *Daily Mail* for ten years. He had ruthlessly made the paper a tabloid after it had lost £32.4 million in its final year as a broadsheet newspaper. Turning to English, Thatcher declared of the *Daily Mail*, bizarrely addressing the newspaper itself, 'You became a great newspaper through will, determination and sheer professionalism.'[21]

Thatcher was impressed by English's ten-year record as editor. She said, almost prophetically, 'I look forward to being around at least as long in my capacity as David English has been in his. He is, of course, the longest serving daily newspaper editor in Fleet Street.' This was an ambitious statement, given that her government was trailing the main opposition Labour party in national opinion polls, but ten years in 10 Downing Street was part of her vision for national renewal. More remarkably, in the draft of the speech she had included the phrase, 'We shall need 10 years really to put this country back on its feet and make it proud, independent and truly self-reliant again.'[22]

Thatcher's notes on her menu card spoke of being 'successful and controversial' and of the *Daily Mail* newspaper itself as being proof of the efficacy of 'strong determined leadership'. She spoke endlessly about 'freedom', 'democracy', the 'rule of law' and 'personal responsibility'. It was this simplicity which endeared her to Ronald Reagan, the newly elected President of the United States. She always had a ready audience of well-wishers and admirers in the United States, all through the Reagan years.

In February 1981, Thatcher had visited the United States for the first time in the Reagan Presidency. Reagan, who had been inaugurated on 20 January, had been a charming host. He had no doubt been sufficiently flattered and impressed when she addressed him in a speech on the White House Lawn on 26 February. 'If we are to succeed in the battle of ideas, if we are to hold fast and extend the frontiers of freedom, we must first proclaim the truth that makes men free.' This was Thatcher in characteristically evangelical mood. The 'truth that makes men free' was more likely to come from the lips of a travelling pastor, or John Wesley himself, than from those of a normal British prime minister.

The trip to the US was highly successful. On 28 February, Thatcher was presented with the Donovan Award at the Waldorf Hotel in New York. The William J. Donovan Award was a prize given by the Office of Strategic Services Society, a society which honoured the memory of the OSS, forerunner of the Central Intelligence Agency (CIA). She used the occasion of her acceptance speech to preach on her favourite subject of freedom. The Donovan Award was presented to 'an individual who has rendered distinguished service to the United States'. It was difficult to see, except in the most general terms, what 'distinguished service' Thatcher had rendered to the United States before 1981, but that seemed to be irrelevant.

Thatcher's status as a special friend to a certain section of the American elite is underlined when one considers such a prize as the Donovan Award. The award had been established in 1961, and Thatcher was only the second British subject to receive it. Today, she remains, with the exception of Earl Mountbatten of Burma, the only British winner. She liked winning prizes and giving speeches accepting them. 'There can only be one theme for the recipient of the Donovan Award. That is why I intend this evening to speak about the Defence of Freedom.' Then she went into the speech that she had given so many times. 'Freedom based on respect for the individual is an idea whose strength and beauty has remained undimmed down the ages.'

It was against the glow of the warm reception she had enjoyed in the US at the end of February that much of 1981 could be understood. For a politician who defined herself in terms of conflict and the 'battle of ideas', having stalwart 'friends' was crucially important. To friends she showed unbending loyalty. To enemies she would be equally steadfast in her hostility and aggression. Thatcher felt no embarrassment in declaring to her hosts in New York, on receiving the award, that freedom was 'the great gift of Western culture to mankind'. Freedom remained 'the driving force of the Western democracies today. It is the source of their strength, of their diversity and of their prosperity.' Freedom, in the mind of Thatcher, contrasted with tyranny. This was why 'tyrants of every kind have fought – still fight – so hard to destroy it'.

Her firm alliance with the Republican right in 1981 was a sustaining source of inspiration and solace when she was beset by so many enemies at home. She reciprocated the hospitality shown her in February with a dinner on Thursday 25 June at 10 Downing Street, held in honour of 'the Vice-President of the United States of America and Mrs Bush'. Once again her brief speech on that occasion has been captured for posterity only by her notes scrawled on the menu card, but those notes suggested the familiar themes of her speeches on the subject of Anglo-American relations. 'One great valiant conviction shared on both sides of the Atlantic' was one of the lines written in the Prime Minister's own hand on the menu. The culinary offering was almost exactly the same as at the *Daily Mail* dinner nearly two months before, except that the dinner was a four-course affair, with chilled mint and cucumber soup as a starter, followed by baked salmon trout, roast fillet of Scotch beef and wild strawberries. The wine was probably much better than at the *Daily Mail* dinner. A ten-year-old claret, Château Talbot 1971, was served alongside some vintage port and champagne.

Thatcher enjoyed entertaining and giving speeches. The other clearly legible sentence from the dinner in honour of Vice President George H. W. Bush was: 'Together there is no problem we cannot solve.'[23] This was a firm statement of the Atlantic alliance, a theme which Churchill had often expounded, and one which was deeply felt by many of the generation who had lived through the Second World War. Thatcher rehearsed her key themes over and over again. Few national leaders have managed to convey their political personalities so effectively over such a long time. Part of this success must surely have been attributable to the narrow focus and the limited range of Thatcher's message.

The constant references to 'freedom', the 'rule of law', 'conviction' and 'personal responsibility' made a Thatcher pronouncement instantly recognisable. It was also a highly effective way of communicating. She reinforced messages until people knew what she was likely to say, and this also served to reassure her core supporters. It inspired them that they had a leader who was so sure of herself, and whose message was so unwavering. This is a characteristic of religion. The message, or 'gospel', is constantly preached and reaffirmed. Any deviation from the core message serves, in many instances, only to confuse an audience which has no need for reflection, no room for doubt.

Thatcher's various homilies often drew enthusiastic plaudits from her supporters. After her speech on Sunday 24 May at the opening of John Wesley's house on City Road, she received a number of congratulatory fan letters. This was telling, given that – as we have seen – her diary secretary Caroline Stephens had tried to dissuade her from attending the opening. The event occurred on the Sunday before the Whitsun bank holiday on 25 May. As Stephens herself had written to the Prime Minister in January, 'I really am in despair about the attached letter from the Speaker. The invitation is for the Sunday of the Whitsun Recess and I am fighting "tooth and nail" to get you some rest over the period.'[24] The next month, Stephens gently reminded Thatcher of her attempts to give the Prime Minister some chance of rest. 'You will remember I tried to dissuade you from accepting this as it is during the Whitsun recess which I am trying to keep free.'[25] Thatcher had earlier, in January, told her diary secretary, 'I think I will have to do it. The day can't be changed because it is Wesley's day,' 24 May being the day in 1738 when John Wesley 'experienced confirmation of his salvation by the grace of God'. Revealingly, Denis Thatcher did not attend this commemoration of the founder of Methodism. 'Do you wish to accompany her on this occasion?' Stephens had asked him on 17 February. 'No, thank you' was the firm reply.[26]

The warm approval from some Methodists perhaps justified her instinct that she should attend the event. One such letter was dated 25 May, the day immediately following Wesley's day: 'together with my wife and two young children, I have just returned from a wonderful day at Wesley's Chapel and your contribution made such an impact on me'. David Rutter from a Methodist church in Brighton wanted to let the Prime Minister know 'what a sheer delight it was for us to meet you and for my wife and I to have the thrill of shaking your hand soon after you had come out of visiting the House and Museum'. What was particularly reassuring to Rutter was the sincerity of Thatcher's Methodist convictions. 'It was so obvious you spoke from the heart, and I rejoice at the influence of your Methodist upbringing.'[27]

Thatcher had been a controversial choice to open the museum. On 15 May, Ronald Gibbins, the superintendent minister of the East End Mission, wrote to the Prime Minister expressing his regret that 'some of our radical brethren do not like the idea of you re-opening Wesley's House'.[28] He was honest, but he reassured the Prime Minister that this was 'really a very small segment of Methodist life throughout the country'.

Five days before the service and the opening of the museum, one supporter wrote in the most glowing terms: 'As a Conservative I have my own corner of pride that you are coming. I have read a lot about Wesley, our founder, and I think you have a lot in common with him.'[29] In Methodist circles, the choice of Thatcher to open the museum had stirred such controversy as to reach the pages of the *Methodist Recorder*, a weekly established in 1861. At the end of April, two letters appeared which questioned Thatcher's selection as the keynote speaker. One slightly unbalanced correspondent wrote to Thatcher enclosing a letter he had sent to the editor, since he doubted whether it would be published in the *Recorder*. '*Someone* [emphasis in original] has to stand up to the Devil when he comes in the guise of Atheistic Communism.'[30]

The controversy, which did not register outside Methodist circles, illustrated Thatcher's almost preternatural ability to divide opinion. It also revealed the semi-religious devotion she inspired in sections of the electorate. 'I warmly encourage you in your duties for this country and may your policies ultimately lead this great country to better days of industrial peace and Christian principles,' David Rutter's letter had concluded.[31] Nationalism and Christianity were a powerful blend. In so far as there has ever been a 'religious right' in Britain, Thatcher uniquely appealed to it.

Perhaps most gratifyingly of all, the Speaker of the House of Commons, George Thomas, a Methodist lay preacher, wrote with great enthusiasm. He was gratified that she had accepted his invitation to perform the task of opening the museum, though as a former Labour MP he was not a natural 'friend', but in his case their strong religious affinity, the shared Methodist background, confirmed their mutual respect. Thomas spoke of his 'heartfelt thanks' for Thatcher's 'overwhelming kindness' in performing 'the re-opening of John Wesley's House'. His effusiveness showed that even people who had nothing to gain from Thatcher's good favour could be as sycophantic as her direct subordinates. Thomas assured Thatcher that the 800-strong audience had been 'thrilled'. More strikingly, the address Thatcher had delivered 'could only have been given by someone whose heritage was in Methodism'.[32] This was undoubtedly true.

The friends Thatcher had cultivated were necessary, given the hostility she often attracted. By the summer of 1981, she had alienated many quite moderate forces. She seemed isolated in her Cabinet. Most of her parliamentary party seemed quite excited about the prospect of the summer recess. July 1981 saw the end of the gruelling civil service strike which had begun in March. Once again, the dispute had pitted Thatcher in her tough uncompromising way against a section of public sector workers in an industrial dispute. Less well remembered, because on a smaller scale, than the miners' strike of 1984–5, the civil service pay dispute formed yet another background of conflict in a turbulent year.

To many on the left, Thatcher's stance over the civil service strike was typical of her intransigence. In July 1981, *Marxism Today* declared that the dispute, which had begun in March, 'with the Government's announcement that the 6% cash limit would determine Civil Service pay in 1981', showed an inflexible line. The government's final offer had been 7 per cent, a figure which became a fixation with Thatcher, who was singularly determined that any pay deal with the striking civil servants should not involve any concession above this proposed level of increase. For the left-wing commentators on *Marxism Today*, Thatcher's government had 'one of the most disastrous records of industrial relations policy' since the war. Thatcher would probably have felt vindicated by the enmity of *Marxism Today*.

The battle of wills between Thatcher and the civil service had been welcomed by both Thatcher and *Marxism Today*, which boasted that there was 'no question that the civil servants possess the "industrial" muscle to win this dispute'. For the magazine, Thatcher's belligerence presented an opportunity for the left to win a victory which could humiliate the Prime Minister. 'The problem is encapsulated by one of Thatcher's "asides": We'll see who is more determined.'[33] In this instance, Thatcherite determination and will proved wanting. The civil servants had demanded 15 per cent, obviously much higher than the 7 per cent which was the government's stated and final offer.

At the beginning of March 1981, just as the budget was receiving its final tweaks, Christopher Soames had written to Thatcher suggesting 'we are now entering a critical phase as we approach the one-day strike called by the Civil Service unions for 9 March as a precursor to further action'. Soames dutifully reported to the Prime Minister that 'we stand absolutely firm' and that 'a 7% pay settlement is the most that can be squeezed out'.[34] A large, engaging and ebullient man, Soames typified the Tory establishment. His instincts were much more conciliatory than those of Thatcher, for whom every political problem became, almost inevitably, a trial of strength, a battle of will and determination, between 'us' and 'them'.

Soames was now the Lord President of the Council, a largely honorific title which gave him a seat in the Cabinet. He also enjoyed a certain prestige within the party for being Winston Churchill's son-in-law. It was Soames who was in charge of the negotiations with the civil service unions on behalf of the government. His desire to find a compromise was obvious. He wanted 'to be able to give the unions some sort of a lifeline in terms of future arrangements for pay determination', even though 'he had no intention whatsoever of conceding anything on the 7% pay figure'. In negotiating the wording of an agreement, Thatcher was reluctant to give 'too much emphasis to the idea that civil service pay should not fall behind' pay outside the public sector.[35]

The strike duly took place on Monday 9 March. On 12 March, Soames wrote to the Prime Minister that 'an estimated 275,000 non-industrial civil servants took part'. This was 52 per cent of the civil service. 'The unions are now taking selective and disruptive action.' After the initial strike, an average 1,300 civil servants went on strike each day. Soames was also telling the Prime Minister in the same letter that 'there is no sign of their weakening and selective and disruptive action will probably be extended next week'.[36]

Throughout the dispute, Thatcher was inevitably supported by her tough, ideologically committed advisers who favoured a hard line. 'Is our objective now to "settle", as Christopher Soames seems to be suggesting?' asked an increasingly belligerent John Hoskyns.[37] At the beginning of April, even Howe was looking for a way out of the dispute. On 2 April, it was reported that the Chancellor agreed with Soames that 'bitterness was growing among the civil servants, and that we should now try to find a way out of the dispute'.[38] The battle between Soames and the group around the Prime Minister centred on the nature of the agreement with the unions. Soames wanted to leave open a possible acceptance of the union demand that there could be some arbitration for the 1982 settlement, once the current dispute had been resolved. Thatcher wanted on no account to accept any arbitration for 1982.

In a note of marked irritation she wrote, 'We could *never agree* [emphasis in original] to accept the result.' By the beginning of May, Soames could scarcely conceal his own slight frustration at the Prime Minister's stubbornness. 'If your view is that we should rule out arbitration, in advance, for 1982 this is a change from what we agreed at Cabinet on 14th April.'[39] If this were true, the one thing Thatcher felt mortified about was the memory of former weakness.

A similar belligerence was displayed by Hoskyns and others. 'How long can we sit out the present level of disruption?' Hoskyns asked in April. The group around Thatcher were once again preparing themselves for a long struggle. Was it 'theoretically possible (provided we can sell it politically) to accept the costs of the present level of disruption almost indefinitely'? Hoskyns was gearing himself up for a period of confrontation and defiance. The way to break the 'strike culture' was defiance. 'As you know, we believe that as a *general* rule (i.e. except where life and limb are endangered) the only way to end the strike-culture is to *let it happen* [emphasis in original].'[40] Hoskyns's approach illustrated Thatcher's own instincts towards confrontation. This was significant because Hoskyns and, by implication, Thatcher wanted to end the 'strike culture'. Theirs was a general, even a philosophical, stance against strikes in themselves. Soames would never have seen this as his role. He was a mediator, a man of goodwill, sent in to perform a certain negotiating function in a specific set of circumstances.

Hoskyns told Thatcher what she wanted to hear: 'We are strongly against compromising on 1982.' The cry of 'no surrender' was one which Thatcher sustained for twenty-one weeks during the entire course of the dispute. It was Soames and not Mrs Thatcher who negotiated the final settlement which, naturally enough, was a slight, but significant, climbdown from the point of view of the Prime Minister. By the beginning of July, Soames wrote to the Prime Minister informing her that 'at our meeting on 2nd July we reverted to the possibility of offering an extra ½% to the civil service'. Soames, a tough and expansive figure, was keen to attribute responsibility for the deal directly to the Prime Minister, an action which probably did not endear him to her during this period. 'You suggested', Soames wrote, 'that we should say to the Unions that we would go to 7½%,' adding that he was simply following the Prime Minister's recommendations.[41]

This was not far from the final deal reached at the end of the month. Soames, of course, had reassured Thatcher at the beginning of March, only four months previously, that 'we stand absolutely firm' on the 7 per cent. Thatcher herself had, in a mood of extreme petulance, told Whitelaw 'quite crisply', according to Hugo Young, the left-wing journalist, 'that she would resign if the civil servants were given 7½%'.[42] This had been in June. This climbdown was the kind of 'U-turn' Thatcher had prided herself on avoiding. She was embarrassed and more likely to lash out and prove herself more defiant in her subsequent behaviour. This, after all, had been one of the lessons of the 1981 budget. The settlement of the civil service pay dispute on terms which she had explicitly repudiated was, at the time, a major setback. It showed, revealingly, that there were limits to what could be achieved through blind willpower.

The strike had been financially expensive and politically damaging. Christopher Soames had been sent out as a sacrificial lamb. He had been put in charge of negotiations and told, in no uncertain terms, that he could not under any circumstances retreat from the 7 per cent offer. 'We stand absolutely firm,' he had said. In the course of the dispute, benefits claimants were not paid and the government suffered in so far as 'income tax revenue was not collected'. It was estimated that the strike had cost between £500 and £1,000 million in lost revenues.

It also became clear that the strike could have been ended by getting to the 7½ per cent deal in early June, which would have saved about 'half of the projected costs'.[43] Many felt that, once again, the Prime Minister's intransigence had been unnecessarily costly.

The civil service dispute showed Thatcher at her most belligerent. The outcome of the dispute in which her wishes had been flouted suggested that the Thatcher method was not universally successful, but no political tactic can infallibly bring about excellent results. If this were the case, political leadership would be a simple affair. It was perhaps lucky that the Prime Minister had a summer recess in which to gather her energy and launch her fresh assault on the enemies and dragons she felt compelled to slay in her quest to make Britain great once again. For her and her Cabinet, July 1981 probably was the nadir. Bernard Ingham, Thatcher's chief press secretary, identified July as the most difficult month in the political calendar.

Ingham, a straight-talking Yorkshireman, was an indispensable player in Margaret Thatcher's team. At the beginning of the fateful month, July 1981, he wrote a cogent and incisive note to the Leader of the House of Commons, Francis Pym. 'Historically', he declared, July was the month of 'crisis measures'.[44] This July, as far as he could identify in his note, the usual problems were compounded by riots in 'Southall, Toxteth, Wood Green, Moss Side (and where next?)'. Riots clearly put pressure on the credibility of the government's economic policies, and they detracted, according to Ingham, from the government's 'good law and order reputation'. He surveyed the prospect of the Warrington by-election and worried about the 'appalling' prospect of an SDP win and a Tory 'lost deposit'. He worried too that the undoubted enthusiasm and feeling of national pride aroused by the Royal Wedding, of the Prince of Wales to Lady Diana Spencer, which was due to take place on 29 July, would be diminished by industrial action and civil discord.

Ingham believed that there was a high likelihood that the government would be 'propelled into the recess in a state of profound

agitation, depression and gloom'.[45] Yet July, although it had started
badly with riots and images of riot police quelling crowds, would prove
to be auspicious for the government and for many people in Britain
generally. A surprising victory in the cricket test match at Headingley,
which took place between the 16th and the 21st, in which England
achieved a highly improbable win over Australia, appeared to lift
the national mood. Over and above this sporting success, the Royal
Wedding seemed to have been, in Ingham's own words, a 'national
tonic'. Ingham's report to Francis Pym, dated 31 July, was much more
upbeat than had been the case little more than three weeks previously.
His conclusion was that 'we had emerged from a most difficult month,
even at the best of times, in far better shape than we might have reason-
ably expected'. There were still 'no grounds for euphoria', but 'contrary
to all our expectations, we have ended July and entered Recess – on a
higher rather than a lower note'. This was 'gratifying'.[46]

July 1981 had indeed been difficult. At the beginning of the month,
John Hoskyns had written to the Chancellor of the Exchequer suggesting that the government try 'implicitly and subtly' to 'link in people's
minds the moral similarity between high pay claims demanded with
menaces and other forms of anti-social behaviour, including rioting
and looting'. Connecting riots and other forms of violent anti-social
behaviour with public sector workers exercising their legal right to
strike was a bold political move. Hoskyns's plan had in fact been real-
ised by a cartoon in the *Sun* which appeared on 9 July. The drawing showed Arthur Scargill, the President of the NUM, wearing a
miner's hat and throwing an axe through a pastry-shop window. Howe,
wearing an apron, says, 'Maggie! They're on the rampage again!' The
link between strikes, riots and general civil disorder was one which
Thatcher's friends in the media often made 'implicitly and subtly', as
Hoskyns recommended.[47]

For Thatcher, the trials of the second quarter of 1981 had been bruising and potentially career-ending. Her standing among her Cabinet

colleagues and within the country at large was not at the commanding level she would subsequently attain. As Hugo Young wrote in 1989, 'two years after the election, she was not yet secured in place as part of the permanent furniture of British life'. She was vulnerable in the summer of 1981 as never before or afterwards until the moment when she was finally ousted in 1990. On 23 July, the strong objections of her Cabinet colleagues to further cuts in public spending had shaken her authority, even if they had failed to dent her overwhelming sense of mission and inner confidence.

Purge of the 'Wets'

Monday 14 September 1981 – It was a busy day. Reshuffle day, when Prime Ministers try to inject some energy into a government by sacking ministers who have not performed or whose face somehow doesn't fit, while promoting others, more energetic and more thrusting, to give the government the air of renewal. Thatcher's diary was full of meetings, on a one-to-one basis, with people she would be promoting or asking to leave her government.

In her memoirs Thatcher stated that she 'always saw first those who were being asked to leave the Cabinet'.[1] This was not strictly true. Her diary shows that after Ian Gilmour, who was indeed asked to leave the government, she saw Humphrey Atkins, who was demoted from Secretary of State for Northern Ireland to become Lord Privy Seal, the number two to Lord Carrington in the Foreign Office. She then saw Jim Prior, who was shuffled out of the Employment brief to Northern Ireland as Atkins's replacement. The meetings were short, brusque affairs lasting no more than fifteen minutes. The draft of the diary indicates that Thatcher's meeting with Ian Gilmour began at 9.40 a.m. Her last face-to-face appointment of that morning was Janet Young at 11.40. The diary reveals the despatch with which Thatcher hoped to conclude the business of remaking her government. Twelve ministers were given personal interviews over a period of two hours and ten minutes.

'I began with Ian Gilmour and told him of my decision.' Gilmour's reaction, as Thatcher remembered it, was 'huffy'. Gilmour, in his account, gave more details of what must have been an awkward meeting for him. He remembered being ushered upstairs at Number 10 and Mrs Thatcher asking him if he 'minded the presence of her private secretary'. Being polite, Gilmour said he had no objection, though he found the request 'oddish'. What was even more disconcerting for Gilmour was that 'the Prime Minister remained standing throughout the interview'. For Gilmour, a tall man, this presented a dilemma. He did not know whether to stand up or sit down. He sat down and as 'the room was small and we were only a few feet apart this gave me the feeling of being addressed at a public meeting with the speaker too near the audience'.[2]

Gilmour's short interview was not the most difficult meeting of the morning. At eleven o'clock or thereabouts, Christopher Soames was summoned for his interview with Thatcher. Thatcher remembered Soames being furious at the news of his imminent departure from government, 'but in a grander way' than Gilmour. Soames had enjoyed a life of privilege, but had had a political career of considerable distinction. His sacking was a notable scalp for the daughter of a Lincolnshire grocer. To Margaret Thatcher, who was not so often as obviously class conscious, Soames gave 'the distinct impression' that he felt the natural order of things was being 'violated' and that he was, in effect, 'being dismissed by his housemaid'.[3]

Other accounts of Soames's dismissal are more extreme and dramatic than Thatcher's own cursory description. Soames decided to give Thatcher a piece of his mind and is reported to have 'assailed her for twenty minutes for her various shortcomings'. His irritation was manifest and it was said that his 'thunderous' and booming voice 'could be heard out of the open window halfway across Horseguards Parade'.[4] Soames was appalled at his sacking. He felt that he had done his best in the civil service strike. The final deal, which included the 7½ per cent pay deal for the unions, had been reached under his influence and, he might have added, it would have been accomplished weeks earlier if the Prime Minister had not been so intransigent.

The reason for his sacking was probably more to do with his tone and style than any lack of competence. Soames had been forceful and direct in his dealings with Thatcher, probably under the mistaken impression that she valued strength and decisiveness. This assessment of Thatcher's character was probably true as far as it went, but she hated, above all else, to be patronised. The man who immediately followed Soames in this series of interviews was another minister whose Cabinet career was about to be terminated. In contrast to Soames, Mark Carlisle did not have a grand manner or significant connections. In Thatcher's recollection, he 'had not been a very effective Education Secretary' and had 'leaned to the left'. He managed to leave the Cabinet 'with courtesy and good humour', but this did not avail him much, as he was never shown any preferment again under Mrs Thatcher and left the House of Commons in 1987. Carlisle came from the respectable middle classes. He was a tall, 'imposing figure with a friendly, easy-going manner'. He had been educated at Radley and had followed that with a degree at Manchester University, after which he had been called to the Bar.

The removal of Soames, Gilmour and Carlisle was accompanied by the 'resignation' of Peter Thorneycroft from the position of party Chairman. Although his removal was skilfully presented as a voluntary resignation, Thorneycroft had been pushed out. Thatcher had deputed Ian Gow to travel to Venice towards the end of August to tell him the news in person.[5] Thorneycroft was clearly disappointed to be excluded in this way. Although now seventy-one, he felt himself to be a significant player in the rarefied world of Conservative politics. On 7 August from the comfort of a villa in San Marino, he had written a letter to Francis Pym, Leader of the House of Commons, clearly outlining his hopes for the future.

In this letter Thorneycroft cleverly presented himself as a centrist figure who could act as an arbiter between the warring Cabinet factions. 'During July,' he wrote, 'a number of our colleagues had kept me informed of their mounting anxieties, of the deteriorating political situation.' He spoke of the growing tensions in the Cabinet. Like many politicians of a certain age, Thorneycroft portrayed himself as a disinterested figure, above the petty ambitions of normal politics, doing what he had to do for the sake of the party. 'I am at least beyond ambition and regard myself as expendible [sic].' He claimed that he had been asked 'to do something'. He confronted Thatcher, probably before the end of July, with Ian Gow in attendance. 'I told her that she led one of the most divided and unhappy Cabinets that I had ever seen – that its divisions imperilled the future of the Party and that steps had to be taken to find unity and common cause.' Thorneycroft then referred to the meeting he had held with the Sunday lobby (the political editors of the Sunday newspapers) in early August. He admitted to Pym that in this briefing he had indulged in a 'certain amount of overkill'.[6] He had spoken very openly about the government's difficulties. When asked by one of the journalists present whether he was a 'wet or a dry', he described himself as a 'rising damp'. The pressmen believed he was talking off the record, and no notes were taken. At the end of the meeting, however, one journalist asked speculatively whether the conversation had been on or off the record. To the astonishment of all present, Thorneycroft said 'on, of course'.[7]

The Sunday papers gave large coverage to Thorneycroft's hesitant support for the government. It was especially hard for him as he had made similar remarks at a speech to the Press Gallery on 11 February. On that occasion, he had said, 'I confess I like the centre ground amid the wets and drys: I like to consider myself as a reluctant example of rising damp.'[8] As is often the case in politics, a remark made on one occasion may make little impact, while exactly the same remark on another occasion can attract adverse headlines. Thorneycroft's various indiscretions were felt to be too excessive for him to remain in Thatcher's government. Even Peter Shore, the Labour shadow Chancellor, had noticed the tepid nature of Thorneycroft's enthusiasm. Writing to Thatcher on 3 August, Shore referred to a radio interview in which

Thorneycroft had reportedly suggested that 'there is no sign of it [the economy] picking up'.[9]

Despite this wayward approach to message discipline and loyalty to his leader, Thorneycroft did not believe himself to be in any danger. He blithely told Pym, from the Villa Malagola in San Marino, that the senior members of the party had 'a few weeks in which to devise an improved scenario'. In his experience, 'much' would turn 'on Margaret's conference speech'. He felt this could be influenced by senior party people, the old establishment, in which he included Pym, 'Willie [Whitelaw]', 'Peter [Carrington] and others'. He intended 'to remain here in Italy' before moving to Venice 'about the 1st September'.[10] In a rather self-satisfied conclusion Thorneycroft remarked, 'I think that I have for the moment done all that I can to influence events.'

Events had overtaken Thorneycroft, but his letter to Pym shows the extent to which many of the 'wets' were surprised by the rather brutal termination of their political careers. Thatcher ruthlessly dismissed them from office. She recalled in her memoirs how she had ensured that she had discussed the details of the reshuffle at Chequers the weekend before with her 'closest advisers', Willie Whitelaw, Michael Jopling (the Chief Whip) and Ian Gow who had all come over to Chequers on the 'weekend of 12/13 September'.[11]

Thatcher's instincts were to make sure that Willie Whitelaw, a figure with whom the 'wets' could identify, would be implicated in the decision to remove a number of them from government. Whitelaw's involvement in the 1981 reshuffle was something which, interestingly enough, he did not even mention in his own memoirs published in 1989. This omission may have been an oversight, but may well have reflected the painful process in which he became directly associated with the removal of friends and colleagues whose outlook and values he shared.

Whitelaw's involvement in the demise of the 'wets' was viewed by some of them as a betrayal. Gilmour, in his agonised recollection of the events of September 1981, asked himself, 'Why did the moderates lose?' His answer was that 'their "captains" were non-playing members of the team'. 'For a variety of reasons,' he slyly suggested, 'none of them discreditable, the most powerful moderates declined to challenge the Prime Minister or her economic policy.' The people Gilmour was referring to can be guessed at, but Willie Whitelaw no doubt would have been at the head of that list. Carrington and Pym were probably the other two prominent establishment figures whom he had in mind.

Most of the 'wets' who were sacked in September 1981 (Gilmour, Thorneycroft and Soames) and their allies in Cabinet (Whitelaw, Pym and Carrington) were from a remarkably tight-knit social group and, perhaps even more importantly, were all roughly the same age. Of the six mentioned, Thorneycroft was by far the oldest, having been born in 1909. He had served as Harold Macmillan's Chancellor of the Exchequer, from which post he had resigned as long ago as 1958. The others – Soames, Gilmour, Pym, Whitelaw and Carrington – had all been born between 1919 and 1926. Each of them had served in the Second World War, four of them in the elite Brigade of Guards, with Pym being the odd man out in this respect, since he had served in a cavalry regiment. Four of the five had been educated at Eton, while Whitelaw had been an academically undistinguished pupil at Winchester College. He was generally regarded as being 'more interested in golf than in books' and it had come as 'a surprise to all when he passed the examination for Winchester College'.[12]

The uniform background and age of most of the leading 'wets' was something which was remarked on at the time, though, in a British way, few dwelt on this aspect of Thatcher's reshuffle. It should be remembered that the experience of the 'wets' in both war and peacetime, their patrician background and their sense of fair play coloured their politics and set them at odds with Thatcher. Their style, rather languid and debonair in the form of Ian Gilmour, or full of bluff bonhomie in the manner of Christopher Soames and Willie Whitelaw, could not have been more starkly contrasted with that of the Prime Minister. The shrill insistence on principle, her dogmatic inflexibility, seemed too much for them. Gilmour himself was like a creature from another age. His *Guardian* obituarist would refer to him as an 'intellectual' and also a 'toff'. Educated at Eton and Balliol College, Oxford, with a three-year stint in the Grenadier Guards, Gilmour was simply never flexible enough to accommodate himself to the Thatcher phenomenon. 'The element of hysteria latent in Thatcher and her compulsive adversarialism was alien to him,' was one judgement on the ending of his political career.[13]

Alongside Gilmour, Soames had also been educated at Eton and had served in the Second World War as an officer in the Coldstream Guards. He had been first elected to the House of Commons in 1950, where he acted as Parliamentary Private Secretary to his father-in-law Winston Churchill from 1952 to 1955. 'At 6-foot-4, with a waistline to match, he had an eye for the good life and was seldom far removed from a bottle of champagne or a fine vintage wine.'[14] He had used his gifts for social life and good living to great effect when he served as Ambassador to Paris from 1968 to 1972, where his chief duty was to persuade the French to admit Britain into the EEC. He had led a charmed life in politics, where he was a popular figure, enjoying admiration from all sides of the House of Commons. It had been a Labour Prime Minister, Harold Wilson, who had appointed him Ambassador to France. The posting was appropriate because Soames had won the Croix de Guerre in the Second World War, as a liaison officer with the French Foreign Legion. He had met his wife, Mary Churchill, the youngest daughter of the Prime Minister, in Paris.

Thatcher's sacking of such a popular figure showed the extent of her ruthlessness. Characteristically, she was too cunning an operator to exclude all the 'wets' in one blow. She probably did not have the strength to eliminate Walker, Prior and Pym at the same time. She had come to rely on Whitelaw and was charmed by Carrington. Despite her nonconformist roots, she had a residual admiration for the institution of the hereditary peerage. Carrington was an hereditary peer, a 6th baron no less. He sat in the House of Lords and did not pose an immediate threat to her. Besides, as Foreign Secretary, he had shown little interest in the economic questions which had defined the position of the 'wets' and the 'drys'. Another Etonian, a landowner from a family which had been involved at the highest level of politics for at least two centuries, he was the quintessential political aristocrat.

Carrington had served with distinction in the Grenadier Guards, winning the Military Cross for action at Nijmegen in March 1945. Whitelaw had served in the Scots Guards during the Second World War, winning the Military Cross in 1944. 'There can be no doubt that our wartime experiences had a profound effect on the lives of all those who took part,' Whitelaw wrote. He spoke of 'special feelings of comradeship and loyalty to each other which come naturally from mutual experiences, happy and unhappy'.[15] Either consciously or unconsciously, Thatcher used the 'natural' sense of loyalty, strongly developed in Whitelaw, against his erstwhile comrades in arms, Soames and Gilmour.

The shared experiences of wartime, the honour of serving as a Guards officer, the responsibilities which officers had towards the men under their command, their Etonian background, shaped many of the 'wets'. As a woman from a lower-middle-class background, Thatcher was doubly excluded from those tight circles of privilege in which many of the 'wets' operated. A cursory look at *Who's Who*, the documentary record of the members of the British establishment, would reveal how close knit those circles were. In their *Who's Who* entries, Whitelaw, Soames, Carrington and Gilmour all revealed their membership of White's, the oldest of gentlemen's clubs.

It mattered that all four men had also served as Guards officers in the Second World War. In a book admittedly describing the Guards in the First World War, one writer has described the significance of service in this elite fighting brigade. 'To serve in the Guards was to have a very specific experience of the war.' The Guards regiments themselves were 'socially elitist, officered by aristocrats or by those who aspired to be like aristocrats'. These men were also 'a combat elite'. They had 'an unshakeable esprit de corps'. As Oliver Lyttelton, a member of Churchill's peacetime Cabinet in the early 1950s, recalled, members of his unit were 'all Guardsmen first', they had 'the same standards of discipline, the same professional training, the same pride'.[16] It was, of course, no accident that Harold Macmillan, whom many of the 'wets' admired as their political godfather and an ideal prime minister, had served in the Grenadier Guards in the First World War.

It was Thatcher's genius to divide this strongly knit cadre of politicians. For their replacements, she turned to younger, more dynamic, more meritocratic figures who had come from markedly different backgrounds. For Whitelaw, above all others, the September 1981 reshuffle must have been a trying period. His whole character, upbringing and experience made him rather sceptical of Thatcherism, yet he displayed an impressive and unfaltering loyalty to her, which was exactly the reason that prompted some of his natural allies within the party to 'accuse him of betrayal'.[17]

Cecil Parkinson, who replaced Peter Thorneycroft as party Chairman, was the son of a railwayman in Lancashire. By means of Lancaster Grammar School and Cambridge University, which he had represented in athletics, the tall and dapper Parkinson had a touch of the dash and energy that Margaret Thatcher found appealing. 'Who'd believe he was once working class?' asked the *Daily Mail* in a flattering profile of him.[18] Above all else, Thatcher was pleased with Parkinson's outlook on the social and economic problems facing Britain. It was almost as if she had an ideological test to allow certain people specific jobs within her administration. Parkinson also had the right technocratic background. 'I appointed Cecil Parkinson to succeed him [Thorneycroft] – dynamic, full of common sense, a good accountant, an excellent presenter and, no less important, on my wing of the Party.'[19] What evidence Thatcher had of Parkinson's accounting ability is unknown, but he had the right profile and was ideologically compatible with the Prime Minister.

Parkinson celebrated his promotion with another of the newly promoted ministers, Norman Tebbit, who had been described by Michael Foot, the Labour leader, as a 'semi-house-trained polecat'.[20] Parkinson and Tebbit 'drank a glass of champagne to celebrate the fact that we were joining the Privy Council and the Cabinet on the same day'.[21] Tebbit and Parkinson had been born in 1930 and 1931 respectively. They were naturally too young to have had direct experience as combatants in the Second World War. In social terms, they were both grammar-school boys, who had won themselves a first-class academic education by dint of passing exams and study. Unlike Parkinson, Tebbit had not followed his grammar-school education by a spell at Cambridge, or any other university. He remained a rather unpolished figure, full of Thatcherite zeal and a sense of mission.

Tebbit's own trajectory into politics had been unusual for a Conservative politician. He had served in the Royal Air Force for his National Service and had then pursued a career as a pilot in civil aviation, before his election to parliament in 1970. He was a thrusting right-wing populist, with a streak of menace. He had been involved in the pilots' union and had been politicised by these experiences. Parkinson, as an accountant and executive for Metal Box – as the name suggested, a tin-can manufacturer – had a background in industry, which was unusual for the post-war generation of Conservative leaders. He had then trained as an accountant and established his own securities firm.

The third easily identifiable Thatcherite promoted to Cabinet that September was Nigel Lawson. The son of a Jewish tea merchant, Lawson was born in 1932 and was educated at Westminster and Christ Church, Oxford. Of the three obviously Thatcherite appointments to the Cabinet, he had arguably the most conventional background in

politics, yet he was younger than the 'wets' and his social provenance
was from the mercantile and immigrant middle classes. He could in no
way be described as having the aristocratic connections or pretensions
of many of the 'wets'. He too had been too young to fight in the Second
World War and, although only six years younger than Gilmour, these
subtle differences in age and youthful experiences were important. For
people interested in such things, it was noteworthy that Parkinson had
done his National Service as an NCO in the Royal Air Force, while
Lawson had served in the Royal Navy. A commission in the British
Army, especially in the Guards regiments, was in the 1950s perceived
to be a mark of social distinction.

It had been rumoured that Thatcher was considering Tebbit for the
post of party Chairman, but he nursed reservations about accepting
this role. It was an 'unpaid job', and he liked 'ministerial life too much'
to want to change. According to Tebbit's account, he 'went to see
Margaret' and told her that the 'man for the job was Cecil Parkinson'.[22]
Lawson's background was in financial journalism. He had an ideological commitment to free markets and had proved an articulate defender
of the monetarist ideas which became fashionable in Conservative
circles during the 1970s. Lawson would now be the Energy Secretary
replacing David Howell, who had been moved to be Secretary of State
for Transport. Tebbit replaced Prior as Employment Secretary.

Jim Prior had been the most belligerent and outwardly self-confident
of the 'wets'. He was a farmer who, although too young to fight in
the Second World War, came from a solidly middle-class background.
He too had been educated at a famous public school, Charterhouse,
followed by Cambridge. He was born in 1932, so did not fit exactly
into the mould of his other 'wet' colleagues. Neither did Peter Walker,
a self-made businessman who had been the 'rising star' of the party
under Heath's leadership. Yet these two 'wets' remained. It seemed to
Harold Macmillan, now aged eighty-seven, that Mrs Thatcher had an
especial animus against alumni of his old school, Eton. 'Out go the

Etonians, in come the Estonians,' he is supposed to have remarked in an unguarded aside.[23] The Etonians were easy enough to identify. The term 'Estonians' was probably a reference to the Jewish provenance of people like Nigel Lawson and Leon Brittan. Brittan, although already in the Cabinet since January 1981, was clearly a favoured protégé of the Prime Minister.

Press reports of the reshuffle at the time suggested that a major change had taken place. Thatcher and her acolytes had succeeded in taking over the party, it was reported. Jim Prior had been shuffled sideways to become the Secretary of State for Northern Ireland, a post which he had publicly insinuated that he would not take. He believed he had an affinity with the trade unions and presented a friendly face to them. Thatcher, it would appear from her account, took a special relish in moving him sideways. 'Jim Prior was obviously shocked to be moved from Employment, where he had come to consider himself all but indispensable.' Of course, Thatcher proved that he was not the 'indispensable' man he believed himself to be.

She wanted Prior's post for the 'formidable Norman Tebbit'. Jim Prior could not 'intimidate me by threatening himself', she remarked. She was tougher, and she had to show she was tougher, than everybody else in the government. Thatcher's *The Downing Street Years* is an extraordinary account of the passions and enmities she nursed during her period as Prime Minister. Tebbit was 'a true believer in the kind of approach Keith Joseph and I stood for'. He 'understood how trade union reform fitted into our overall strategy'.[24] The reference to one's own supporters as 'true believers', in an autobiography written for public consumption, would be astonishing from any other British politician. Thatcher was, in retrospect, sometimes obsessed with ideological considerations. It was certainly something that, with hindsight, she valued. Phrases such as 'my wing of the party' and 'true believers', and lengthy accounts, sometimes laced with bitterness, of the differences between 'wets and drys', are frequently encountered in her record of her years as Prime Minister.

Thatcher's account of the 'wets' bristles with indignation and resentment at the treatment she felt that they had given her. They were, in her view, sexist, patronising and snobbish. It was uncharacteristic of her to use such terms, which she probably would have felt to be too self-pitying. Those men, however, were 'quite prepared to make every allowance for "the weaker sex", but if a woman asks no special privileges and expects to be judged solely by what she is and does this is found gravely and unforgivably disorienting'. In this remarkably frank, and somewhat vituperative, account of being a woman right at the very top of politics, Thatcher disclosed her belief that there were 'certain kinds of men who simply cannot abide working for a woman'. She went on to complain that 'in the eyes of the "wet" Tory establishment I was not only a woman, but "that woman", someone not just a different sex, but of a different class, a person with an alarming conviction that the values and virtues of middle England should be brought to bear on the problems which the establishment consensus had created'.[25]

The press portrayed Thatcher's strike against the 'wets' in narrow ideological terms. The move was presented frequently in terms of 'left' and 'right', 'wets' and 'drys'. 'Mrs Thatcher defiantly reinforced the right wing of her Government yesterday when she dropped three "wets" from her Cabinet, brought in three loyalists and exiled Mr James Prior to Stormont Castle,' reported Michael White of the *Guardian*. White was astute enough to see that Thorneycroft had been 'dropped' and had not simply resigned voluntarily. A feature of the reporting of the reshuffle was the public trial of strength between Thatcher and Jim Prior who had 'publicly stated' in 'a protracted series of manoeuvres this summer that he would prefer to stay put'. Prior had suggested that he 'might resign rather than go to Northern Ireland to replace Mr Humphrey Atkins'.

The victorious 'drys' did not exult blatantly over their triumph. Tebbit went around telling friends, apparently, that there was 'little difference between him and Mr Prior on the key union question. "I am a hawk not a kamikaze. Jim is a dove not a chicken.'"[26] The *Guardian* was dismissive of the 'extraordinarily messy performance' of Thatcher's reshuffle and denounced her skills as a manager of people. 'This reshuffle falls utterly at the first test of good man management.' Lord Soames, 'a wet, is out'. Sir Ian Gilmour, 'a wet, is pitched bitterly into the cold'. Mark Carlisle, 'a dampish fellow, finds oblivion'. These were some of the staccato sentences with which the editorial page of the *Guardian* proclaimed Thatcher's ruthlessness. The paper quoted Sir Ian Gilmour's parting remarks. He had decided not to 'go gently into that good night'. He used his mordant wit and sarcasm to skewer the Prime Minister: 'It does no harm to throw the occasional man overboard,' but 'it does not do much good if you are steering full speed ahead for the rocks'. Gilmour was sniffily dismissive of the reshuffle itself. It was all very well changing personnel, but what was needed was a change of policy. The *Guardian* wholeheartedly agreed with him. 'Sir Ian believes that it is far more important to change the policy than to change the Cabinet.' Said Gilmour, 'Changes in the government can buy a little time. They give an appearance of movement and control. But that will not last long.'[27]

While the left-wing newspapers wrote enthusiastically about the brilliance of Sir Ian Gilmour who, in the *Guardian*'s words, had been removed 'wholly on ideological grounds', more abrasive figures lurked in the background. These people would later become bogeymen, part of the demonology built up by the left around Thatcher and her government. In September 1981, however, it seemed that Thatcher's rule, as well as that of her henchmen, would be short lived. Thatcher herself was viewed as a diminishing force. With 'every twist and turn, the base of her influence shrinks'. Her corrosive grip had shrivelled the power of her government. 'The disloyal are condemned, the narrow band of the like-minded promoted. And so to the winter of Mr Norman Tebbit.'[28] The *Guardian* predicted Thatcher's demise, from the ripples of the botched reshuffle, at the hands of the party establishment. 'The exercise has not enhanced Mrs Thatcher's own rule. It has in all probability accelerated the day when those across the swathe of the governing party who have never quite believed that "there is no alternative" will come to feel . . . that there must be some alternative.'[29]

It suited the *Guardian* to portray the likes of Norman Tebbit as ghoulish troglodyte figures from a repressive past, while the newspaper eulogised the statesmanlike Gilmour. 'No practising Conservative politician', it gushed, 'in modern times has written more thoughtfully or originally about the evolving role of the party.' Of course, the 'evolving role of the party' no doubt implied an evolution in the direction favoured by the *Guardian*. Gilmour, the newspaper acknowledged candidly, had not been 'a dominant Westminster performer', neither did his rhetoric 'rouse Tory conferences'.[30] His sacking was a convenient rod with which to beat Thatcher. Here was a highly intelligent, cultivated man being sacked for merely ideological reasons, yet there was a mild irony in the fact that it was Tebbit, not Sir Ian Gilmour, who represented a new social force within the Conservative party. It was the former civil aviation pilot, and not the wealthy Old Etonian baronet, who seemed, in those days of September 1981, to be the more dynamic, 'modern' figure.

The Times presented another view of the Thatcher reshuffle. In an editorial headed 'Prima inter pares', the Murdoch-owned paper pointed out that 'at the crucial Cabinet on July 17th to consider future public expenditure cuts the Prime Minister and the Chancellor lost the argument'. They 'even lost the vote of such normally loyal supporters as Mr Nott and Mr Biffen'. The crucial meeting of the Cabinet had taken place on 23 July, not the week before as *The Times* had suggested, but the broad picture was right.[31] Now, the *Times* editorial suggested, the Cabinet which had emerged was 'clearly more to Mrs Thatcher's personal taste' and was more 'likely to share her policy instincts'. This was something Thatcher herself later acknowledged in her memoirs. 'After the new Cabinet's first meeting I remarked to David Wolfson [chief of staff of the Political Office at Number 10] and John Hoskyns what a difference it made to have most of the people in it on my side.'[32] This comment, which implied that a number of the members of the Cabinet were still not on her side was another extraordinary statement from the head of a government. Thatcher's ability to contain contradictory, and often openly hostile, elements within the same Cabinet was unusual.

The *Times* editorial, which appeared on Tuesday 15 September, a day after the reshuffle, offered an acute analysis of the Prime Minister's leadership style. Although the paper acknowledged that the Cabinet was more in her image than ever before, it questioned whether such a Cabinet would indeed 'support her policies through thick and thin, regardless of political popularity, whatever the levels of unemployment or business bankruptcies'. The *Times* recognised that 'most politicians, even some of her personal supporters, are less dogmatic than the Prime Minister'. Most normal politicians, it suggested, did not have 'her courage, or her impetuosity'. They did 'not necessarily share all of her vision'. Dogmatism, courage, impetuosity – these were all traits which had been identified early in her first term as Prime Minister. It was, after all, that staid newspaper the *Economist* which had compared her, after the 1981 budget, to an impetuous driver who 'wrenches the steering wheel from side to side, trying to drive single-handedly a machine that wants to go the other way'.[33]

Now, in September, her leadership style was directly compared to that of a head teacher or an evangelical preacher rather than to that of a leader of a team. 'She clearly does not view her Cabinet as a team to be guided and led, but rather as a class to be instructed or a religious army to be ordered into battle.' In a remark which would characterise her entire tenure as Prime Minister, the editorial observed that she 'makes too little attempt to persuade'. The Thatcher style was based on personal conviction and courage. It left little room for persuasion or 'consensus-building'. As the paper noted, the question of Prime

Ministerial style was of particular interest, because the Conservative party remained 'deeply divided over its general philosophy, its broad strategy and particular policies'.

The Thatcher style was a high-risk enterprise both for the Prime Minister herself and for her nervous party. 'If she succeeds,' concluded the broadly admiring editorial, 'and by success we mean regenerating the British economy and winning the next election for the Conservative Party – it will be a remarkable personal triumph. If she fails, the fault will be laid at her door, though the damage and the casualties will spread wide through the political and economic landscape.'[34] Thatcher herself accepted this judgement. She quotes the end of the editorial fully in her own memoirs. 'I would accept that,' she admitted.[35] Indeed the appearance of that last paragraph of the *Times* editorial in her memoirs is redolent of a prize pupil quoting a school report with glowing pride.

To many who preferred a quieter life, such high stakes were not really what politics, or the political life, were about. What was particularly galling for those who sought a consensus in politics was the overtly 'sectarian' nature of her leadership. It was true that the Cabinet was still a 'coalition of the different strands of present-day Conservatism'. There remained members of the Cabinet who had led 'the criticism of what they see as a divisive economic strategy'. Prior, Pym and Walker were still in the Cabinet, as were 'Mr Whitelaw and Lord Carrington who are also critical if more circumspect'. In essence, however, Thatcher had accomplished a reshuffle which bore the 'indelible stamp and style of the Prime Minister herself'. She had, according to the *Times* tribute, 'reasserted her political dominance and restated her faith in her own policies'. More ruthlessly, she had 'rewarded those who do, and punished some of those who do not share that faith'.[36]

This description, with its mock-religious overtones, portrayed Thatcher almost as a kind of vengeful pagan god, rewarding pet favourites with earthly rewards while hurling others to political damnation. It seemed reasonable to make her out to be an all-powerful figure in the weeks after the reshuffle. The reality had been different. Thatcher had been buffeted and goaded all through the summer by press reports and by some of her own supporters. The image of the commanding, self-assured leader, mistress of all she surveyed, was only partially reflective of reality. Throughout August, Thatcher received a barrage of advice from well-wishers and supporters which, if anything, urged her to be even tougher on the 'wets' than was eventually the case on 14 September.

Charles Douglas-Home, a nephew of the former Prime Minister, and deputy editor of *The Times*, wrote to Thatcher from King's Lynn on 18 August reporting that he had been talking to her senior colleagues – 'Prior, Pym, Nott and Whitelaw himself'. Douglas-Home found their tone 'pretty depressing'. He recommended that she face each of her critics individually. Even more harshly, John Hoskyns had sent her a stern message, informing the Prime Minister that she had poor management skills. In what Charles Moore, Margaret Thatcher's authorised biographer, has described as 'quite possibly the bluntest official document ever seen in Downing Street', Hoskyns recognised that Thatcher's government had achieved 'the beginnings of a near-revolution in the private sector and especially in Industry'. He told her in stark terms that her 'own credibility and prestige are draining away very fast'. More woundingly, he declared, in various paragraph headings, '*You lack management competence*', '*Your own leadership style is wrong*'. He added, 'You break every rule of good man-management. You bully your weaker colleagues.' These were all sentiments which the 'wets' themselves would not dispute.[37]

Hoskyns's words would have been hurtful to Thatcher. He had a rebarbative style which antagonised many civil servants, for whom he had a contempt that was assuredly reciprocated. A self-made businessman, he was an archetypal Thatcherite figure. He also understood the nature of Thatcher's highly idiosyncratic appeal. He expressly did not want to be like other parties. As was demonstrated by his frank note to the Prime Minister, he was a man who favoured telling 'hard truths' to the electorate. 'We therefore should play down further tax cuts for the present,' was one unorthodox pearl of wisdom for a Conservative, which he recorded in his notes on a strategy meeting that took place at Chequers on 24 July. Another starkly contrarian opinion, from the point of view of more classical theories of attracting political support, was Hoskyns's view that 'we must take every opportunity of showing the electorate how *utterly different* (morally, socially, economically) our *objectives* are from the other parties, and thus how different our *means* often have to be [emphasis in original]'.[38] These thoughts chimed harmoniously with Thatcher's own instincts.

More seriously, the need for a major overhaul of the Cabinet was a constant theme among MPs, journalists and the tribe of people who inhabit what would later be called the 'Westminster village'. It was clear that some drastic change would have to be made. Thatcher's own soundings of the backbenches, conducted by her ever thorough Parliamentary Private Secretary Ian Gow, also suggested that a considerable shake-up of the leadership team was desired by the junior ranks of the party. The role of Parliamentary Private Secretary to the Prime Minister is, like many things in the British constitution and political institutions, loosely defined. There is no doubt, however that, in the respectable form of Ian Gow, Thatcher had one of the best in the history of the role.

Gow was only in his early forties when Thatcher became Prime Minister in 1979, but he had the mien and mannerisms of a man considerably older. He was described as a man of 'principle, determination and humour'. He had a keen sense of where the party's heart lay on certain issues. For four years he served as Mrs Thatcher's 'eyes and ears' in the House of Commons, which of course is what a good Prime Minister's Parliamentary Private Secretary should be. Nicknamed 'Supergrass' by Thatcher's critics, he was generally polite and courteous. He was a staunch and unyielding Unionist who would lose his life in 1990 at the hands of the IRA. Not only did Gow share many of Thatcher's advanced economic views, such as monetarism and a belief in the free market, he was personally loyal to her, almost to the point of devotion.[39]

Gow would have widely canvassed backbench opinion about the possible direction and character of a reshuffle. He was particularly assiduous in attending the various smoking bars within the Palace of Westminster and the gentlemen's clubs outside it which were then still a feature of the social life of Conservative Members of Parliament. In his *Who's Who* entry Gow proudly listed his clubs as the 'Carlton, Pratt's, Beefsteak, and the Cavalry and Guards' and by all accounts he frequented those establishments conscientiously. His wife Jane was often invited along with him to Chequers, and the couple were both present there on the fateful weekend when Thatcher put the last touches to her reshuffle. 'It was incredibly kind of you to have had us both to stay at Chequers last weekend,' Jane wrote on 17 September, the Thursday after the reshuffle. 'It was a most amusing and luxurious 24 hours.' No other Prime Minister, according to a grateful Jane Gow, would 'even think of inviting their PPS's wife'.[40] Gail Jopling, the Chief Whip's wife, who also spent the weekend at Chequers, wrote more directly about how 'fascinating' it had been 'to be on the fringe of the decision making'. She added charmingly that 'I hope today', meaning 14 September, the day of the reshuffle itself, 'isn't as grim as you expect and that you weren't awake all night.'[41]

Soundings from the backbenches would have revealed to both Gow and Thatcher that an overhaul was required. In a series of backbench judgements on Cabinet members before the recess on 16 July, presented by Derek Howe, a Conservative party official described as Mrs Thatcher's 'political secretary', it was found that Sir Ian Gilmour 'would not be missed'. He was not 'known for his enthusiasm for government policies'. Soames was viewed as projecting 'hardly the right image'. He was condemned as 'another non-communicator'. There were also 'doubts'

about his 'wholehearted support for Government'. There was in addition a campaign to suggest 'that the Home Secretary should make way
for someone else'. In Whitelaw's case there was 'no specific reason' to
shift him, 'just vague criticism' which was not confined 'to one section
of the Parliamentary Party'. By contrast, it was suggested that Jim
Prior's move to Northern Ireland would be 'counter-productive' and
might 'cause some backbench friction'.[42]

Derek Howe reported in his missive of 16 July that the 'unanimous
view of the group, and this encapsulates the views of others, is that the
Party would welcome changes ahead of the Party Conference'.[43] This was
due to take place, as always, at the beginning of October. As was often the
case, Thatcher had prepared the ground carefully before she struck. She
was meticulous and thorough, and the people she summarily dismissed
were precisely those people who did not command a following within
the parliamentary party. She had done her homework about that.

The rumours of the reshuffle dominated the press in the usually
fallow months of July and August. Towards the end of August, the
Economist lucidly described the difficulties of the Prime Minister's position. So widespread were rumours of the reshuffle that the magazine
actually had 'Thatcher to Shuffle' as its cover story in its 22 August
edition. If Thatcher had not gone through with it, she would have been
described as the weakest Prime Minister in history.

The *Economist* set the scene, in a challenge to the Prime Minister.
'Mrs Thatcher is going to create a new cabinet. It had better be in
her own image,' it provocatively declared. Thatcher now faced 'one of
the most important decisions of her career, since her present cabinet
is a vessel too full of confusion and disunity to be sailed safely into
the next general election'.[44] The impression of Cabinet disunity was
now almost universal. Hoskyns had made much the same point in his
notes on the strategy meeting when he asked, 'How can we achieve
and then demonstrate greater cabinet unity? To the public, a visibly
divided cabinet suggests a divided country.'[45] The *Economist*, at the end

of August, seemed to be fully briefed about the nature of the reshuffle and gave decent hints about the direction of Thatcher's thinking. Lord Carrington and 'Mr William Whitelaw' were correctly identified as 'Mrs Thatcher's closest lieutenants'. This was a shrewd surmise since Thatcher needed them in order to perform the hatchet job on the other 'wet' grandees who closely resembled them in style, outlook and values. It was a case of keeping one's enemies even closer than one's friends.

The problem the *Economist* identified was one which had bedevilled Thatcher's Cabinet from the very beginning. It had been too broad to begin with. This was 'probably Thatcher's biggest error'. Her problem was that her Cabinet had up till now 'persistently hobbled her own radicalism without succeeding in converting it into a gentler "one-nation" Toryism'. Thus her Cabinet combined the worst of both worlds; it was insufficiently radical, but neither did it present the gentle side of Toryism projected by the 'one-nation' strand of the party. The article correctly identified Thatcher's intended victims: 'She is keen to drop altogether three prominent wets.' These were 'Lord Soames (leader of the Lords), Sir Ian Gilmour (foreign) and Mr Mark Carlisle (education)'. The *Economist* also correctly identified those tipped for promotion. 'The most likely newcomers are Mr Norman Tebbit, Mr Nigel Lawson, Mr Tom King and Lady Young.' Three of the four would enter the Cabinet for the first time in September.

The precision with which the *Economist* identified the winners and losers suggested a reliable source at the highest levels of the government. Gilmour complained that the reports of 'the coming purge were so pervasive' that 'even the day was known'.[46] The briefing was no doubt extensive. Even Tebbit mentioned that there 'had been plenty of speculation about the reshuffle'.[47] The reshuffle's purpose was clear. Thatcher, according to the *Economist*, expressing a view shared by nearly every commentator at the time, was 'never going to be a leader of the Tory consensus'.[48] She had stated a number of times, 'I am not a consensus politician.'[49] It was unrealistic to expect anything else. Her 'party cannot now ask her to be that'. If Thatcher was to find unity, it would have to be 'round her own ideas and not round some vague compromise'.

It was inevitable that, when Thatcher finally performed what everybody had expected, there would be a backlash. The *Economist*, which had so accurately predicted the nature of the reshuffle, then described the move, which it had heralded, as a 'mid-term upheaval'. The September reshuffle showed a government 'which, halfway through its life, has rejected compromise'.[50] This was a stark judgement and not strictly true, but it reflected a widely held view. Her supporters in the country were ready to rally round her.

This support sometimes came from unusual quarters. She received a letter dated 13 September from the eccentric Marquess of Bath, the seventy-six-year-old proprietor of Longleat House in Wiltshire. He thanked her for contributing a 'Teddy' for one of the teddy-bear picnics he often arranged at his stately home. He then paid a 'personal tribute' to the Prime Minister. 'Top politicians are divided into two groups – the "good politicians" and the "great politicians".' While Wilson, Macmillan and Attlee had been 'good', Winston Churchill and Margaret Thatcher were 'great'. 'I can't say more.'[51] Her cult of personality was already established. It would also be crude to divide her support on class lines. Many of the 'wets' were patrician members of the upper class and gentry, while some 'wets' were not. It was also true that there were elements of the old aristocracy, the people living in country houses, and members of the old political right who were genuinely excited by Thatcher, and were enthused by her anti-socialist crusading zeal.

The 10th Earl of Bessborough, from his Edwardian stately home Stansted Park in Hampshire, recounted a meeting with Renaud de La Genière, the Governor of the Bank of France, while staying in Provence over the summer. A notable cultural figure, and one of three founder-members of the Chichester Theatre board, Lord Bessborough had been a Conservative minister under Edward Heath.[52] At the very end of August, he reported that the French central banker had said that under Thatcher's leadership 'La Grande Bretagne est sur la bonne voie' – 'Britain is on the right road – economically,' Bessborough added by way of translation.[53] The Frenchman was 'fearful about what may happen in France under the Socialists'. The background of the Cold War in Europe meant that Thatcher, at least, in 1981 was viewed as a reliable warrior against any socialist menace.

Thatcher enjoyed support from the elements of her party, and in the wider country, who were frightened by socialism. Her vision was strongly defined by what it was against: socialism, consensus, 'one-nation' Toryism. She also had a positive programme, which was encapsulated by free markets in the economy, an authoritarian streak with regard to 'law and order' and a certain sense of 'British exceptionalism', which some might term nationalism. She had defined her enemies and sought to defeat them, both within and outside her own party.

The leading opponent to Thatcher was arguably Sir Ian Gilmour. He was known to be close to Lord Carrington, whose deputy in the Foreign Office he had been, and whom the *Economist* described as a 'brooding' figure after the reshuffle, 'now shorn of Sir Ian Gilmour'. Gilmour was a political writer of note. He had written a book published in 1977, *Inside Right*, which attacked 'an ideological approach to politics and made a plea for consensus'. Of the victims of Thatcher's reshuffle, he was by far the most articulate and philosophical, even though his influence in the day-to-day bustle of politics was slight. 'Getting to the top? I don't believe I have the combination of skills and traits of character necessary,' he told the *Daily Telegraph*, a short time before his death in 2007.[54] Gilmour's languid and debonair manner reminded Julian Critchley, a Tory MP and friend, of Arthur Balfour, the Prime Minister at the beginning of the twentieth century, who was described by Lloyd George as 'not a man but a mannerism'.[55]

Gilmour took the extraordinary step of writing a lengthy article in *The Times* which appeared on 23 September, a mere nine days after his removal from office. It was an impressive performance in which he railed, in his civilised fashion, against the course which Thatcher was pursuing. The piece was entitled, 'How a move further right will sink the Tories'. He rather pompously asserted that it was 'profoundly unconservative for Tories to denigrate the economic policies of every Conservative government since that of Sir Winston Churchill'. Implicitly criticising Thatcher, he observed that it had 'become fashionable for some Conservatives to say that everything that was done in the past was wrong'.

He attacked Thatcher's notion of conviction politics: 'now we are told that all will be well because the Prime Minister at last has a "conviction Cabinet". I am not sure what this means.' He believed that the 'wets' had convictions too. 'The chief difference in the last Cabinet was not between those who had convictions and those who had not,' but 'between the Wets who had by and large held the same convictions over the years and the Hards who had mostly changed theirs fairly recently. In that sense the Hards had had more convictions than the Wets.' Gilmour made a good case that he and his fellow 'wets' were the actual conservatives, while Thatcher was a dangerous radical. He also observed that, even after the reshuffle, the Cabinet was still not wholly united behind the 'convictions of the Prime Minister'. He pleaded the case of the 'pragmatic' politician through the ages: 'the Tory Party should now be sloughing off its ideology not sharpening it up'. He denounced the very notion of ideology. 'Ideology, as Baldwin wisely foresaw, divides the country, and that is something the Conservatives should seek to avoid at almost any cost.'[56]

Gilmour was rational and articulate. 'For the Tory Government to move to the right now would be a defiance of the laws of political gravity.' He raised the fearful prospect of the SDP taking the place of the Conservative party. The Labour party was in a 'state of incipient civil war'. It was 'manifestly unfit to govern', but Labour was still 'well ahead of the Conservatives' in the polls. Meanwhile, the 'Social Democrats and Liberals' gave the 'Tories every reason for moving towards the centre'. Gilmour's eminently sensible analysis was that the

SDP had arisen 'because both the Conservative government and the Labour opposition have left the centre ground of politics wide open'. As a consequence, 'many Conservative seats always previously regarded as safe are safe no longer'. Those seats were impregnable to Labour, 'but they could fall to the SDP'.

Gilmour's piece was a lucid and plausible account of normal political conditions under normal, average, middle-of-the-road leaders. 'Scepticism about fashionable orthodoxies, emphasis on the importance of the centre ground' were all fair and pragmatic notions. The Conservative party was 'very unpopular', as he reminded his readers. He had objected to the Thatcherite cry of 'TINA' (There is no alternative). He wrote hopefully that 'there will presumably be great enthusiasm when alternatives are produced. I look forward to seeing it.' When he wrote the article, Gilmour presumably expected Thatcher to be defeated if not by the 'unfit' Labour party, then by the SDP: 'if Conservative unpopularity continues, the election will be won not by a left wing Labour Party but the SDP Liberal alliance'. Gilmour was notoriously close to Roy Jenkins, who it was believed had conducted an affair with Gilmour's wife, Caroline.[57] It was unlikely that he thought, at only fifty-five, that his Cabinet career had been ended for good.

It was equally unlikely that Thatcher paid much attention to Gilmour's wise and balanced objections. Lucidity and elegance of phrase were not qualities she especially valued. She was a lady of conviction, of fervent political passion, who had a job to do, and enemies to overcome. By background, temperament and conviction, she was radically different from Gilmour, although she was less than nine months older than him. Gilmour's education and background, his literary abilities and general breadth of mind made him a natural antagonist. In the end, it was Gilmour who left the Cabinet for the last time in 1981 never to return, while Thatcher would be Prime Minister for another nine years. The odds of such an occurrence happening would have seemed remote in September 1981.

Thatcher had given an interview to the *News of the World* which was due to appear on 20 September. In her notes for the interview, which were dated 16 September, Thatcher gave a clear, even blistering account of her philosophy and principles of leadership. The reasonableness of Gilmour was not something to which she now aspired, given the difficulties which the country faced. 'Britain today has a conviction government' was a favourite mantra. 'Not a consensus government. Not a confrontation government.' Hers was now, in her own words, 'a Cabinet of unity and singleness of purpose'. She was happy to characterise the Cabinet as 'right wing'. She did not 'mind taking a bit of stick provided we get through'. She was happy to get 'the blame for the difficulties faced by industry and our people'. This was, after all, part of the job.

She portrayed herself in a typically embattled mood. The 'There is no alternative' theme was also played. 'I have not heard any alternative policy which will take Britain through to prosperity.' She referred to her theory of mobilising support. 'If you have conviction people are more likely to come out and support you.' This had been the view of Lord Salisbury, British Prime Minister at the end of the nineteenth century. Thatcher then spoke of the 'great faiths' upon which 'our own moral values are founded'. 'Most of those great faiths', she argued, 'would never have got started if their prophets had gone out to the people and said: "Brothers I believe in consensus."' This was perhaps true, but nobody believed that Thatcher was a prophet starting a new religion. She was Prime Minister of the United Kingdom, and the comparison of a British prime minister with Old Testament prophets would have struck people in 1981 as highly unusual.

The interview rehearsed all the favourite themes of Thatcher's political credo. The prophets had turned to their followers and said, 'Brothers, these are the things I believe in. This is why I hope you will agree and come with us.' She was bold; she was tough. 'What I am doing are the things which absolutely had to be done. Things which have been ducked by one government after another for about 30 years.' She spoke of 'moral values'. Her policies were based 'not on some economic theory but on things I and millions like me were brought up with. "An honest day's work for an honest day's pay. Live within your means. Put by a nest egg for a rainy day. Pay your bills on time. Support the police."'[58] The injunction to 'support the police' may have been a little jarring, in the light of the disturbances of the summer. She had put taxpayers' money where her mouth was in relation to the police, giving them a 13.2 per cent rise at the end of July, which had been described by the Labour MP Bob Cryer as a 'slap in the face for nurses and civil servants when they see that the police get virtually what they want without asking'.[59]

Thatcher's style towards the end of 1981 was still not bearing any fruit in the polls. According to the Gallup survey, the Conservatives plumbed new depths at the very beginning of September, when they polled 23 per cent, with Labour on 37 per cent and the SDP–Liberal Alliance on 29 per cent.[60] There seemed to be no respite, but her inner conviction remained, outwardly at least, defiant and resolute. Thatcher posed as a prophetic figure, even though she was prepared to compromise, as we have seen, in the face of some opposition. Her unbending public stance may have been different from the pliancy she sometimes showed under pressure, but it was a personality she consciously projected. If the idea of the 'Iron Lady', an uncompromising chain-mailed crusader, was a myth, it was one which she self-consciously helped to create.

Against the force of Thatcher's Christian moralism, Ian Gilmour's plea for moderation, and his appeals to stick to the 'centre ground', did not make much impact. Outwardly, Thatcher was in no mood to compromise. She lashed out at politicians promising jam today who, she suggested, had no 'moral values'. 'How anyone with any moral values can stand up before an audience or say to the electorates, "I am an honest politician but I am going for dishonest money because I haven't got enough to spend so I am going to print it," beats me.'[61]

Epilogue

Sunday 5 June 1983 – Wembley Conference Centre in north-west London was 'filled to capacity'. The Prime Minister was in confident mood. She opened her speech in front of the party Chairman, Cecil Parkinson, and addressed 'fellow Young Conservatives' to rapturous applause and cheering. The youth rally was something of an innovation. Figures from the world of entertainment were present as cheerleaders and presenters. Such luminaries as Bob Monkhouse, the veteran comedian, Jimmy Tarbuck, a comedian and presenter, and the world snooker champion Steve Davis attended the event. The popular disc jockey and comedian Kenny Everett stole the show. Wearing giant foam hands, he yelled, 'Let's bomb Russia!' and 'Let's kick Michael Foot's stick away!'[1] The comedians joked that the sartorially challenged Michael Foot, who would celebrate his seventieth birthday in 1983, had been unfortunate; his tailor had died in 1937.[2] Everett's performance made some cringe with embarrassment. He was ridiculed in the press.[3]

The Prime Minister herself was in full electioneering mode. She was ebullient, brash and pugnacious in her thirty-five-minute speech to the young faithful. She was sure that what 'Britain's young people' wanted was 'another Tory Government'. She struck a libertarian note. Addressing the audience in the hall, she said, the young were individuals 'who want to live your own lives, in the way you choose, with a style which is your own within the law'. Above all, 'young people want to stay free'.[4] She had tailored her message of freedom to her audience, giving it a more socially liberal tinge than she was comfortable with, but the theme of freedom was something she had spoken about, with force and conviction, from the mid-1970s. Thatcher was addressing more than 2,500 Young Conservatives at an event described by the *Daily Mail* as having the 'razzamatazz of an American political convention'.[5]

The Prime Minister attacked Labour in her usual uncompromising and aggressive manner. She was not a politician who gave any quarter. She always questioned the motives of her opponents, even accusing them of being unpatriotic. Labour had 'no pride in Britain's achievements'. Instead, the Labour party indulged in 'a compulsive concentration on failure and a kind of envy which resents success'. Labour had 'no hope for Britain'. It had 'no faith in the British people'.[6] She was highly effective at discrediting her opponents, and questioning their motives. This approach stirred her followers. It also created clear dividing lines, but, as was inevitable, it infuriated her political opponents.

The essential duality of Thatcher's mind was expressed in the contrast she drew between the Conservatives and Labour. 'Where Labour's pessimistic, we are full of hope. Where they are bitter, we are determined to succeed. Where they fear the future, we rise to the challenge and the excitement and the adventure.' Thatcher could not resist referring to Kipling in her remarks. 'Do you remember Kipling's famous verse?' she asked hopefully. She spoke of Kipling as though the young of 1983 were familiar with his work. What the young activists made of Kipling's 'famous verse', 'At Runnymede, at Runnymede / Your rights were won at Runnymede', is unrecorded. 'No freeman shall be fined or bound / Or dispossessed of freehold ground.' She concluded, 'Well, you would under Labour.' The audience applauded. In her own mind Thatcher stood for the ancestral freedoms of the English people. The implication was that Labour, as a party, was hostile to the basic rights of Englishmen, won at Runneymede and enshrined in Magna Carta. 'Conservatives give you the chance to choose.' Conservatives, as she had said so many times, 'believe in freedom'. Kipling's verse was as familiar to Thatcher as the Bible, long ago memorised in her childhood and young adolescence. Addressing Cecil Parkinson, she observed that 'freedom cannot survive without personal responsibility'.[7] She had said this hundreds of times.

In an equally bizarre reference, given the youth of the audience, Thatcher spoke from the heart about the nation having been 'built on the success of merchant adventurers'. 'Men', she said without any irony, given her status as Britain's first female Prime Minister, 'who were willing to sail out into the unknown to carry our trade and bring back wealth to our people.' The imperialist note was also there, remarkable given that many of the audience would have known absolutely nothing about the British Empire. 'Men who took our ways of freedom and law to countries who would never otherwise have known them and some who would wish they still have them.'[8]

Four days after the rally, on Thursday 9 June 1983, the general election took place. Thatcher was re-elected with a majority of 144 in the House of Commons. This was a personal triumph. Given the difficulties of 1981 especially, nobody could have predicted such an astonishing result eighteen months before the election. Thatcher was presented as a human dynamo who had single-handedly crushed her political foes. One commentator in 1983 wrote that 'Margaret Thatcher, to an increasing degree, towered over the political scene, over a government that lacked any strong alternative figures, and over an opposition that was in disarray.'[9] *The Times* spoke in reverential terms of her 'famous stamina'. Ominously, as far as her opponents both within and outside the Conservative party were concerned, Thatcher made it clear that she now saw her government 'extending well into the 1990s'. She told party workers in Conservative Central Office that they should 'start work straightaway on winning the next general election'.[10] There was an air of dominance and triumphalism. She wanted a mandate to transform Britain which, she had even said in the dark days of 1981, would take 'ten years'. Nineteen-eighty-three seemed to vindicate her long-term vision. Thatcher was unembarrassed about talking of the long term, of 'going on and on'.[11]

The 1983 election was the last British general election before the real thawing of the Cold War took place. 'By 1987 Margaret Thatcher was taking tea with Gorbachev in Moscow.'[12] Unsurprisingly, Reagan hailed her victory, while the Kremlin 'criticized the British "winner takes all" electoral system' for distorting the 'real position of the political parties in the country'.[13] It was extraordinary that Soviet leaders, who presided over a one-party state, should offer insights into the relative merits of the 'first past the post' electoral system and proportional representation.

The cartoon caricature of Thatcher at this point was widely known. The impression, as David Butler wrote in 1983, was of an 'Iron Lady', a Boudicca, TINA (There is no alternative). Thatcher, unlike other recent Prime Ministers, had already by 1983 given her own name to a broad philosophy, a set of ideas. Thatcherism and Thatcherite meant very different things to different people and were used as terms of praise and as terms of opprobrium. But they were the terms and ideas on which the election was fought. They were perceived and, in varying measure responded to, by the British public: 'Victorian values', 'paying your own way', 'no easy solutions', 'reducing the size of government', 'making Britain great' were winning slogans.[14] It must be remembered that David Butler's assessment of Thatcher was written in 1983 without any benefit of hindsight.

Of course, the Falklands War of 1982 had played an important role in defining Thatcher in the public mind, as an embattled and determined leader. This was something which she herself acknowledged. 'It is no exaggeration to say that the outcome of the Falklands War transformed the British political scene.' She acknowledged, plausibly enough, the connection between the 'resolution' she had shown in 'economic policy' and 'the handling of the Falklands crisis'.[15] In this judgement, she was coherent and persuasive. The strength Thatcher showed in the

Falklands crisis simply reinforced an image she had already burnished as a tough, uncompromising and resolute leader. It was 1981 which had helped to imprint this image on the public mind.

The Falklands and Thatcher's leadership style raise the notion of 'charismatic leadership'. If such a thing really exists, Thatcher, more than any Prime Minister since Winston Churchill, was such a leader. Her character and personality were always at the forefront of any judgement about her government. As William Keegan, the left-leaning commentator, observed about Thatcher's control of economic policy, 'the crucial strategic decisions on economic policy' were 'taken at No. 10 Downing Street'. 'This heavy prime-ministerial involvement was intrinsic to the nature of the Thatcher economic experiment.'[16] Thatcher was at the centre of her government. She talked of the economy in the terms of her Methodist upbringing, in terms of 'freedom', moral certainties and 'battles' against various evils.[17] Max Weber, the originator of the idea of 'charismatic leadership', had defined charisma as 'a certain quality of an individual personality by virtue of which he is considered as endowed with supernatural, superhuman, or at least specifically exceptional powers or qualities'.[18] The notion of 'exceptional powers or qualities' animated Thatcher's own view of what leadership involved.

Weber himself had borrowed the term charisma from Christian theology, 'ultimately from the New Testament'. It was no surprise that such a concept had its origins in theology and religion. The characteristic mark of charismatic authority is that it is 'extraordinary'. It typically emerged when the 'regular holders of authority, whether legal or traditional, seem to be incapable of rising to the situation'. Charismatic leaders often emerge 'in opposition to the established authorities' of their society. Charisma is 'usually a force for social change and innovation'.[19] These observations, in all probability, would have received spontaneous assent from Margaret Thatcher. In Weber's conception, the charismatic leader was often a religious figure, a prophet who relied on the force of his personality and the simplicity of his message to win adherents. Thatcher, consciously or unconsciously, fitted this mould. She saw herself as the head and centre of a movement whose purpose was nothing less than the transformation of Britain.

The style of leadership which led to her victories was idiosyncratic in the extreme. It must also be remembered that the times in which Thatcher lived were unusual. As a historical phenomenon she was the product of the perceived economic failure of the 1970s and a shrinking national confidence. Her uncompromising style, the sharp simplicity of her ideas, offered consolation to a demoralised British public. All of this was shown to remarkable effect in the Falklands conflict, where Thatcher, once again, displayed a belligerence wholly alien to the British establishment, the Foreign Office mandarins who sought peace and conciliatory discussions.

The Argentinian junta which invaded the Falkland Islands did Thatcher a great service. Despite pleas to the contrary, her leadership style was confrontational. She always defined herself and her philosophy against enemies who were sometimes real and sometimes imaginary. Allusion has been made in this book to John Bunyan's *The Pilgrim's Progress*. It was significant that the 1906 English hymnal version of the John Bunyan hymn 'He who would true valour see' was sung at Margaret Thatcher's funeral. The hymn is popular in the English-speaking world, but few would know that it is Mr Valiant-for-Truth in whose mouth the original hymn appears in the second part of *The Pilgrim's Progress*.[20]

The notion of puritan struggle is a common theme in Anglo-American political discourse. Thatcher would probably have agreed with Theodore Roosevelt when he said in 1899 in Chicago that 'I wish to preach, not the doctrine of ignoble ease, but the doctrine of the strenuous life, the life of toil and effort, of labor and strife.'[21] This was a Protestant vision which has been more commonly expressed in American politics than has been the case in Britain.

The formation of Thatcher's mind and character was unusual. With the notable exception of Neville Chamberlain, Thatcher was the first Conservative leader to spring from a nonconformist tradition. It is striking that Tony Benn, her left-wing contemporary, chose the Bunyan hymn as one of his records on BBC Radio 4's *Desert Island Discs*. Nonconformist politicians were found in the ranks of the Liberal party and, subsequently, the Labour party. A Conservative leader from this background was unusual and, when combined with the popular nationalism Thatcher espoused, it became a powerful political tool.

The other intellectual influences on Thatcher were science and the law. She was a good chemist, even if she did not have the flair of a really great scientist. She liked to think of herself as empirical and logical, even though she was essentially an instinctive politician. As a tax lawyer, she had been meticulous and painstaking. She had a well-developed eye for detail, and relished arguments. She enjoyed victory of all kinds, both intellectual and, in the case of the Falklands, in war. Her aggressive personality was one of the key features of her style. Her best form of defence was always attack. She was always looking for more enemies to fight, for more dragons to slay.

It was this aggression that gave her energy and purpose. It inspired her followers with a sense of mission, and her enemies were always on the defensive. The nature of Thatcher's appeal, though, should not be exaggerated. She aroused equally strong feelings of antipathy among large sections of the population. This was perhaps inevitable, given her style of leadership. A preacher who claims to have a sole monopoly on truth will create enemies. Her speaking style, which seems to her enemies self-righteous and hectoring, did not lend itself to universal acceptance. But Thatcher never set out to be popular. Towards the end of her interview with the *News of the World* in September 1981, she quoted words which purported to be advice given to Earl Mountbatten of Burma by his mother. This, it was reported, had now been adopted by Thatcher as a guiding text. 'Don't worry what people think now.

Don't ever work for popularity. Above all, don't care what the newspapers say. What is important is that your decisions should be clear, and stand up to history. All you have got to think about is whether your children and grandchildren will think you have done well.'[22]

Nineteen-eighty-one was the crucial year of Thatcher's first government. As Norman Fowler said, 'it was also during 1981 that Margaret Thatcher really showed her style of leadership. It was decisive and at times attracted public support because she seemed to be taking action which the public overwhelmingly thought was right but never thought any government would have the nerve to carry out.'[23] But 1981, it must be remembered, did not see a marked improvement in the government's fortunes. As she herself remembered, on the eve of the Conservative party conference she was 'being described in the press as "the most unpopular prime minister since polls began"'.[24]

A Gallup poll conducted on behalf of the *Daily Telegraph* on 14 December 1981 revealed support for the SDP–Liberal Alliance at 50 per cent, while Labour and the Conservatives hovered at 23 per cent each.[25] It was a particularly trying period for Thatcher and her followers, but, even at the time, there was a sense that a corner had been turned. As Ian Gow, her Parliamentary Private Secretary, wrote on 29 September to the Prime Minister, 'It's been quite a year: and although the economic clouds should begin to lift slowly we both know that the most severe political struggles, within and without our own party, lie ahead.' Gow was sycophantically loyal to Thatcher. He accurately captures the notion of a leader being surrounded by enemies 'within and without' her 'own party'. This suggests a 'bunker mentality' shared by Thatcher and her entourage. The sense that the atmosphere around the Prime Minister resembled a 'siege' is vividly portrayed by Matthew Parris, who worked in her office before the 1979 election. 'In the Opposition leader's office I joined in 1976 it always felt like a kind of siege. Siege from the impossible workload she and all of us faced. Siege from the press who, while not universally hostile, were incredulous and finding grave difficulty in taking the new leader seriously.'[26] Such feelings were probably even more acute during 1981.

Gow's effusive letter at the end of the year showed impressive loyalty, engendered by the experience of 1981. 'We have been told', he wrote, 'that "familiarity breeds contempt". My experience over the past two and a half years has been the opposite. The longer I serve you, the greater is my regard and respect. You have been a giant among pygmies.' He also remarked how pleased he had been when Thatcher told him in September that she would like to see him 'through to the end'. Gow concluded his adulatory letter: 'Thank you . . . for being such a marvellous boss; and above all thank you for leading the British people with such honesty and dauntless courage.'[27]

Nineteen-eighty-one more than any other single year revealed Thatcher's character and personality. There is no sense in which she grew during that period. She simply relied upon her own instincts and many of the truths which she had learnt as a child. The striking thing about Margaret Thatcher as a political personality was how little, in fact, she developed from her assumption of the Tory leadership in 1975 to her last days in Number 10 in 1990. The 'rule of law', 'personal responsibility', 'freedom' were all part of her vocabulary from the beginning of her leadership and sustained her right to the end.

Other leaders may be said to have grown in office, or to have changed their point of view in the course of their political careers. In the context of Britain, one could mention William Gladstone, Benjamin Disraeli and perhaps Sir Robert Peel. Churchill's political career went through many phases and different parties. It is impossible to conceive Margaret Thatcher ever changing political parties. It could be argued that most leaders are substantially different at the end of their careers as Prime Minister, or President, from how they were at the start. The same cannot be said of Thatcher. Her style and her language show a remarkable consistency, not only of theme but of imagery. It was, after all, as early as January 1976, in her first year as party leader, that she was dubbed the 'Iron Lady' after a speech that she gave at Kensington Town Hall.[28]

In looking at her political career, there is something monolithic about Thatcher that is impressive and somewhat daunting. It is highly likely that her mental stock of ideas had been fully furnished by the time she had left Oxford in 1947, certainly by the time she had entered parliament in 1959. Her full schedule precluded her reading extensively, and there is no real evidence that she spent any time as Prime Minister reading much at all, other than official papers and memoranda relating to government affairs. Her mind had been set at a young age on certain principles from which she never deviated.

Thatcher was described when she became Prime Minister as 'Britain's fighting lady'. The cover of *Time* magazine on 14 May 1979 showed an embattled blonde with intense blue eyes, a hint of red lipstick on her pursed lips, with a Union Jack as a background.[29] Her combative style seemed to contradict notions of femininity, but that was all part of the paradox and the glamour. Images of Boudicca, the Celtic warrior queen who fought the Romans, and the mythic figure of Britannia mingled with notions of Queen Victoria and Elizabeth I to shape British conceptions of female leaders.

In terms of class, Thatcher had clearly come up in the world. She had adopted the somewhat strangulated vowels of the Southern middle classes, even though her roots were in the East Midlands. She had married a solidly middle-class professional in the oil business, who ran his own family company. She sent her son to Harrow, a school of privilege and wealth. Yet, despite her social aspirations, she cleverly, even if unconsciously, associated herself with shopkeepers and traditional lower-middle-class values.

Valéry Giscard d'Estaing, the President of France from 1974 to 1981, is reported to have dismissed Margaret Thatcher as 'une fille d'épicier', a grocer's daughter.[30] Her story was one of social mobility driven by determination and hard work. It seemed that there was a kind of destiny propelling her from the obscurity of a provincial town in the East Midlands onward to Number 10 and the global stage, where she became one of the most famous women in the world. The whole notion of *The Pilgrim's Progress* was that of a journey from a doomed town to the celestial city. The pilgrim encounters many temptations and enemies on the way. As the words of the modern version of Bunyan's hymn suggested, 'No foes shall stay his might, though he with giants fight, He will make good his right to be a pilgrim.' In her own mind, Thatcher's career had been a kind of pilgrimage, fighting error and seeking to spread truth. She had fought passionately for absolute values in a world which seemed diffident and uncertain of purpose. Her response to the challenges of 1981 had, more than any period in her public career, demonstrated this.

Notes

Abbreviations

DNB   *Oxford Dictionary of National Biography*
FCO   Foreign and Commonwealth Office, London
PREM   Prime Minister's Office files, The National Archives, Kew
TFW   http://www.margaretthatcher.org/ – website of the Margaret Thatcher Foundation
THCR   The Thatcher Papers, Churchill College, Cambridge

Preface

1 *Guardian*, 'The Lady and the People', 5 May 1979.
2 Norman Fowler, *Ministers Decide: A Personal Memoir of the Thatcher Years*, London, 1991, p. 145.
3 Margaret Thatcher, *The Downing Street Years*, London, 1993, p. 302.
4 *Guardian*, 'Margaret Thatcher tributes: Ed Miliband's speech', 10 April 2013.

Chapter 1: Portrait of a Lady

1 Speech at St Lawrence Jewry, 4 March 1981, TFW.
2 *Guardian*, 5 March 1981.
3 Speech at St Lawrence Jewry, 4 March 1981, TFW.
4 *DNB*, J. R. Green.
5 Russell Lewis, *Margaret Thatcher: A Personal and Political Biography*, London, 1975, p. 10.
6 Speech at St Lawrence Jewry, 4 March 1981, TFW.
7 Speech at Intercontinental Hotel, on 21st anniversary as MP for Finchley, 18 October 1980, TFW.
8 Patricia Murray, *Margaret Thatcher: A Profile*, London, 1980, pp. 12, 13.
9 Alfred Roberts (extract from Sermon Notes), TFW.
10 Ibid.

11 Maldwyn Edwards, *Methodism and England: A Study of Methodism in its Social and Political Aspects during the Period 1850–1932*, London, 1943, pp. 168, 179.

12 Ibid., p. 204, quoting the *Methodist Recorder*, 29 December 1918.

13 Ibid.

14 *Grantham Journal*, 8 May 1942, TFW.

15 Murray, *Thatcher*, p. 13.

16 Eliza Filby's *God and Mrs Thatcher: The Battle for Britain's Soul*, London, 2015, is an excellent account of Margaret Thatcher's religious inspiration.

17 William F. May, 'Manichaeism in American Politics', found on www.religion-online.org.

18 *Independent*, Andy McSmith, 'For and against Maggie: when the Iron Lady stood (almost) alone', 21 March 2013.

19 Alfred Roberts (extract from Sermon Notes), TFW.

20 *Economist*, Letters, 5 May 1979.

21 In fact she was elected to the House of Commons on 8 October 1959, five days before her thirty-fourth birthday on 13 October.

22 Speech at the Conservative Political Centre, Blackpool, 11 October 1968, TFW.

23 *Spectator*, Patrick Cosgrave, 'Mrs Thatcher and the Leadership', 14 December 1974, THCR 7/1/12.

24 *Daily Telegraph*, Obituary, Patrick Cosgrave, 17 September 2001.

25 *Spectator*, Patrick Cosgrave, 'Mrs Thatcher and the Leadership', 14 December 1974, THCR 7/1/12.

26 David Wood, *The Times*, 30 December 1974, THCR 7/1/12.

27 *Evening Standard*, 30 December 1974, THCR 7/1/12.

28 *Scotsman*, 7 January 1975, THCR 7/1/12.

29 Ibid.

30 *Spectator*, Patrick Cosgrave, 'Getting the Priorities Right', 18 January 1975, THCR 7/1/12.

31 Ibid.

32 *Evening Standard*, Londoner's Diary, 'Hotting up', 24 January 1975, THCR 7/1/12.

33 Lewis, *Thatcher*, p. 127.

34 *Daily Mirror*, 24 January 1975, THCR 7/1/12.

35 *Observer*, Woodrow Wyatt, 'Would you cry on her shoulder?', 2 February 1975, THCR 7/1/12.

36 *Observer*, 2 February 1975, THCR 7/1/12.

37 Ben Pimlott, *Hugh Dalton*, London, 1985, p. 445.

38 *Western Mail*, Nora Beloff, 5 February 1975, THCR 7/1/12.

39 *Daily Express*, 23 January 1975, THCR 7/1/12.

40 *Daily Express*, 1 February 1975, THCR 7/1/12.

41 *Economist*, 1 February 1975, THCR 7/1/12.

42 *Daily Mirror*, 5 February 1975, THCR 7/1/12.

43 *Daily Mirror*, Marjorie Proops, 'The Iron Maiden', 5 February 1975, THCR 7/1/12.

44 *Daily Telegraph*, 4 February 1975, THCR 7/1/12.
45 *Daily Telegraph*, 5 February 1975, THCR 7/1/12.
46 *Guardian*, 'First Lady will put the Tories right', 12 February 1975.
47 *Financial Times*, 12 February 1975, THCR 7/1/12.
48 Ibid.
49 *Guardian*, 'First Lady will put the Tories right', 12 February 1975.
50 Ibid.
51 *Economist*, 'Not quite Disraeli', 23 July 1977.
52 *Daily Mirror*, Marjorie Proops, 'The Iron Maiden', 5 February 1975, THCR 7/1/12.
53 *Sunday Telegraph*, 'Tory Facts and Faces', Peregrine Worsthorne, 2 February 1975, THCR 7/1/12.
54 Speech in Finchley (adoption), 'The Britain I want to see', 11 April 1979, TFW.
55 Ibid.
56 *Guardian*, Obituary, Lord Callaghan, 28 March 2005; *Daily Telegraph*, Obituary, Lord Callaghan of Cardiff, 28 March 2005.
57 Speech in Finchley (adoption), 11 April 1979, TFW.
58 Speech to Conservative Rally in Cardiff, 16 April 1979, TFW; quoted in Charles Moore, *Margaret Thatcher: The Authorized Biography*, vol. 1: *Not for Turning*, London, 2013, pp. 408–9.
59 *Sun*, Katherine Hadley, 'My Face, My Figure, My Diet', 16 March 1979, TFW.
60 *Guardian*, 5 May 1979.
61 *Guardian*, 'The Lady and the People', 5 May 1979.
62 *Guardian*, 5 May 1979.
63 *Economist*, 'Up the hill', 11 October 1975.
64 Hugh Stephenson, *Mrs Thatcher's First Year*, London, 1980, p. 7.
65 *Economist*, 'Cabinet Maker', 12 May 1979.
66 *Guardian*, 7 May 1979.
67 *Guardian*, Anthony Arblaster, 'Did the Tsarina of Finchley deserve to win?', 7 May 1979.
68 Murray, *Thatcher*, p. 101.
69 *Economist*, 'Doing it her way', 22 September 1979.
70 Ibid.
71 Ibid.
72 Murray, *Thatcher*, p. 126.
73 TV interview for Granada *World in Action*, 27 January 1978, TFW.
74 Murray, *Thatcher*, p. 127.
75 *Economist*, 'Doing it her way', 22 September 1979.
76 Stephenson, *Mrs Thatcher's First Year*, p. 7.
77 Ibid., p. 94.
78 Ibid., p. 95.
79 Speech at Press Association lunch, 11 January 1980, TFW.
80 Stephenson, *Mrs Thatcher's First Year*, p. 101.
81 *Economist*, 'Doing it her way', 22 September 1979.

82 Ibid.
83 Murray, *Thatcher*, p. 92.
84 *Economist*, 'Doing it her way', 22 September 1979.

Chapter 2: Friends, Foes and the '81 Budget

1   Speech at *Guardian* Young Businessman of the Year Award, 11 March 1981, TFW.
2   Geoffrey Howe, *Conflict of Loyalty*, London, 1994, pp. 197, 204.
3   *Glasgow Herald*, 'Chancellor spares no one in struggle to beat inflation', 11 March 1981.
4   John Sparrow, Letter to Margaret Thatcher, 20 February 1981, PREM 19/436.
5   www.bbc.co.uk/onthisday.
6   Norman Fowler, *Ministers Decide: A Personal Memoir of the Thatcher Years*, London, 1991, pp. 145–6.
7   *Financial Times*, 'Thatcher defends "swift and decisive" action on pit closures', 20 February 1981.
8   *Financial Times*, 'The leading lady handles the script change with aplomb', 20 February 1981.
9   Speech to the House of Commons, 28 February 1980, TFW.
10 William Keegan, *Mrs Thatcher's Economic Experiment*, London, 1984, p. 131.
11 Quoted in ibid., p. 134.
12 Hansard, 10 March 1981.
13 Margaret Thatcher, *The Downing Street Years*, London, 1993, p. 136.
14 Tim Lankester, 'Note for the Record', 13 February 1981, PREM 19/438.
15 Ibid.
16 Note written for PM by Walters, Wolfson and Hoskyns, 20 February 1981, PREM 19/439.
17 *Daily Telegraph*, Obituary, Sir Alan Walters, 5 January 2009.
18 *Guardian*, Obituary, Sir John Hoskyns, 20 October 2014.
19 John Hoskyns, *Just in Time: Inside the Thatcher Revolution*, London, 2000, p. 279.
20 Ibid., pp. 280–1.
21 *Glasgow Herald*, 'Chancellor spares no one in struggle to beat inflation', 11 March 1981.
22 Hansard, 11 March 1981.
23 Ibid.
24 Ibid.
25 Ibid.
26 *DNB*, Peter Shore.
27 *Guardian*, 16 March 1981.
28 *The Times*, 12 March 1981.
29 *Sun*, 13 March 1981.
30 *Independent*, Obituary, Lord Pennock, 8 March 1993.
31 Nigel Lawson, *The View from No. 11*, London, 1992, p. 98.

32 Note written to Margaret Thatcher, 30 March 1981, PREM 19/441.
33 Press release embargoed 24 hours, 29 March 1981, TFW.
34 Howe, *Conflict of Loyalty*, p. 209.
35 Thatcher, *The Downing Street Years*, p. 51.
36 Jim Prior, *A Balance of Power*, London, 1986, p. 134.
37 Ibid., p. 140.
38 Ian Gilmour, *Dancing with Dogma*, London, 1992, p. 40.
39 Thatcher, *The Downing Street Years*, p. 51.
40 *Sun*, 'Cabinet Men Warn on Budget', 13 March 1981.
41 *The Times*, Geoffrey Smith, 'Inside the Cabinet: The Men who Said No to the Budget', 13 March 1981.
42 Prior, *A Balance of Power*, p. 134.
43 Bernard Ingham, Note to Mrs Thatcher, 11 March 1981, TFW.
44 *Sun*, 'Cabinet Men Warn on Budget', 13 March 1981.
45 Ibid.
46 Howe, *Conflict of Loyalty*, p. 208.
47 *Sun*, 'Cabinet Men Warn on Budget', 13 March 1981.
48 Hoskyns, *Just in Time*, p. 288.
49 *Herald*, Obituary, Sir Ronald Millar, 18 April 1998.
50 *Financial Times*, 'The Thatcher Cabinet', 16 March 1981.
51 *Financial Times*, 'Thatcher Defends Budget as Tory Discontent Grows', 12 March 1981.
52 *Financial Times*, 'Walker hits out cautiously at Thatcher's policies', 23 March 1981.
53 *Financial Times*, 'Mrs Thatcher reassures the Tory faithful', 30 March 1981.
54 Ibid.
55 Speech to Conservative Central Council, 28 March 1981, Cardiff, TFW.
56 *Sun*, 'Cabinet Men Warn on Budget', 13 March 1981.
57 Hoskyns, *Just in Time*, p. 288.
58 Prior, *A Balance of Power*, p. 133.
59 Lawson, *The View from No. 11*, pp. 26–7.
60 *Economist*, 'Charging the Guns', 21 March 1981.
61 Ibid.

Chapter 3: Civil War on the Left

1 *Guardian*, 'Pleasant Party's Rosy Dawn', 27 March 1981.
2 Ibid.
3 Bill Rodgers, *Fourth among Equals*, London, 2000, p. 211.
4 Ivor Crewe and Anthony King, *SDP: The Birth, Life and Death of the Social Democratic Party*, Oxford, 1995, p. 102.
5 *Guardian*, 'Not just another player, but more a new game', 27 March 1981.
6 *Guardian*, 'Democrat in the Classroom', 31 March 1981.
7 *Guardian*, Obituary, Lord Jenkins of Hillhead, 6 January 2003.
8 *Guardian*, 'Not just another player, but more a new game', 27 March 1981.

9 *Guardian*, Obituary, Lord Jenkins of Hillhead, 6 January 2003.
10 Ibid.
11 *Guardian*, 'Not just another player, but more a new game', 27 March 1981.
12 Hugh Stephenson, *Claret and Chips: The Rise of the SDP*, London, 1982, p. 6.
13 'Press Statement – SDP launched', 26 March 1981, SDP Archives, McGivan Papers, Essex University.
14 Stephenson, *Claret and Chips*, pp. 6–7.
15 *South Wales Echo*, Interview with Margaret Thatcher, 30 March 1981, TFW.
16 Hugo Young, *The Hugo Young Papers: A Journalist's Notes from the Heart of Politics*, ed. Ion Trewin, London, 2008, pp. 162–3.
17 *Independent*, Obituary, Richard Negus, 4 July 2011; *Who's Who*, Michael Thomas.
18 Rodgers, *Fourth among Equals*, p. 211.
19 *DNB*, Michael Foot; Denis Healey, *The Time of my Life*, London, 1989, p. 477.
20 Henry Pelling, *A Short History of the Labour Party*, 8th edn, London, 1985, p. 179.
21 *Guardian*, '"Gang of Three" bid to save Labour', 1 August 1981.
22 Shirley Williams, *Climbing the Bookshelves*, London, 2009, p. 275.
23 Tony Benn, *The End of an Era: Diaries 1980–1990*, ed. Ruth Winstone, London, 1992, p. 23.
24 Williams, *Climbing the Bookshelves*, p. 276.
25 Ibid., pp. 278–9.
26 Benn, *The End of an Era: Diaries 1980–1990*, p. 69.
27 Roy Hattersley, *Who Goes Home? Scenes from a Political Life*, London, 1995, p. 222.
28 Ibid., pp. 222–33.
29 Michael Foot, *Loyalists and Loners*, London, 1986, p. 122.
30 Williams, *Climbing the Bookshelves*, p. 281.
31 David Owen, *Time to Declare*, London, 1991, p. 481.
32 David Owen Papers, Liverpool University, D709.
33 David Owen, Letter to Councillor Harold Luscombe, 9 October 1980, David Owen Papers, Liverpool University, D709.
34 Glen Barnham, Letter to Bill Rodgers, 19 January 1981, SDP Archives, Lord Rodgers Collection, Essex University.
35 John Parker, Letter to Bill Rodgers, 20 January 1981, SDP Archives, Lord Rodgers Collection, Essex University.
36 Jeremy Bray, Letter to 'Bill and Shirley', 20 January 1981, David Owen Papers, Liverpool University, D709.
37 *Guardian*, Obituary, Jeremy Bray, 5 June 2002.
38 Jeremy Bray, Letter to 'Bill and Shirley', 20 January 1981, David Owen Papers, Liverpool University, D709.
39 Roy Jenkins, *A Life at the Centre*, London, 1991, p. 535.
40 Ibid.
41 Stephenson, *Claret and Chips*, p. 9.
42 Tim Hough, Letter to David Owen, 30 March 1981, SDP Archives, McGivan Papers, Essex University.

43 Alec McGivan, General Letter to members, Council for Labour Victory, 11 March 1981, SDP Archives, Lord Rodgers Collection, Essex University.

44 Stephenson, *Claret and Chips*, p. 8.

45 Ibid., pp. 8–9.

46 Brian McGillan, Letter to Alec McGivan, 12 March 1981, SDP Archives, McGivan Papers, Essex University; Alastair Reid, Letter to Alec McGivan, 11 March 1981, SDP Archives, McGivan Papers, Essex University.

47 David Owen, Letter to Janet Knowles, 31 March 1981, David Owen Papers, Liverpool University, D709.

48 *Economist*, 'Born to Lead', 28 March 1981.

49 www.ukpollingreport.co.uk/voting-intention-1979–1983.

50 *Guardian*, 'Foot castigates the "SDP Bubble"', 11 April 1981.

51 Article for *NOW!* magazine by the Rt. Hon. Dr David Owen MP, Tuesday 24 March 1981, David Owen Papers, Liverpool University, D709.

52 David Owen, Article for the *Parliamentary Year Book*, written in the summer of 1981, David Owen Papers, Liverpool University, D709.

53 Roy Jenkins, Speech at Metropole Hotel, Brighton, 29 May 1981, SDP Archives, McGivan Papers, Essex University.

54 David Owen, Speech to a Social Democrats Students Meeting at Liverpool University, 29 April 1981, SDP Archives, McGivan Papers, Essex University.

55 David Owen, Speech to SDP meeting in Cardiff at the Park Hotel, 2 June 1981, SDP Archives, McGivan Papers, Essex University.

56 Shirley Williams, Speech to Third World Lobby in the House of Commons, 5 May 1981, SDP Archives, McGivan Papers, Essex University.

57 Shirley Williams, Speech at the Technical College, Gloucester, 11 April 1981, SDP Archives, McGivan Papers, Essex University.

58 Stephenson, *Claret and Chips*, p. 57.

59 Williams, *Climbing the Bookshelves*, p. 288.

60 Ibid., p. 289.

61 Stephenson, *Claret and Chips*, p. 60; Jenkins, *A Life at the Centre*, pp. 539–41.

62 David Owen, Article for the *Daily Express*, 13 July 1981, David Owen Papers, Liverpool University, D709.

63 Margaret Thatcher, Letter to Stan Sorrell, 9 July 1981, TFW.

64 *Guardian*, 'Jenkins fails to beat Hoyle by 1,759 votes', 17 July 1981.

65 Stephenson, *Claret and Chips*, p. 63.

66 David Owen, Interview with *Company*, July 1981, David Owen Papers, Liverpool University, D709.

67 Roy Jenkins, Speech at the Summer Luncheon of the Merseyside Chamber of Commerce at the Adelphi Hotel, Liverpool, 18 June 1981, SDP Archives, McGivan Papers, Essex University.

Chapter 4: Death in Ireland

1 *Financial Times*, 'Ripper evaded police 9 times', 6 May 1981

2 *Daily Mail*, 'Yorkshire Ripper: My mission to kill', 6 May 1981.

3 Hansard, 5 May 1981.

4 Ibid.

5 www.cain.ulst.ac.uk.

6 *DNB*, Bobby Sands.

7 *People*, 'In Bobby Sands the IRA finds a martyr – and his family finds a hero', 18 May 1981.

8 Ibid.

9 *Economist*, 'American condolences', 9 May 1981.

10 Ibid.

11 Thomas Hennessey, *Hunger Strike: Margaret Thatcher's Battle with the IRA 1980–1981*, Sallins, Co. Kildare, 2014, p. 163.

12 Humphrey Atkins, Letter to Margaret Thatcher, 3 April 1981, TFW.

13 *Daily Telegraph*, Obituary, Harry West, 7 February 2004.

14 Ibid.

15 Bobby Sands, *Skylark Sing your Lonely Song: An Anthology of the Writings of Bobby Sands*, ed. Ulick O'Connor, Dublin 1982, pp. 153, 156.

16 Humphrey Atkins, Letter to Margaret Thatcher, 3 April 1981, TFW.

17 *DNB*, Humphrey Atkins.

18 *Independent*, Obituary, Humphrey Atkins, 8 October 1996.

19 Humphrey Atkins, Letter to Margaret Thatcher, 3 April 1981, TFW.

20 *Guardian*, 'Tight security for by-election ballots', 10 April 1981.

21 *Guardian*, 'Poll coup for IRA a blow to Thatcher', 11 April 1981.

22 Telegram from Washington to Foreign Office, 10 April 1981, TFW.

23 Humphrey Atkins, Letter to Francis Pym, 8 April 1981, TFW.

24 Ibid.

25 *Guardian*, 'A Political Sort of Status', 15 April 1981.

26 Riyadh Press Conference, 21 April 1981, TFW.

27 www.bbc.co.uk/news, 8 April 2013.

28 Riyadh Press Conference, 21 April 1981, TFW.

29 John Hume, *Personal Views: Politics, Peace and Reconciliation in Ireland*, Dublin, 1996, p. 92.

30 N. Harington, Letter to PM, 3 April 1981, TFW.

31 M. W. Hopkins, Letter to N. Sanders, 21 April 1981, TFW.

32 Ian Paisley, Letter to Margaret Thatcher, 6 March 1981, TFW.

33 Mike Hopkins, Letter to Michael Alexander, No. 10, 2 April 1981, TFW.

34 Ibid.

35 Ibid.

36 Lord Carrington, Letter to the Prime Minister, 16 April 1981, TFW.

37 Dermot Nally, Telegram to the FCO, 22 April 1981, TFW.

38 From J. Raymond Application no. 9338/81, Robert Sands v The United Kingdom, TFW.

39 Statement issued by ECHR Commissioners, Belfast, enclosed in Lankester minute to Margaret Thatcher, 25 April 1981, TFW.

40 Outline of Statement allegedly brought out of the Maze by members of hunger striker Bobby Sands's family, enclosed in Lankester minute to Margaret Thatcher, 25 April 1981, TFW.

41 *Guardian*, Obituary, Charles Haughey, 14 June 2006; *Economist*, Obituary, Charles Haughey, 22 June 2006.

42 T. Ryle Dwyer, *Charlie: The Political Biography of Charles James Haughey*, Dublin, 1987, p. 140.

43 Leonard Figg, Telegram from Dublin to the FCO, 29 April 1981, TFW.

44 Prime Minister's Telephone Conversation with the Secretary of State for Northern Ireland on Saturday Evening, 25 April 1981, TFW.

45 M. W. Hopkins to No. 10 Downing St., 27 April 1981, PREM 19/504.

46 Telegram from UKRep Brussels to the FCO, 29 April 1981, TFW.

47 Dwyer, *Charlie*, p. 143.

48 Telegram from Delhi to the FCO, 7 May 1981, TFW.

49 Telegram from Bonn to the FCO, 6 May 1981, TFW.

50 *New York Times*, Obituary, Tip O'Neill Jr, 7 January 1994.

51 *New York Times*, Obituary, Daniel Moynihan, 27 March 2003.

52 Edward Kennedy, Statement after Sands's death, 5 May 1981, TFW.

53 *New York Times*, Obituary, Edward Kennedy, 26 August 2009.

54 Telegram from Washington to the FCO, 6 May 1981, TFW.

55 Marie E. Howe, Letter to Margaret Thatcher, The Commonwealth of Massachusetts House of Representatives – Assistant Majority Leader, 12 May 1981, TFW.

56 Telegram from Washington to the FCO, 14 May 1981, PREM 19/504.

57 Record of a meeting between the Prime Minister and the Leader of the Opposition, Mr Michael Foot, at the House of Commons on 14 May 1981 at 2025, PREM 19/504.

58 Ian Paisley, Telegram to Margaret Thatcher, 14 May 1981, PREM 19/504.

59 Message of 14 May from the British PM, The Rt. Hon. Margaret Thatcher MP, to Senator Kennedy, Speaker O'Neill, Senator Moynihan and Governor Carey, TFW.

60 Walden to Mike Pattison, 19 May 1981, TFW.

61 John Bew, 'The Lady was for Turning', review of Thomas Hennessey, *Hunger Strike: Margaret Thatcher's Battle with the IRA 1980–1981*, *New Statesman*, 14 March 2014.

62 Message of 14 May from the British PM, The Rt. Hon. Margaret Thatcher MP, to Senator Kennedy, Speaker O'Neill, Senator Moynihan and Governor Carey, TFW.

63 Speech to Conservative Women's Conference, Methodist Central Hall, Westminster, 20 May 1981, TFW.

64 Remarks on becoming a grandmother, 3 March 1989, TFW.

65 Speech to Scottish Conservative Conference, City Hall, Perth, 8 May 1981, TFW.

66 Speech at reopening of Wesley's House in the presence of George Thomas, Speaker of the House of Commons, City Road, London, 24 May 1981, TFW.

67 Speech at Stormont Castle, 28 May 1981, TFW.

68 Interviews with ITN, Ulster TV, RTE, 28 May 1981, THCR 2/1/5/98.

69 John J. Louis, Letter to Margaret Thatcher, 29 June 1981, TFW.

70 Dwyer, *Charlie*, p. 143.

71 Ibid.

Chapter 5: Riots

1 Meeting with Chief Constable of Merseyside in Police Headquarters Liverpool, Monday 13 July 1981, at 0930 hours, TFW.
2 Margaret Thatcher, *The Downing Street Years*, London, 1993, p. 143.
3 *Liverpool Echo*, 'Leroy Cooper: The Toxteth Riots were a wake-up call and did some good', 4 July 2011.
4 www.bbc.news.co.uk, 4 July 2001.
5 Ibid.
6 *DNB*, Kenneth Oxford.
7 www.racquetclub.org.uk.
8 www.bbc.news.co.uk, 4 July 2001.
9 Ibid.
10 David Owen, Article on the SDP for the *Parliamentary Year Book*, David Owen Archive, Liverpool University, D709.
11 Martin Kettle and Lucy Hodges, *Uprising: The Police, the People and the Riots in Britain's Cities*, London, 1982, p. 183.
12 Ibid., pp. 182–3.
13 Ibid., p. 186.
14 www.socialistalternative.org/liverpool/chapter-3-the-road-to-power/; Doyle described herself as a 'socialist agitator' on a website of the charity Afghan Mother & Child Rescue, www.amcr.org.uk.
15 Kettle and Hodges, *Uprising*, p. 186.
16 Ibid., p. 184.
17 Meeting with the representatives of the Liverpool City Council and the Merseyside County Council, 13 July 1981, TFW.
18 Tristram Hunt, *Ten Cities that Made an Empire*, London, 2014, p. 386.
19 Meeting with Liverpool Community Leaders in the Liverpool Town Hall on 13 July 1981, TFW.
20 *Independent*, Obituary, The Most Rev. Derek Worlock, 9 February 1996.
21 Meeting with the representatives of the Liverpool City Council and the Merseyside County Council, 13 July 1981, TFW.
22 Thatcher, *The Downing Street Years*, p. 145.
23 Kathryn A. Manzo, *Creating Boundaries: The Politics of Race and Nation*, London, 1998, p. 153.
24 Ibid., p. 147.
25 Kettle and Hodges, *Uprising*, p. 9.
26 *Guardian*, 'How smouldering tension erupted to set Brixton aflame', 13 April 1981.
27 *Guardian*, Darcus Howe, 'New Cross: the blaze we cannot forget', 17 January 2011.
28 Ibid.
29 Ibid.
30 Tony Jefferson and Roger Grimshaw, *Controlling the Constable: Police Accountability in England and Wales*, London, 1984, p. 81; Kettle and Hodges, *Uprising*, p. 20.

31 www.georgepadmoreinstitute.org.
32 Jefferson and Grimshaw, *Controlling the Constable*, p. 101.
33 Ibid., p. 85.
34 Kettle and Hodges, *Uprising*, pp. 91–2.
35 *Time*, 'Britain: Bloody Saturday', 20 April 1981.
36 *Guardian*, 'How smouldering tension erupted to set Brixton aflame', 13 April 1981.
37 Hansard, 27 July 1981.
38 TV interview for ITN, 13 April 1981, TFW.
39 www.bbc.co.uk, 'In pictures, Tory conference classics'.
40 TV interview for ITN, 13 April 1981, TFW.
41 No. 10 record of conversation, 13 April 1981, TFW.
42 *Guardian*, Obituary, Leslie Scarman, 10 December 2014.
43 *DNB*, Leslie Scarman; *Guardian*, Obituary, Leslie Scarman, 10 December 2014; *DNB*, Leslie Scarman.
44 Kettle and Hodges, *Uprising*, p. 168.
45 Hansard, 16 July 1981.
46 TV interview for Granada *World in Action*, 27 January 1978, TFW.
47 Kettle and Hodges, *Uprising*, p. 105.
48 TV interview for Granada *World in Action*, 27 January 1978, TFW.
49 Thatcher, *The Downing Street Years*, p. 145.
50 Ibid., p.143.
51 *Economist*, 'Doing it her way', 22 September 1979.
52 Alan Clark, *Diaries*, vol. 2: *In Power 1983–1992*, London, 1993, p. 350.
53 Thatcher, *The Downing Street Years*, p. 144.
54 Ibid., p. 145.
55 Michael Heseltine, *Life in the Jungle: My Autobiography*, London, 2000, p. 228.

Chapter 6: 'Among Friends'

1 *Guardian*, 'It's now or never, Thatcher tells MPs', 24 July 1981.
2 *DNB*, Anthony Barber.
3 Margaret Thatcher, *The Downing Street Years*, London, 1993, p. 148.
4 Ian Gilmour, *Dancing with Dogma*, London, 1992, p. 38.
5 Thatcher, *The Downing Street Years*, pp. 148–9.
6 Gilmour, *Dancing with Dogma*, p. 38.
7 Thatcher, *The Downing Street Years*, p. 149.
8 Charles Moore, *Margaret Thatcher: The Authorized Biography*, vol. 1: *Not for Turning*, London, 2013, p. 638.
9 Hugo Young, *One of Us: A Biography of Margaret Thatcher*, London, 1989, p. 219.
10 Allan Meltzer and Brian Griffiths, Letter to Margaret Thatcher, 19 May 1981, PREM 19/441.
11 Tim Lankester, 'Note for the Record', 15 July 1981, PREM 19/441.

12 Paul Johnson, 'Freedom – the *Moral* Foundation', speech given 7 April 1981, published in the *Free Nation*, June 1981.

13 Menu card from the Fourth Ross McWhirter Memorial Dinner, 7 April 1981, THCR 1/7/5.

14 *DNB*, Ross McWhirter.

15 *DNB*, Norris McWhirter.

16 Speech opening Automan '81, 18 May 1981, TFW.

17 Charles Dickens, *Hard Times*, London, 1854.

18 Harold Wilson, Speech at the Labour party conference, 1 October 1963, quoted in www.guardian.com, 'Harold Wilson's "white heat of technology" speech 50 years on', 1 October 2013.

19 Moore, *Margaret Thatcher*, p. 48.

20 *Independent*, Obituary, David English, 12 June 1998.

21 Speech at *Daily Mail* Tabloid 10th Anniversary Banquet, 1 May 1981, TFW.

22 Draft Speech for the PM, *Daily Mail* 10th Anniversary, 1 May 1981, THCR 1/3/5A.

23 Menu card from Dinner at No. 10 Downing Street in honour of The Vice-President of the United States of America and Mrs Bush, 25 June 1981, TFW.

24 Caroline Stephens, Note to Margaret Thatcher, 15 January 1981, THCR 6/2/2/25.

25 Caroline Stephens, Note to Margaret Thatcher, 16 February 1981, THCR 6/2/2/25.

26 Caroline Stephens, Note to Denis Thatcher, 17 February 1981, THCR 6/2/2/25.

27 David Rutter, Letter to Margaret Thatcher, 25 May 1981, THCR 6/2/2/25.

28 Ronald Gibbins, Letter to Margaret Thatcher, 15 May 1981, THCR 6/2/2/25.

29 Geoffrey Tower, Letter to Margaret Thatcher, 19 May 1981, THCR 6/2/2/25.

30 Rupert Brown, Letter to Margaret Thatcher, 25 April 1981, THCR 6/2/2/25.

31 David Rutter, Letter to Margaret Thatcher, 25 May 1981, THCR 6/2/2/25.

32 George Thomas, Letter to Margaret Thatcher, 1 June 1981, TFW.

33 *Marxism Today*, July 1981, p. 5.

34 Christopher Soames, Letter to Margaret Thatcher, 2 March 1981, TFW.

35 T. P. Lankester, Note from 3 March 1981, TFW.

36 Christopher Soames, Letter to Margaret Thatcher, 12 March 1981, TFW.

37 John Hoskyns, Letter to Margaret Thatcher, 8 April 1981, TFW.

38 Clive Whitmore, Note to John Wiggins (at No. 10), 2 April 1981, TFW.

39 Christopher Soames, Letter to Margaret Thatcher, 1 May 1981, TFW.

40 John Hoskyns, Letter to Margaret Thatcher, 8 April 1981, TFW.

41 Christopher Soames, Letter to Margaret Thatcher, 6 July 1981, TFW.

42 Young, *One of Us*, p. 228.

43 Colin Pilkington, *The Civil Service in Britain Today*, Manchester, 1999, p. 60.

44 Bernard Ingham, Note to the Chancellor of the Duchy of Lancaster, 8 July 1981, PREM 19/424.

45 Ibid.

46 Bernard Ingham, Note to the Chancellor of the Duchy of Lancaster, 31 July 1981, PREM 19/424.

47 John Hoskyns, Letter to Geoffrey Howe, 9 July 1981, PREM 19/424.

Chapter 7: Purge of the 'Wets'

1 Margaret Thatcher, *The Downing Street Years*, London, 1993, p. 151.

2 Ian Gilmour, *Dancing with Dogma*, London, 1992, p. 38.

3 Thatcher, *The Downing Street Years*, p. 151.

4 Hugo Young, *One of Us: A Biography of Margaret Thatcher*, London, 1989, p. 221.

5 Charles Moore, *Margaret Thatcher: The Authorized Biography*, vol. 1: *Not for Turning*, London, 2013, p. 642.

6 Peter Thorneycroft, Letter to Francis Pym, 7 August 1981, uncatalogued, Thatcher Papers, Churchill College, Cambridge.

7 Cecil Parkinson, *Right at the Centre: An Autobiography*, London, 1992, p. 173.

8 Extract from a speech by The Rt Hon. The Lord Thorneycroft, CH, Chairman of the Conservative Party, speaking at the Press Gallery Luncheon, on Wednesday 11 February 1981, THCR 2/14/1/22.

9 Peter Shore, Letter to Margaret Thatcher, 3 August 1981, PREM 19/424.

10 Peter Thorneycroft, Letter to Francis Pym, 7 August 1981, uncatalogued, Thatcher Papers, Churchill College, Cambridge.

11 Thatcher, *The Downing Street Years*, p. 151.

12 *DNB*, William Whitelaw.

13 *Guardian*, Obituary, Ian Gilmour, 24 July 2007.

14 *Philadelphia Inquirer*, Obituary, Christopher Soames, 18 September 1987.

15 William Whitelaw, *The Whitelaw Memoirs*, London, 1989, p. 10.

16 Simon Ball, *The Guardsmen*, London, 2004, pp. 27, 388.

17 *Guardian*, Obituary, William Whitelaw, 2 July 1999.

18 *Daily Mail*, 15 September 1981.

19 Thatcher, *The Downing Street Years*, p. 152.

20 Simon Hoggart, *A Long Lunch*, London, 2010, p. 263.

21 Parkinson, *Right at the Centre*, p. 175.

22 Norman Tebbit, *Upwardly Mobile: An Autobiography*, London, 1988, pp. 180–1.

23 *Times Educational Supplement*, 'Anti-Semitism still an issue', 24 February 2006.

24 Thatcher, *The Downing Street Years*, p. 151.

25 Ibid., pp. 129–30.

26 *Guardian*, 'Thatcher drops three "wets"', 15 September 1981.

27 *Guardian*, 'Reshuffling: much motion as time runs out', 15 September 1981.

28 Ibid.

29 Ibid.

30 Ibid.

31 *The Times*, 'Prima inter pares', 15 September 1981.

32 Thatcher, *The Downing Street Years*, p. 152.

33 *Economist*, 'Charging the Guns', 21 March 1981.

34 *The Times*, 'Prima inter pares', 15 September 1981.

35 Thatcher, *The Downing Street Years*, p. 153.

36 *The Times*, 'Prima inter pares', 15 September 1981.

37 Moore, *Margaret Thatcher*, pp. 640–1.

38 John Hoskyns, Note on Strategy Meeting Chequers, 24 July 1981, PREM 19/424.
39 *DNB*, Ian Gow.
40 Jane Gow, Letter to Margaret Thatcher, 17 September 1981, THCR 1/3/6.
41 Gail Jopling, Letter to Margaret Thatcher, 14 September 1981, THCR 1/3/6.
42 Derek Howe, Note to the Prime Minister, 'Fox and Goose', 16 July 1981, TFW.
43 Ibid.
44 *Economist*, 'Thatcher to Shuffle', 22 August 1981.
45 John Hoskyns, Note on Strategy Meeting Chequers, 24 July 1981, PREM 19/424.
46 Gilmour, *Dancing with Dogma*, p. 38.
47 Tebbit, *Upwardly Mobile*, p. 180.
48 *Economist*, 'Thatcher to Shuffle', 22 August 1981.
49 *Time*, 'A Tory Wind of Change', 14 May 1979.
50 *Economist*, 'Mrs Thatcher repairs the dykes for the rainy season', 19 September 1981.
51 Marquess of Bath, Letter to Margaret Thatcher, 13 September 1981, THCR 1/3/6; *Independent*, Obituary, The Marquess of Bath, 1 July 1992.
52 *Independent*, Obituary, The Earl of Bessborough, 18 December 1993.
53 Earl of Bessborough, Letter to Margaret Thatcher, 29 August 1981, THCR 1/3/6.
54 *DNB*, Ian Gilmour.
55 Ibid.; Travis L. Crosby, *The Unknown David Lloyd George: A Statesman in Conflict*, London, 2014, p. 62.
56 Ian Gilmour, 'How a move further right will sink the Tories', *The Times*, 23 September 1981.
57 John Campbell, *Roy Jenkins: A Well-Rounded Life*, London, 2014, pp. 190–2.
58 Interview with the *News of the World*, Notes, 16 September 1981, TFW.
59 *The Times*, 25 July 1981.
60 D. K. Britto, Note to Derek Howe, 16 September 1981, TFW.
61 Interview with the *News of the World*, Notes, 16 September 1981, TFW.

Epilogue

1 Jo-Anne Nadler, *Too Nice to be a Tory: It's my Party and I'll Cry if I Want to*, London, 2004, p. 76.
2 *Daily Mail*, 'Thatcher-matazz', 6 June 1983.
3 Nadler, *Too Nice to be a Tory*, p. 76.
4 Speech to Wembley Youth Rally, 5 June 1983, TFW.
5 *Daily Mail*, 'Thatcher-matazz', 6 June 1983.
6 Speech to Wembley Youth Rally, 5 June 1983, TFW.
7 Ibid.
8 Ibid.

9 David Butler and Dennis Kavanagh, *The British General Election of 1983*, London, 1983, pp. 1–2.

10 *The Times*, 'Day in the Life of the Winner', 11 June 1983.

11 John Cole, 'Going on, and on, and on', *Independent*, 1 April 1995.

12 Nadler, *Too Nice to be a Tory*, pp. 76–7.

13 *The Times*, 'Reagan hails victory, East block dismayed', 11 June 1983.

14 Butler and Kavanagh, *The British General Election of 1983*, pp. 1–2.

15 Margaret Thatcher, *The Downing Street Years*, London, 1993, p. 264.

16 William Keegan, *Mrs Thatcher's Economic Experiment*, London, 1984, p. 133.

17 See Eliza Filby, *God and Mrs Thatcher: The Battle for Britain's Soul*, London, 2015, for the role of religion in Thatcher's economic arguments.

18 Justin Taylor, 'Max Weber Revisited: Charisma and Institution at the Origins of Christianity', *Australian eJournal of Theology*, 19.3 (December 2012), pp. 195–208, at p. 196.

19 Ibid., p. 197.

20 John Bunyan, *The Pilgrim's Progress*, ed. W. R. Owens, Oxford, 2003 [1684], p. 275.

21 Theodore Roosevelt, 'The Strenuous Life', Speech before the Hamilton Club, Chicago, 10 April 1899, quoted in www.bartelby.com.

22 Interview with the *News of the World*, Notes, 16 September 1981, TFW.

23 Norman Fowler, *Ministers Decide: A Personal Memoir of the Thatcher Years*, London, 1991, p. 150.

24 Thatcher, *The Downing Street Years*, p. 153.

25 www.ukpollingreport.co.uk/voting-intention-1979–1983.

26 Matthew Parris, *Chance Witness: An Outsider's Life in Politics*, London, 2002, p. 188.

27 Ian Gow, Letter to Margaret Thatcher, 29 December 1981, THCR 1/3/6.

28 Speech, Kensington Town Hall, 19 January 1976, TFW.

29 *Time*, 'Britain's Fighting Lady', 14 May 1979.

30 This phrase formed part of the title of John Campbell, *Margaret Thatcher: The Grocer's Daughter*, London, 2000.

Bibliography

Archives

National Archives, Kew
SDP Archives, McGivan Papers, Essex University
David Owen Papers, Liverpool University
Thatcher Papers, Churchill College, Cambridge University

Newspapers and Magazines

Daily Express
Daily Mail
Daily Mirror
Daily Telegraph
Economist
Evening Standard
Glasgow Herald
Guardian
Independent
Liverpool Echo
New Statesman
New York Times
Observer
Philadelphia Inquirer
South Wales Echo
Sun
Sunday Telegraph
The Times
Time
Times Educational Supplement
Western Mail

Books and Articles

Ball, Simon, *The Guardsmen*, London, 2004

Benn, Tony, *The End of an Era: Diaries 1980–1990*, ed. Ruth Winstone, London, 1992

Bunyan, John, *The Pilgrim's Progress*, ed. W. R. Owens, Oxford, 2003 [1684]

Butler, David, and Dennis Kavanagh, *The British General Election of 1983*, London, 1983

Campbell, John, *Margaret Thatcher: The Grocer's Daughter*, London, 2000

—, *Roy Jenkins: A Well-Rounded Life*, London, 2013

Crewe, Ivor, and Anthony King, *SDP: The Birth, Life and Death of the Social Democratic Party*, Oxford, 1995

Crosby, Travis L., *The Unknown David Lloyd George: A Statesman in Conflict*, London, 2014

Dwyer, T. Ryle, *Charlie: The Political Biography of Charles James Haughey*, Dublin, 1987

Edwards, Maldwyn, *Methodism and England: A Study of Methodism in its Social and Political Aspects during the Period 1850–1932*, London, 1943

Filby, Eliza, *God and Mrs Thatcher: The Battle for Britain's Soul*, London, 2015

Foot, Michael, *Loyalists and Loners*, London, 1986

Fowler, Norman, *Ministers Decide: A Personal Memoir of the Thatcher Years*, London, 1991

Gilmour, Ian, *Dancing with Dogma*, London, 1992

Hattersley, Roy, *Who Goes Home? Scenes from a Political Life*, London, 1995

Healey, Denis, *The Time of my Life*, London, 1989

Hennessey, Thomas, *Hunger Strike: Margaret Thatcher's Battle with the IRA: 1980–1981*, Sallins, Co. Kildare, 2014

Heseltine, Michael, *Life in the Jungle: My Autobiography*, London, 2000

Hoggart, Simon, *A Long Lunch*, London, 2010

Hoskyns, John, *Just in Time: Inside the Thatcher Revolution*, London, 2000

Howe, Geoffrey, *Conflict of Loyalty*, London, 1994

Hume, John, *Personal Views: Politics, Peace and Reconciliation in Ireland*, Dublin, 1996

Hunt, Tristram, *Ten Cities that Made an Empire*, London, 2014

Jefferson, Tony and Roger Grimshaw, *Controlling the Constable: Police Accountability in England and Wales*, London, 1984

Jenkins, Roy, *A Life at the Centre*, London, 1991

Keegan, William, *Mrs Thatcher's Economic Experiment*, London, 1984

Kettle, Martin and Lucy Hodges, *Uprising: The Police, the People and the Riots in Britain's Cities*, London, 1982

Lawson, Nigel, *The View from No. 11*, London, 1992

Lewis, Russell, *Margaret Thatcher: A Personal and Political Biography*, London, 1975

Manzo, Kathryn A., *Creating Boundaries: The Politics of Race and Nation*, London, 1998

May, William F., 'Manichaeism in American Politics', found on www.religion-on-line.org

Moore, Charles, *Margaret Thatcher: The Authorized Biography*, vol. 1: *Not for Turning*, London, 2013

Murray, Patricia, *Margaret Thatcher: A Profile*, London, 1980

Nadler, Jo-Anne, *Too Nice to be a Tory: It's my Party and I'll Cry if I Want to*, London, 2004

Owen, David, *Time to Declare*, London, 1991

Parkinson, Cecil, *Right at the Centre: An Autobiography*, London, 1992

Parris, Matthew, *Chance Witness: An Outsider's Life in Politics*, London, 2002

Pelling, Henry, *A Short History of the Labour Party*, 8th edn, London, 1985

Pilkington, Colin, *The Civil Service in Britain Today*, Manchester, 1999

Pimlott, Ben, *Hugh Dalton*, London, 1985

Prior, Jim, *A Balance of Power*, London, 1986

Rodgers, Bill, *Fourth among Equals*, London, 2000

Roosevelt, Theodore, *The Strenuous Life: Essays and Addresses*, New York, 1900

Sands, Bobby, *Skylark Sing your Lonely Song: An Anthology of the Writings of Bobby Sands*, ed. Ulick O'Connor, Dublin, 1982

Stephenson, Hugh, *Claret and Chips: The Rise of the SDP*, London, 1982

—, *Mrs Thatcher's First Year*, London, 1980

Taylor, Justin, 'Max Weber Revisited: Charisma and Institution at the Origins of Christianity', *Australian eJournal of Theology*, 19.3 (December 2012), pp. 195–208

Tebbit, Norman, *Upwardly Mobile: An Autobiography*, London, 1988

Thatcher, Margaret, *The Downing Street Years*, London, 1993

Whitelaw, William, *The Whitelaw Memoirs*, London, 1989

Williams, Shirley, *Climbing the Bookshelves*, London, 2009

Young, Hugo, *The Hugo Young Papers: A Journalist's Notes from the Heart of Politics*, ed. Ion Trewin, London, 2008

—, *One of Us: A Biography of Margaret Thatcher*, London, 1989

Acknowledgements

As is only to be expected, while writing this book I have incurred many debts of gratitude. I would especially like to thank, in no particular order, Allen Packwood and Andrew Riley at the Churchill Archives Centre at Churchill College, Cambridge; the staff at the National Archives in Kew; Sarah Knight in my office; and Kate Summerscale.

I have also been greatly assisted by the many politicians and public figures with whom I have conversed about aspects of Mrs Thatcher's personality and her government. It would be invidious to name them all individually, but I thank them all.

Finally, I would like to thank Anna Simpson and Michael Fishwick at Bloomsbury, as well as Peter James, my excellent copy editor. I am also immensely grateful to my agent, Georgina Capel, for her encouragement and support.

Index

Adams, Gerry, 113–14
Aitken, Ian, 24
Arthur, King, 32
Atkins, Humphrey, 102–5, 107–8,
    110, 116, 180, 192
Attlee, Clement, 35, 82, 202
authority
    'charismatic', 212
    respect for, 136, 140–1

Bagehot, Walter, 20
Baldwin, Stanley, 71, 204
Balfour, Arthur, 203
Barber, Anthony, 155
Barron, Sergeant Alan, 135
Bath, Marquess of, 202
Beckett, Samuel, 102
Beloff, Nora, 17–18
Benn, Tony, 75–80, 87, 91, 165, 214
Bessborough, Earl of, 202–3
Bevan, Aneurin, 78
Bible
    misquotation, 125–6, 156
    Old Testament, 2–3, 28, 32, 206
Biffen, John, 33, 195
Bismarck, Otto von, 20
Blaney, Neil, 110
Bonar Law, Andrew, 15
Boudicca, 211, 217
Bray, Jeremy, 84
British Empire, 210
Brittan, Leon, 158, 191

Brixton riots, 133, 135, 141–6, 149–50
Brown, Wally, 132, 137–9, 147
Budd, Alan, 160
budget (1973), 155
budget (1981), 40–65, 141, 176
    background, 42–4
    and Cabinet disunity, 57–8
    Conservative party response to,
        58–64
    and economists' letter, 53–5
    opposition to, 49–55
    public reception of, 64–5
    'wets' and, 55–7
Bunyan, John, 6, 63, 127, 140,
    213–14, 218
Burmah Oil, 38
Burnet, Alastair, 144
Bush, George H. W., 169
Butler, David, 211
Butler, Joyce, 24
Butt, Ronald, 13, 134

Cabinet disunity, 57–8, 156–7, 178–9,
    183, 194–6, 200–1, 204
Cabinet reshuffle, 180–207
    backbenchers and, 198–200
    and criticisms of Thatcher, 197–8
    and ideological politics, 191–4, 203
Callaghan, James, 27–9, 51, 67, 71,
    74–5, 78, 85, 87
capital punishment, 34–6, 151
Carey, Governor Hugh, 118–20

Carlisle, Mark, 57, 182, 193, 201
Carrington, Peter, 38, 57, 60, 119
    and Cabinet reshuffle, 180, 184–7,
        196, 201
Carron, Owen, 106, 108
Carter, Jimmy, 66
Centre for Policy Studies, 49
Chamberlain, Neville, 214
'charismatic leadership', 212
Charles, Prince of Wales, 177
Churchill, Mary, 186
Churchill, Winston, 20, 45, 96, 165,
        169, 174, 186, 188, 202, 204,
        212, 216
City of London, 4, 163–4
civil servants, 38, 67, 197, 207
civil service pay dispute, 172–7, 181
Coleraine, Lord, 15–16
Company magazine, 97
comprehensive schools, 81, 162
Concannon, Don, 105
Confederation of British Industry
    (CBI), 50, 52–3
consensus politics, 11, 28, 71–2, 196,
        201, 203, 206
Conservative Central Council, 62
Conservative party
    backbenchers, 154–6, 198–200
    leadership contest, 12–25
    response to budget, 58–64
    'wets', 55–8, 61, 63, 133, 157,
        183–8, 190–2, 197, 201–2, 204
Conservative Women's Conference,
    123–4
'conviction politics', 9, 11, 31–2, 71,
    204–7
Cooke, Archbishop Terence, 116
Cooper, Leroy, 130–1
Cosgrave, Patrick, 12, 14–15
cricket, 178
Criminal Attempts Act (1981), 144
Criminal Law Act (1967), 104
Cripps, Francis, 52

Critchley, Julian, 203
Cromwell, Oliver, 93
Cryer, Bob, 207

Daily Express, 19, 95, 143
Daily Mail, 19, 21, 98, 134, 166–7,
        169, 188, 209
Daily Mirror, 16, 21–2, 25
Daily Telegraph, 15, 23, 64, 88,
        159–60, 203, 215
Dalton, Hugh, 17
Davis, Steve, 208
de Valera, Éamon, 110
de Valera, Sile, 110
democracy, 124, 129, 149–50, 167
    Labour party and, 76–7, 83
Diana, Princess of Wales, 177
Dickens, Charles, 164
Die Welt, 118
Disraeli, Benjamin, 25, 216
Donovan Award, 168
Douglas-Home, Charles, 197
Douglas-Home, Sir Alex, 34, 45
Downing Street Years, The, 44, 55, 191
Doyle, Clare, 135
du Cann, Edward, 60, 63, 154
Duffy, Brendan, 123
Duffy, Patrick, 98–9
Dunwoody, Gwyneth, 24

Easter Rising, 102, 110
economic policy, Prime Ministers and,
    44–5
Economist, 9, 20–1, 25, 31, 53, 65–7,
        88, 151
    and Cabinet reshuffle, 195, 200–3
Eden, Sir Anthony, 45, 63, 96
Eden, Sir John, 63
Elizabeth I, Queen, 217
English, David, 166–7
European Commission, 69–70
Evening Standard, 13, 15
Everett, Kenny, 208

Falkender, Marcia, 84
Falklands War, 211–14
Fermanagh and South Tyrone by-
    election, 102–6, 111
Financial Times, 52, 61, 159
Foot, Jill, 75
Foot, Michael, 43, 49–51, 61, 90, 189,
    208
    and Bobby Sands's death, 98–9,
        120–1
    and launch of SDP, 88–9
    and leadership contest, 75–7, 79–81
Fowler, Norman, 42, 215
Franco, General Francisco, 18
free enterprise, 27, 34
freedom, 11, 25–6, 124, 161, 167–70,
    208–10, 212, 216

general election (1979), 27–32
general election (1983), 210–11
gentlemen's clubs, 36, 95, 187, 199
Gibbins, Ronald, 171
Gilmour, Caroline, 205
Gilmour, Ian, 55–6, 157–8
    and Cabinet reshuffle, 180–2,
        184–7, 190, 193–4, 199, 201,
        203–7
Giscard d'Estaing, Valéry, 66, 217
Gladstone, William Ewart, 7, 216
Godley, Wynne, 52
Good Samaritan, parable, 11
Goodson, Alan, 135
Gorbachev, Mikhail, 211
Gow, Ian, 60, 159, 182–4, 198–9,
    215–16
Gow, Jane, 199
Green, J. R., 2
Griffiths, Brian, 158–60
Grosvenor, Lord, Robert, 102–3
Grunwick dispute, 147
Guardian, 24, 31, 33, 52, 76, 96, 108,
    159, 186
    and Cabinet reshuffle, 192–4

Guardian Young Businessman of the
    Year Awards, 40
Guards regiments, 152, 185–8, 190

Hadley, Katherine, 29
Hahn, Frank, 54
Hailsham, Lord, 158
Hamilton, Marquess of, 103
Harris, Ralph, 160
Hattersley, Roy, 80–1
Haughey, Charles, 111–15, 117, 122,
    128
Healey, Denis, 18, 65, 87, 91
    and leadership contest, 75–6, 80
Heath, Edward, 32–4, 39, 41, 63, 67,
    96, 155, 165, 190, 202
    and economic policy, 45, 51
    friendships and loyalty, 36
    and leadership contest, 12, 15–17,
        19, 21–4
    sacks Powell, 151
    Thatcher serves under, 10–12
Henderson, Nicko, 106
Henshall, Bishop Michael, 139
Heseltine, Michael, 142, 152–3
Hodges, Lucy, 134
Hoggart, Simon, 33
Hoover, Herbert, 158
Hoskyns, John, 41, 44–6, 48–9, 53,
    59–60, 174–5, 178
    and Cabinet reshuffle, 195, 197–8,
        200
Hough, Tim, 86
Howe, Derek, 199–200
Howe, Geoffrey, 35, 55, 87, 158,
    178
    and budget, 40–1, 44–50, 53, 59,
        64–5, 67
    relationship with Thatcher, 45
Howe, Marie, 119
Howell, David, 43, 190
Hoyle, Doug, 96
Hughes, Hugh Price, 77

Hume, John, 120–1
Humphreys, Mrs, 31

ICI, 53
immigration, 'new Commonwealth',
    149–51
inflation, 44, 48–9, 51, 62, 155
Ingham, Bernard, 58, 177–8
inner-city riots, 130–53, 177–8
    and policing, 130–2, 135, 138–9,
        141, 143–4, 147–8, 152, 207
    and race relations, 134–5, 137–45,
        147–51
    and unemployment, 132–3, 135–8,
        145, 147
International Monetary Fund (IMF),
    46
IRA
    Gow assassination, 199
    and hunger strikes, 100, 105–7,
        110–11, 115–16, 118, 120,
        122–3, 127, 133
    McWhirter assassination, 162–3
    Neave assassination, 35

Jenkins, Clive, 75
Jenkins, Roy, 69–71, 73–4, 81–2, 84,
    90–1, 93, 165, 205
    and Warrington by-election, 94–7,
        136
John Paul II, Pope, 125
Johnson, Paul, 161–2
Jopling, Gail, 199
Jopling, Michael, 146, 184
Joseph, Sir Keith, 20, 33, 96, 158, 191

Keegan, William, 212
Kennedy, Senator Edward, 118–19
Kennedy, John F., 4, 118
Kennedy, Joseph, 118
Kennedy, Senator Robert, 118
Kettle, Martin, 134
Keynesian economics, 47, 52, 54, 57–8

King, Tom, 201
Kipling, Rudyard, 13, 209
Kissinger, Henry, 60
Knowles, Janet, 88

La Genière, Renaud de, 202
La Pasionaria, 18
Labour party, 204–5, 207, 209, 215
    and internationalism, 76–7
    and launch of SDP, 75–90
    leadership contest, 75–81
    and Thatcher's leadership victory,
        16, 23
Lamont, Norman, 49
Lankester, Tim, 46
Lansbury, George, 76
law and order, 20, 27, 132–4, 136–7,
    151–3, 155, 203
Lawson, Nigel, 41, 48, 54, 64, 189–91,
    201
Listener, 93
Liverpool, 136–9, 152–3
    see also Toxteth riots
Lloyd, Selwyn, 65
Lloyd George, David, 7, 203
Londonderry, 108–9
Louis, John J., 128
Luther, Martin, 6, 62, 140
Lyte, Henry Francis, 102
Lyttelton, Oliver, 188

McAliskey, Bernadette, 106
McGillan, Brian, 88
McGivan, Alec, 88
McGuire, Frank, 102
McLachlan, Charles, 135
Maclennan, Bob, 74
McManus, Frank, 103
Macmillan, Harold, 20–1, 23, 34, 37,
    39, 51, 60, 63, 67, 96, 185, 202
    and Cabinet reshuffle, 188, 190–1
Macmillan, Maurice, 63
McWhirter, Ross and Norris, 160–3

Magee, Father, 116
Magna Carta, 209
Manning, Cardinal Tim, 116
Marquand, David, 70
Martin, H. A., 9
Marxism Today, 173
Meltzer Allan, 158–9
merchant adventurers, 210
meritocracy, 20, 165
Methodism, 5–7, 12, 20, 171–2, 212
   see also Wesley, John and Charles
Methodist Recorder, 171–2
Methodist Times, 7
Militant Tendency, 135
milk, free school, 14
Millar, Ronnie, 59–60
miners, capitulation to, 42–4, 46–7,
   49, 66
Minford, Patrick, 160
Molyneaux, James, 120
monetarism, 51, 77, 159, 190, 199
Monkhouse, Bob, 208
Moore, Charles, 197
Moss Side riots, 130, 133, 135, 177
Mountbatten, Earl, 105, 168, 214
Moynihan, Senator Daniel, 118
MPs' pay, 38
Murdoch, Rupert, 52, 73–4, 134, 194
museum charges, 14

Nally, Dermot, 112
Napoleon III, 20
National Coal Board, 42–3
National Health Service, 81
nationalisation, SDP and, 72–3
nationalised industries, 155
nationalism, 2–4, 31, 172, 203, 214
Neave, Airey, 35
Negus, Dick, 74–5
Neild, Robert, 54
New Cross fire, 142
New Statesman, 161
News of the World, 206, 214

Newton, John, 4
Northern Ireland, 98–129, 147, 151
   Bobby Sands's death and interna-
     tional protests, 117–23
   European commissioners visit,
     113–14, 121–2
   and 'four horsemen', 118–23
Nott, John, 157, 195, 197
Notting Hill Carnival, 142
NOW! magazine, 89
Nuffield, Lord, 27

Observer, 17, 36
O'Connell, John, 110
O'Fiaich, Cardinal Tomas, 116
O'Neill, Speaker Tip, 118–19
opinion polls, 64, 72, 88–9, 167, 204,
   207, 215
Orwell, George, 89
Owen, David, 69, 73, 76, 82–3, 85–6,
   88–93, 95, 97, 133
Oxford, Kenneth, 130–2, 138–9

Paisley, Rev. Ian, 111–12, 121
Pannell, Lord, 38–9
Parker, John, 83
Parkinson, Cecil, 49, 64, 208, 210
   and Cabinet reshuffle, 188–90
Parris, Matthew, 215
Peel, Sir Robert, 20, 216
Pennock, Sir Raymond, 53
personal responsibility, 13, 167, 170,
   210, 216
police pay, 207
Police Review, 135
policing, 130–2, 135, 138–9, 141,
   143–4, 147–8, 152
   and 'sus' law, 143–4
Powell, Enoch, 148, 151
PPE graduates, 165
Prior, Jim, 35, 55–7, 64
   and Cabinet reshuffle, 180, 186,
     190–3, 196–7, 200

private education, 69–70
Private Eye, 12
Proops, Marjorie, 22, 25
Protestant individualism, 127, 140–1
Public Sector Borrowing Requirement
    (PSBR), 45–6, 49
public spending cuts, 66, 152, 157, 159,
    179, 194
Pym, Francis, 35, 57–8, 107–8, 177–8
    and Cabinet reshuffle, 182–6, 196–7

race relations, 36, 134–5, 137–45,
    147–51
'radical right', 37
Raphael, Adam, 36
Reagan, Ronald, 4, 103, 122, 125, 128,
    167, 211
Red Lion Square disturbances, 147
Reece, Gordon, 60
Reid, Alastair, 88
Revolutionary Communist Tendency,
    135
Richardson, Michael, 63–4
Roberts, Alfred, 3, 5–8, 30
Roberts, Muriel, 5
robots, 163–5
Rodgers, Bill, 69, 73, 76, 83–5, 87, 93
Roosevelt, Theodore, 213
Royal Ulster Constabulary (RUC),
    100, 104
Royal Wedding, 177–8
rule of law, 11, 117, 127, 163, 167,
    170, 216
Rutter, David, 171–2
Ryder, Richard, 59, 163

St Francis of Assisi, 30
St John Stevas, Norman, 61
St Lawrence Jewry, Thatcher's speech,
    1–5, 51
Salisbury, Lord, 7, 16, 206
Sanders, Nicholas, 110
Sands, Bobby, 98–123

Sands, John, 100
Sands, Marcella, 100, 113–15
Scargill, Arthur, 178
Scarman, Lord, 146–7, 151–3
Scotsman, 14
Shore Peter, 50–2, 87, 183
Short, Renée, 24
Skinner, Dennis, 80
Soames, Christopher, 57, 173–6
    and Cabinet reshuffle, 181–2,
        185–7, 193, 199, 201
Social Democratic Party (SDP), 68–97,
    204–5, 207, 215
    collective leadership, 93
    and inner-city riots, 132–3
    Limehouse Declaration, 82–3, 85
    pragmatism, 91–2
    and Warrington by-election, 93–7,
        136, 177
socialism, 23, 53, 80, 87, 203
    SDP and, 72–3, 77
Sorrell, Stan, 96
South Sea Bubble, 89
South Wales Echo, 72–3
Southall riots, 130, 138, 177
Spanish Civil War, 18
Sparrow, John, 42–3
Spectator, 12
Steel, David, 89
Stephens, Caroline, 125, 163, 170
Stephenson, Hugh, 37, 71, 87
Sun, 27–9, 52–4, 57, 143
Sunday Times, 13, 73
Sutcliffe, Peter, 98

Tapsell, Peter, 58–9
Tarbuck, Jimmy, 208
taxation, 10, 40, 46, 49–50, 91
    petrol duty, 49, 60–1
    SDP and wealth tax, 74
    tax cuts, 66, 155, 157, 198
Tebbit, Norman, 64, 145, 189–94, 201
Thatcher, Denis, 9, 157, 166, 170

Thatcher, Margaret
    and advisers, 48–9, 53, 60, 67,
        158–60, 174–5
    aggression, 27, 38, 67, 169, 214
    ambitions for political longevity,
        166–7, 210–11
    binary cast of mind, 8, 26–7, 30, 55,
        91, 158, 209
    bunker mentality, 215–16
    choice of diary engagements, 163
    courage, 13, 91, 124, 159, 162, 195,
        216
    cult of personality, 202
    deposed as Prime Minister, 152
    distaste for diplomacy, 38
    and economic policy, 44–5, 59,
        212
    elected to parliament, 10–11
    fascination with clothes, 23
    and gender, 10, 15–19, 24, 28–30
    ideological conviction, 34, 38–9,
        57–8, 157
    inflexibility, 119, 121–2, 127–8,
        155, 186
    'Iron Lady' persona, 22, 207, 211,
        217
    lack of hinterland, 13–14
    lack of political development,
        216–17
    lack of sense of humour, 18
    leadership style, 57–8, 63–7, 195–7,
        212–15
    menu card notes, 160–1, 166–7, 169
    moralistic view of economics, 47,
        51, 97
    outsider status, 12, 42
    political isolation, 35–8, 157–8, 172
    political philosophy, 20–1
    poor communication skills, 16
    scientific training, 9, 163–6, 214
    and sexism, 192
    social aspirations, 217–18
    speaking style, 109, 124, 214
    suburban personality, 17–18, 22–3,
        217
    as tax lawyer, 214
    'There is no alternative' mantra,
        205–6, 211
    triumphalism, 37, 44, 210
    upbringing and early experiences,
        5–8
    work habits, 21, 139
Thatcherism, 45, 50–1, 55, 72–3, 91,
    188, 211
Third World Development, 92
Thomas, George, 125, 172
Thomas, Mike, 68, 74–5
Thorneycroft, Peter, 37, 60
    and Cabinet reshuffle, 182–5, 188,
        192
Time magazine, 144, 217
Times, The, 13, 37, 52, 73, 159, 197,
    210
    and Cabinet reshuffle, 194–6
    economists' letter, 53–5
    Gilmour article, 203–4
    and inner-city riots, 134–6
Tory Reform Group, 61
Toxteth riots, 130–3, 135–8, 141–2,
    147, 177
trade unions, 33, 48, 79, 83, 191, 193
Trades Union Congress (TUC), 50, 52

U-turns, 41, 43, 176
unemployment, 50–1, 61, 77, 92–3,
    96, 156, 158, 165
    and inner-city riots, 132–3, 135–8,
        145, 147
United States, 167–9
    and Northern Ireland, 118–23
Utley, T. E., 3

Vagrancy Act (1824), 143–4
VAT, 50
Victoria, Queen, 217
'Victorian values', 140, 164, 211

Walker, Peter, 55, 61, 186, 190, 196

Walters, Alan, 44–9, 53, 159–60

Warrington by-election, 93–7, 136, 177

Watson, Rev. Basil, 1

Weber, Max, 212

Weimar Germany, 158

Wellbeloved, James, 136

Wesley, John and Charles, 6, 63, 125–7, 170–2

West, Harry, 102–3, 105–6

Western Mail, 17

White, Michael, 192

Whitelaw, William, 22, 35, 146, 148, 151, 158, 176
    and Cabinet reshuffle, 184–8, 196–7, 200–1

Who's Who, 187, 199

Wilde, Oscar, 102

Williams, Bernard, 94

Williams, Shirley, 24, 68–70, 73–4, 76–82, 84, 87, 92, 94, 165

Williams, Sir Thomas, 93–4

Wilson, Harold, 12, 34, 36, 51, 67, 69, 76, 186, 202
    compared with Thatcher, 165

Winter of Discontent, 28

Wolfson, David, 194

Wood Green riots, 177

World in Action, 22, 36, 149

Worlock, Archbishop Derek, 139, 151

Worsthorne, Peregrine, 26

Wyatt, Woodrow, 16–17

Young, Hugo, 176, 179

Young, Janet, 180, 201

Young Communist League, 1

Young Conservatives, 208–9

Younger, George, 57

A NOTE ON THE TYPE

The text of this book is set in Adobe Garamond. It is one of
several versions of Garamond based on the designs of Claude Garamond.
It is thought that Garamond based his font on
Bembo, cut in 1495 by Francesco Griffo in collaboration with
the Italian printer Aldus Manutius. Garamond types were first
used in books printed in Paris around 1532. Many of the
present-day versions of this type are based on the *Typi
Academiae* of Jean Jannon cut in Sedan in 1615.

Claude Garamond was born in Paris in 1480. He learned how to
cut type from his father and by the age of fifteen he was able
to fashion steel punches the size of a pica with great precision.
At the age of sixty he was commissioned by King Francis I
to design a Greek alphabet; for this he was given the
honourable title of royal type founder. He died in 1561.

ALSO AVAILABLE BY KWASI KWARTENG
WAR AND GOLD

'A fascinating, lucid and serious history of money' *The Times*

In the sixteenth century, Spanish conquistadors discovered the New World. The vast quantities of gold and silver would make their country rich, yet the new wealth, which was plunged into multiple wars, would eventually lead to the economic ruin of their empire. Here, historian and politician Kwasi Kwarteng shows that this moment in world history has been echoed many times, from the French Revolution to both World Wars, right up to the present day, when our own financial crisis saw many of our great nations slip into financial trouble.

Kwarteng reveals a pattern of war-waging, financial debt and fluctuations between paper money and the gold standard, and creates a compelling study of the powerful relationship that has shaped the world as we know it, that between war and gold.

'Meaty, thoughtful and well-written'
Literary Review

'Here is a book that explores the financial cost of war, rather than the human ... Kwarteng is thorough and insightful, weaving a narrative that transports the reader convincingly through time and place'
Evening Standard

'Enormously entertaining'
Sunday Times

BLOOMSBURY

GHOSTS OF EMPIRE

'Original, stimulating and insightful' *Times Literary Supplement*

The ghosts of the British Empire continue to haunt today's international scene and many of the problems faced by the Empire have still not been resolved. In Iraq, Kashmir, Burma, Sudan, Nigeria and Hong Kong, new difficulties, resulting from British imperialism, have arisen and continue to baffle politicians and diplomats.

This powerful book addresses the realities of the British Empire from its inception to its demise, skewering fantasies of its glory and cataloguing both the inadequacies of its ideals and the short-termism of its actions.

'Refreshing, original and well-researched ... brilliant'
A. N. Wilson, *Evening Standard*

'Smart, witty and personable ... This is a book alive with wild and wonderful characters ... A cracking debut from a very accomplished historian'
Daily Telegraph

'It won't please jingoists, but this unsparing account of the British Empire, written by a Tory MP with Ghanaian roots, exposes the dangerous folly of imperial pretensions'
Sunday Telegraph

ORDER YOUR COPY:

BY PHONE: +44 (0) 1256 302 699

BY EMAIL: DIRECT@MACMILLAN.CO.UK

DELIVERY IS USUALLY 3–5 WORKING DAYS.

FREE POSTAGE AND PACKAGING FOR ORDERS OVER £20.

ONLINE: WWW.BLOOMSBURY.COM/BOOKSHOP

PRICES AND AVAILABILITY SUBJECT TO CHANGE WITHOUT NOTICE.

BLOOMSBURY.COM/AUTHOR/KWASI-KWARTENG

BLOOMSBURY